URBAN STRUCTURE

URBAN

Consulting Editor: CHARLES H. PAGE, *University of Massachusetts*

STRUCTURE

*The Social and
Spatial Character of Cities*

RALPH THOMLINSON
California State College, Los Angeles

RANDOM HOUSE   New York

First Printing

Copyright © 1969 by Random House, Inc.

All rights reserved under International and Pan-American
Copyright Conventions. Published in the United States
by Random House, Inc., and simultaneously in Canada
by Random House of Canada Limited, Toronto.

Library of Congress Catalog Card Number: 67–30749

Manufactured in the United States of America
by the American Book-Stratford Press, Inc.
Designed by Richard-Gabriel Rummonds.

To those I have loved—
My parents, wife, son and daughter,
And most deeply cherished friends—
For making life such an enjoyable trip.

PREFACE

Urban sociology is a long-established field for research and teaching, yet its importance and even its existence as a specialty are in jeopardy. As increasing numbers of people come to live in urban places and as those remaining on the farm become urban or semi-urban in their outlook and behavior, urban sociology is coming to be nearly synonymous with general sociology. What then is the justification, if any, for the continuation of urban sociology as a special subject within sociology? What contribution to man's knowledge can urban sociology make that cannot be made as well by another field? If no answer can be offered and supported, then urban sociologists, urban sociological research, and urban sociology courses perforce merge conceptually with other sociologists and sociologies.

Fortunately there is an answer: urban ecology. Human spatial distribution in and around cities as an influent and mediator of social relationships is probably the only major urban phenomenon that remains sufficiently separable to provide a legitimate intellectual rationale for the continuance of urban sociology as a distinct field. To condense: The only unique integrant of urban sociology is urban ecology.

These assertions are not meant to imply that all the facts, ideas, and interpretations found in traditionally designed books on urban sociology are cold-heartedly expunged from this volume. On the contrary, quite a bit of the material accords in a limited way with the classic content of urban sociology. The difference between this book and its fellows lies in two circumstances: the primary emphasis on ecological matters and the subordination of nonecological material by weaving it into an ecological framework. Someone who simple-mindedly tabulated the number of facts presented on each subtopic might wonder at the authenticity of my claim to differentness, but comprehension of the principal message of this book should convince readers that it is not just another rehash of urban sociology.

I hope that readers will agree that this book is sufficiently different from the run-of-the-mill book on cities to avoid that worst of all intellectual sins: boredom. In the preface to his 1958 translation of Max Weber's *The City*, Don Martindale complained that students trapped into reading "the ordinary city book" are so bored that they "would sooner face the prospect of failing the course"—a solution so nearly unprecedented as to be unbelievable; Martindale further criticized books about cities for inducing in readers a feeling of being in "the necropolis, the city of the dead from which all life has vanished." After this unflattering evaluation of the efforts of other scholars, I venture no more than to pray that the present volume will not be regarded as contributing to the urban-book necropolis.

No book is an island, and there have been many influences on this one. Easily overlooked because taken for granted is the understanding gained from my having lived in a variety of cities and city parts, from fetid slums to immaculate suburbs. One virtue consequent upon having spent the first forty years of a largely urban life without ever remaining in any one residence for more than two years or in any one city for more than three years consecutively is the diversity of experiences thereby afforded. Assuming it can be done without spurious personification, I should like to express my appreciation to the dozens of large cities and small towns in which I have lived, especially the municipalities in which I worked as a city planner—Montclair and Paterson, New Jersey; the great metropolis in which I grew up—New York; the exciting ascendant in which I now choose to live—Los Angeles; the city that best met my enthusiastic expectations—Paris; and the classic community in which I have spent so many armchair hours—Athens. If I were not a lover of cities, I would never have written this book. As the rock-and-roll song "Downtown" expresses it, that is where the lights are bright and where all the people go. In the vibrant idiom of the late 1960s, cities are "where things are happening" and "where the action is." And, without action, we are dead.

Individuals as well as agglomerations have made their contributions. Surpassing the indebtednesses expressed in footnotes are others too great to be relegated to the small print at the bottom of a page. Herman J. Loether and Charles H. Page manfully struggled through the entire manuscript, Robert C. Eidt read critically the geographic material, William G. Byron supplied valuable cartographic advice, Donald N. Clement and Elsa R. Shafer prepared figures, Margaret W. Thomlinson acted as a superlative secretary, and Estelle Whelan of the Random House staff edited out the worst of my indiscretions. Given all this expert assistance, it is with both a qualified egotism and a persistent and doubtless justified expectation of error that I repeat the naïvely boastful refrain from Thomas D'Urfey's ribald 1707 collection of songs, *Pills to Purge Melancholy:* "My thing is my own, and I'll keep it so still."

R. T.

CONTENTS

part three. HOW URBAN AREAS MIGHT BE
ARRANGED

List of Tables

List of Illustrations

part one

SETTING THE URBAN SCENE

chapter 1

SPACE AS A SOCIAL FORCE

MEN LIVE IN A WORLD THAT HAS SPACE, DISTANCE, AND PHYSICAL features. We manipulate and modify the earth's topographic features and are currently doing a good job of trying to overcome distance, but our actions and feelings, our likes and dislikes, are still closely associated with the spatial characteristics of the areas we inhabit. If it is cold, we shiver; if it is mountainous, we climb or go around; if there is an ocean, we sail or stay put; and if it is a long way home, we may even cry a little.

That space and distance are fundamental and influential parts of man's environment would go without saying—except for the current vogue of ignoring nonsocial factors in attempting to understand human thoughts and activities. But here is one case in which the unlettered may instruct the intellectuals, who sometimes need to be reminded that man is not yet in complete control of his environment.

This book attempts to recognize the importance of these geographic properties of the planet we inhabit, explicitly accepting them in order to analyze and evaluate their potency in affecting human behavior. Yet it remains a work of sociology, insisting that space is what men make of it. People are not passive adapters to their environments, but they do inhabit environments, and it is the very active and often inventive adaptations to these environmental conditions that make up the substance of this volume.

Man's complex territorial behavior is not unique; many animal species regularly subdivide the territory they inhabit, rigorously respecting boundaries often invisible to human beings. Each family or other social group may be allocated a certain space, which may not be violated by members of other groups without permission—or a fight. Sometimes interior parts of the region are set aside for one or more of the various stages of procreation, whereas the less-secure fringe areas are the scenes of wars, mock wars, and other defiant actions. Although some ecological amateurs hold this territorial consciousness to be instinctive, generally on the naïve assumption that all behavioral universals or quasi universals in any nonhuman species must be instinctual rather than learned, the existence of a territorial instinct has never been proved to exist. It has, however, been clearly established that many creatures (homing pigeons are a prominent example) have a powerful, abiding, and seemingly ineradicable spatial orientation. Whatever its provenance, territorial behavior is so widespread among animals of various kinds—and man in particular—that its study is intellectually imperative.

○ *Sources of Ecological Thinking*

The ecology of organisms, the knowledge of the sum of the relations of organisms to the surrounding outer world, to organic and inorganic conditions of existence; the so-called "economy of nature," the correlations between all organisms living together in one and the same locality, their adaptation to their surroundings, their modification in the struggle for existence, especially the circumstances of parasitism, etc. It is just these phenomena in "the economy of nature" which the unscientific, on the superficial consideration, are wont to regard as the wise arrangements of a Creator acting for a definite purpose, but which on a more attentive examination show themselves to be the necessary results of mechanical causes.[1]

This century-old passage offered something new, by coining the word "ecology," and then something old, by making the oft-repeated but still meaningful point that the outcome of serious scholarship is the reduction of the number of phenomena explained by resort to supernatural causes. In a sense, the very purpose of scholarship is to disprove the supernatural, thereby adding to the stock of phenomena that are understood as natural—to the great benefit of man's ability to comprehend and cope with his environment. "God willed it" is a superficial explanation, useless in analysis and prediction. Ernst Heinrich Haeckel, a biologist, replaced theological causation with biological causation, just as today sociologists use social factors rather than supernatural ones to explain social events like the pairing off of couples. This abandonment of supernatural explanation in favor of natural and social-science explanation is a recurring and indeed indispensable part of the history of knowledge; it also goes a long way toward explaining why learning so often seems antireligious, for it diminishes repeatedly the number and scope of intellectual areas belonging to religion.

The opening sentence of Haeckel's statement began the history of the widely used and often misused word "ecology." Taken from the Greek *oikos*, meaning "house" or "place to live," ecology is the study of organisms "at home," in interaction with the living and nonliving parts of their environment. A related neologism taken from the root *oikos* is "ekistics," the study of human settlements.[2]

Ecologists study codfish, for example, by observing and analyzing their interrelations with other fish, various ocean flora, the temperature and rate of flow of currents of water, and other relevant phenomena. Similarly, social ecologists study a primitive tribe in relation to other groups of people, animal predators, food-supplying animals, edible plant life, soil and rainfall, rivers that provide transportation and water supply, and many other circumstances of the tribe's animate and inanimate surroundings. Ecological material, then, consists

[1] Ernst Heinrich Haeckel, *The History of Creation*, II (1868; American ed., New York: Appleton, 1884), 354.

[2] Constantinos A. Doxiadis, *Architecture in Transition* (New York: Oxford, 1963), pp. 96–9.

of the organism (plant, animal, or human being) forming the central subject of study, other organisms that are of interest because of their relations to the primary organism, and various types of inanimate matter that play a part in the survival and way of life of the primary organism.

Systematic ecological reasoning, applicable to all forms of life—plant, animal, and human—was first applied to the study of plants in the late nineteenth century, to animal life early in the twentieth century, and to human beings beginning in the 1920s. The first use of the phrase "human ecology" was apparently by Robert E. Park and Ernest W. Burgess in 1921,[3] since which time the subject has blossomed so rapidly as to have almost reached the prominence of plant and animal ecology as a field for scholarly research.

All three branches are sometimes combined to form the grandiose conception of general or bio-ecology, the study of the relations of all forms of life with all others, as well as with those inanimate objects that happen to be lying around. The sum total of these many relationships among the organisms in a given habitat is called the "biotic community"; the community together with the physical features of its habitat forms an ecosystem. Ecology is the study, not of the ecosystem's creatures and objects themselves, but rather of the relations among them.

Continuation of the community occurs through the cooperative and competitive relations among similar organisms (called "commensalism") and the mutual dependence of dissimilar types (known as "symbiosis"). Men eat rabbits, which eat leaves, which are helped to grow by animal waste, and so forth; certain trees and bushes are normally found together, whereas other bushes will not coexist with those same trees. The fish, frogs, plants, algae, and insects inhabiting a pond each contribute something to the survival of the others, directly or indirectly. Whether it be a pond, a forest, or a central business district, the area of ecological investigation is inspected for both compatible and incompatible inhabitants. Denizens of city sidewalks on a vacation trip to a wild-game refuge may be appalled to discover that the animals that human beings are so anxious to preserve are devot-

---

[3] Robert E. Park and Ernest W. Burgess (eds.), *An Introduction to the Science of Sociology* (Chicago: University of Chicago Press, 1921). See also Park, Burgess, and Roderick D. McKenzie (eds.), *The City* (Chicago: University of Chicago Press, 1925).

ing much of their attention to killing one another. Incensed at this perfidious uncooperativeness, the tourist may strive to correct this destructive situation, only to be informed scornfully that his humanitarian desires, if put into action, would disrupt the balance of nature. If animal A did not kill animal B, animal A would starve to death; either way, one of them dies. Furthermore, animal A constitutes food for animal C, which is essential to keep in check animal D, a terrible pest. And any undue proliferation of animal D might be likened to a plague of locusts, for it would ruin the vegetation of the area, which is necessary to the survival of animals E, F, and G. In this fashion, explains the ecologist, animal A must kill animal B for the sake of animals C, E, F, and G—not to mention the other dreadful consequences that would ensue. For somewhat the same reason, some homeowners welcome otherwise undesirable garden snakes for their role of keeping down the plant-destroying insect population.

Within the ecosystem, these symbiotic and commensal associations of diverse plants and animals tend to determine (subject to modifications by the weather, soil conditions, and other nonliving forces) the population size and density variations of each species—except for civilized man, whose technology gives him such a degree of control over his habitat as to permit "unnatural" manipulations of densities and numbers. Much of the research of ecologists consists of deducing from hypotheses the theoretical density patterns of a given species within an ecosystem and then of going out into the field or pond to count the actual numbers. Most ecologists restrict their investigations to single species or groups of species, but a few have tried to examine entire ecosystems.

This fullest possible attempt to examine nature's intricate web by analyzing the relation of each thing to each other thing lends itself to absurd overextension. Indeed, Walter P. Taylor went so far as to embrace the world with the statement that "ecology is not a restricted subject," covering as it does "all relations of all organisms to all their environment." [4] When ecology is thus broadened to encompass all of life in a single system, its very inclusiveness causes the loss of its special flavor and intellectual point, thereby weakening its contribution to man's knowledge.

Properly restricted in scope, ecology has much to offer to our un-

[4] Walter P. Taylor, "What Is Ecology and What Good Is It?" *Ecology*, 17 (July 1936), 335.

derstanding of plant, animal, and human life. Starting with the vital question of how ever-changing beings maintain and locate themselves in changeable but finite settings, ecology examines the continuous adaptation of organisms to their habitats—the struggle for life. These struggles and adjustments are sometimes individual, sometimes aggregate; for the species, adaptation to environment occurs through a series of consciously or unconsciously communal actions. Unless individuals are physically isolated, survival among higher-order species is a matter of organized, coordinated behavior; in other words, individuals act as a group—the most basic concept of sociology. Not only is the study of ecology based on groups; it is also a dynamic subject that strives to discover the make-up and sequences of change of settlements in various habitats. Ecologists of various academic backgrounds study the group life of bees, the pecking order of chickens, the symbiotic relations between pilot fish and sharks, and the ladder climbing of ambitious men.

⬡ *Human and Urban Ecology*

Since the pioneering work of Park, Burgess, and Roderick D. McKenzie, large numbers of sociologists have incorporated this borrowed term into the body of sociology. "Human ecology—rather than being marginal to sociology—represents one effort to deal with the central problem of sociological analysis." [5] Not that human ecology exhausts the study of social organization, for social-psychological and other nonecological forces contribute much to the understanding of social behavior.

Nor do all sociologists agree that ecological analysis is central to sociology; many pay it scant respect, contending that the spatial factors so dear to ecologists offer very little explanation of how people act and think. These anti-ecologists believe, for instance, that the cliques, marriages, and leadership in a small town are not appreciably influenced by the spatial relations in the community. Ecologists respond to the contrary, demonstrating that propinquity of residence or

[5] Leo F. Schnore, "The Myth of Human Ecology," *Sociological Inquiry*, 31 (Spring 1961), 29.

work plays a major part in determining prospective buddies and marital partners and that a central or peripheral location is a potent factor in leadership potential. They argue further that the size of the area is important: For example, Texas and Rhode Island are unlikely to have the same business and governmental structures (Texas might be expected to contain more branch offices, both because of its larger population and because of its greater territory). And, if two young people are so widely separated in space that they never meet, they are not likely to marry.

A crucial restriction of ecology in sociological analysis is evinced in its most popular prefatory adjective: "urban." Today the greatest sociological use of ecology is in the study of urban structure, ascertaining the "typical constellations of persons and institutions" [6] in cities and their environs—and their multiform variations. Spatial relations are important in this context, as well as in study of the founding of cities. Some cities are located where certain physical features are favorable—a ford in a river or a hospitable mountain valley. In other cases, sheer distance is most significant, as in the railroad towns of Kansas, which are located at intervals suited to refueling with coal or water, or in the small settlements so informatively named "70 Mile House" and "150 Mile House" along the wagon trails traversing Canada's Fraser River Valley, where rest stops were determined by the need for sustenance for horses and men. Whether varied or monotonous, the terrain thus affects man's settlement.

Park posited that "most if not all cultural changes in society will be correlated with changes in its territorial organization, and every change in the territorial and occupational distribution of the population will effect changes in the existing culture." [7] His postulation of an intimate congruity between the social order and physical space, between social and physical distance, and between social equality and residential proximity is the crucial hypothetical framework supporting urban ecological theories.

Such hypotheses focus on one of three levels of aggregation: the neighborhood, the city, or the region. Neighborhood studies concentrate on analyzing primary relations in groups of people living in close proximity in a part of a city block or group of blocks. Ecological studies of the whole city attempt to differentiate sections or districts

[6] Park, *Human Communities* (New York: Free Press, 1952), p. 14.
[7] *Ibid.*, p. 231.

with common properties, to identify attributes of these sections, and to ascertain their changing locations and characteristics. In examining a regional network of cities, ecologists speak of relative size, power, social functions, and role in the marketing system. All three levels are legitimate and fruitful bases for research, and each tends to treat as its smallest ingredient the largest unit of the preceding level. Part Two of this book is organized around these orders of amplitude.

○ *Social Geography*

Data collected for census tracts, blocks, and other small areas have been used to study a number of social phenomena, among them mental derangement, crime, fertility, and social rank. A sociological classic is the 1939 study of psychoses in Chicago by Robert E. L. Faris and H. Warren Dunham. Analysis of the 34,864 cases of mental disorder admitted to state and private hospitals between 1922 and 1934 disclosed:

1. Cases of mental disorders, as plotted by residences of patients previous to admission to public and private hospitals, show a regular decrease from the center to the periphery of the city, a pattern of distribution previously shown for such other kinds of social and economic phenomena as poverty, unemployment, juvenile delinquency, adult crime, suicide, family desertion, infant mortality, communicable disease, and general mortality.
2. Each of the types of mental disorder has a characteristic distribution with reference to the differentiated areas found within the large modern city. Each of the following psychoses had its highest rate of incidence in the indicated type of local community:
   a. paranoid schizophrenia in the rooming-house districts of the city;
   b. catatonic schizophrenia in the neighborhoods of first immigrant settlement which have a high proportion of their population foreign-born or Negro who are the most recent newcomers to the city;
   c. manic-depressive psychoses in areas with higher rentals;
   d. alcoholic psychoses in rooming-house and in certain immigrant areas;

  e. dementia paralytica in lodging and rooming-house districts and Negro communities;
  f. senile psychoses and arteriosclerosis in districts with the lowest percentages of home-owners.
3. There is a high degree of association between different types of psychoses as distributed in different urban areas and certain community conditions, as follows:
  a. paranoid schizophrenia with percentage of hotel residents and lodgers;
  b. catatonic schizophrenia with percentage of foreign-born and Negroes;
  c. manic-depressive psychoses with median monthly rentals;
  d. alcoholic psychoses with per cent of population on relief;
  e. dementia paralytica with distribution of vice resorts and with venereal-disease rates;
  f. senile psychoses with percentage of home-ownership;
  g. senile psychoses combined with arteriosclerosis with percentage of population on relief and with per cent of population of native-white parentage.[8]

This documentation of the association of different types of psychoses with certain sections of the city was a major contribution and an outstanding illustration of fact-finding research. Not content merely to establish these correlations, the authors proceeded to formulate a theoretical explanation, suggesting that communication is essential for normal mental development and that social isolation encourages breakdowns. This hypothesis was tested by E. Gartly Jaco twenty-five years later in his analysis of census tracts of residences of 668 mental patients in Austin, Texas; thirteen of Jaco's eighteen subhypotheses supported the social-isolation thesis.[9]

More recently, Calvin Schmid studied the spatial distribution of crime in Seattle. He found that most types of crime "decreased more or less in direct proportion to the distance from the center of the city" and that both areas where criminals reside and areas where crimes are committed tend to have "low social cohesion, weak family life,

[8] Burgess, "Introduction," in Robert E. L. Faris and H. Warren Dunham, *Mental Disorders in Urban Areas* (Chicago: University of Chicago Press, 1939), pp. ix–x.
[9] E. Gartly Jaco, "The Social Isolation Hypothesis and Schizophrenia," *American Sociological Review*, 19 (October 1954), 567–76.

low socio-economic status, physical deterioration, high rate of population mobility, and personal demoralization." [10] Certain types of crime, however, did not conform to this general pattern. Although Schmid found six relevant and plausible hypotheses in the literature of ecology and criminology, no single one supplies a definitive explanation; as many other factors beside ecology appear to influence crime rates, this indecisive conclusion is to be expected.

A third piece of evidence for geographical sociology is the fertility differential exhibited by residents of various parts of urban areas; for example, fertility is highest in low-rent areas. Otis Dudley Duncan tested the validity of areal variations in fertility by examining differences among residential areas simultaneously with variations in characteristics of married couples. Duncan's findings bolster our confidence in the general validity of areal birth differentials; he points out, however, that not all the spatial differences are attributable to purely spatial (as opposed to familial or individual) factors.[11]

Among the variables most central to sociological analysis is stratification into classes. Socioeconomic status is measured by several observable indicators, one of which is the area in which a person resides. Because the home is a major item of expense and constantly on public display, a person's standing in the community is frequently assessed in terms of where he lives. Residence reflects the inhabitant's background and tastes, both of which are indicators of social position. Because residential proximity affects social interaction by providing opportunity for social relations with one's neighbors while repressing other contacts ("Since they moved to another part of town, we never see them any more!"), people with similar occupations, education, expectations, and consumption patterns often live near one another ("Birds of a feather flock together"). Also, because people tend to take on the coloration of their associates, the character of the immediate neighborhood exerts a potent influence on the personalities and attributes of its members. Residential areas thus acquire well-known status connotations, and spatial distance becomes an indicator of social distance. This ecological observation is supported, for example, by a study of occupations and residences of employed males

---

[10] Calvin F. Schmid, "Urban Crime Areas: Part II," *American Sociological Review,* 25 (October 1960), 655–78.

[11] Otis Dudley Duncan, "Residential Areas and Differential Fertility," *Eugenics Quarterly,* 11 (June 1964), 82–9.

in Chicago, which documents the statement that "spatial distances between ocupation groups are closely related to their social distances." [12]

These four illustrations demonstrate the utility of both spatial and social variables in sociological and ecological explanation. Anyone wishing to comprehend fully the workings of mental illness, crime, birth rates, or social stratification in urban places must take into account distance from the city center and the type of area in addition to the obviously pertinent social-psychological factors.

○ *Segregation of Minorities*

Additional evidence for the salience of spatial forces in urban life is supplied by the segregation of various ethnic groups into separate locations. Whether the minority be defined by religion, race, or nationality; whether the city be in Asia, Europe, or the United States; or whether the group segregated be composed of complete "pariahs" or merely "social inferiors"—some degree of physical separation of undesirables is practiced more or less everywhere. Ethnic quarters are pandemic in Asian cities, Jewish enclaves are so common in Europe as to have spawned the term "ghetto," and Americans are familiar with the designations "Chinatown," "Little Tokyo," "Dagotown," "Brownsville," "Germantown," "Little Sicily," and the like. In the United States, the five most numerous minority racial or religious groups (as identified in the Federal census)—Negroes, Jews, Indians, Japanese, and Chinese—generally reside in separate sections of town, sometimes by choice but more often because of the insistence of the white, Christian majority. Of these sometimes ill-treated minorities, the Negroes are probably the greatest force for potential (and, in view of recent riots, actual) disruption by reason of their large numbers, increasing vocality, long history of maltreatment, and enforced clustering in the least desirable sections of town.

A high degree of racial residential segregation is universal in American cities. Whether a city is a metropolitan center or a suburb; whether it is in the North or South; whether the Negro population is large

[12] Duncan and Beverly D. Duncan, "Residential Distribution and Occupational Stratification," *American Journal of Sociology*, 60 (March 1955), 502.

or small—in every case, white and Negro households are highly segregated from each other. Negroes are more segregated residentially than are Orientals, Mexican Americans, Puerto Ricans, or any nationality group. In fact, Negroes are by far the most residentially segregated urban minority group in recent American history.[13]

This segregation is not simply a manifestation of economic differences, for, regardless of their income levels, Negro families rarely live in white neighborhoods, and whites—no matter how impoverished—rarely settle in Negro areas. Negro residential settlement is far less determined by economics than is the districting of whites. For example, a study of Los Angeles County indicated that the correlation between property values and income in 1960 was very low (.19) among nonwhites (who were four-fifths Negroes and one-fifth Orientals) but high (.78) among whites (excluding Mexican-Americans, who are also treated as a minority group).[14] Figure 1A illustrates graphically that among these Anglos (a term denoting all whites except those of Latin extraction), the higher the income, the higher the value of the property they occupy; by contrast, Figure 1B shows virtually no association between income level and value of property for nonwhites.

Climbing into the upper brackets does not remove a Negro from the prospect of residential segregation, for high-status Negroes often have their own "gilded ghettos." The considerable educational, occupational, and economic gains made by Negroes in recent years have not had ecological correlates, and continued improvements in these three important aspects of life probably will not suffice by themselves to eliminate or even to diminish substantially the prevalent ghettoization of the Negro population. Separation into territorially distinct parts of the city has become so pervasive as to appear almost ineradicable—although in reality segregation is amenable to change in response to tremendous pressure, a long period of time, or certain combinations of events.

In fact, a slight lessening in segregation is observable in cities of

[13] Karl E. Taeuber and Alma F. Taeuber, *Negroes in Cities* (Chicago: Aldine, 1965), p. 2.

[14] Leland S. Burns and Alvin J. Harman, *Profile of the Los Angeles Metropolis: The Complex Metropolis* (Los Angeles: University of California Real Estate Research Program, 1968), p. 7.

⬡ *Practical Applications*

Accretions to knowledge from ecological research are valuable for many purposes, both academic and practical. Ecological generalizations and theories are used by city planners and other policy-making and program-implementing people who must formulate and put into practice decisions concerning the best location of roads, water and sewer lines, schools, fire and police stations, supermarkets, bus lines, apartment buildings, post offices, housing subdivisions, and so forth. There are specialists whose occupational task is the application of ecological knowledge to the location of stores, factories, and even churches and libraries. Obviously, other considerations are involved —cost of the proposed site, zoning regulations, and public opinion— but ecological considerations are much more important and far more frequently applied than is generally supposed.

Both fact-finding and hypothesis-testing research have practical applications. Dot maps showing the location of each fire or burglary or case of tuberculosis in a community are basic to the proper working of fire, police, and public-health departments, for prerequisite to diminishing the frequency and intensity of these ills is a knowledge of which areas pose the greatest danger. More profoundly useful to reformers are the causal explanations of mental illness and crime offered by Faris and Dunham, Jaco, and Schmid, encouraging closer examination of rooming-house districts and other areas of high incidence. Whether we want simply to know the facts or, more ambitiously, to alleviate personal or social disorders, ecological knowledge is often helpful and sometimes obligatory.

Failure to allow for ecological facts and tendencies can be financially disadvantageous. The community that builds a new school in an area that does not grow as rapidly as civic leaders anticipated may find itself with a half-filled schoolhouse that costs taxpayers as much as it would if it were fully utilized. The grocery chain that ignores the socioeconomic level of the residents surrounding its new supermarket may find itself losing money through lack of customers; the type and price of items stocked must fit the educational and income level of persons in the immediate area if customers are to be attracted and kept.

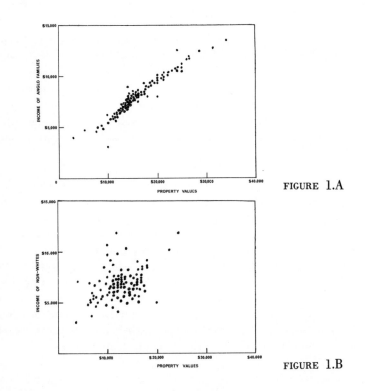

FIGURE 1.A

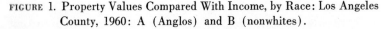

FIGURE 1.B

FIGURE 1. Property Values Compared With Income, by Race: Los Angeles County, 1960: A (Anglos) and B (nonwhites).

Reprinted by permission from Leland S. Burns and Alvin J. Harman, *Profile of the Los Angeles Metropolis: The Complete Metropolis* (Los Angeles: University of California Research Program, 1968), p. 6.

the Northeast and West Coast, and a very small decrease can be seen in midwestern cities; in the urban South, however, segregation is not only rising but shows signs of approaching complete separation into totally distinct residential districts with no intermingling whatever. Of the three principal factors suggested by Gunnar Myrdal to explain the nearly universal prevalence of segregation—poverty, free choice by Negroes, and discrimination[15]—the first two are invalid, and the latter alone offers a sufficient explanation. There is thus no basis for

[15] Gunnar Myrdal, *An American Dilemma* (New York: Harper, 1944), p. 619.

anticipating significant changes in the segregation in American cities unless discriminatory attitudes alter. Such alteration may be in store, however, for opinion surveys of whites over the past quarter-century show increasing acceptance of integration: A majority of northerners now support integration of public transportation, schools, and housing, and southern white acceptance, though still lagging far behind northern egalitarianism, is rising to the level of a large minority view.

The suburbanization of the last several decades has been an almost exclusively white phenomenon: New outlying residential areas have been either formally or—at least as effective and perhaps considerably more so—informally restricted to whites only. This white movement toward the suburbs has had indirect consequences for nonwhites, as areas near the city center lose Caucasian population and Negroes come to have wider ranges of housing alternatives than they did in the early part of the century. The narrow choice of neighborhoods for Negro families seeking housing has expanded, and once-overcrowded Negro areas have spread out in the more permissive housing situation. Nevertheless, the degree of segregation remains high in northern cities and is still higher in southern ones.

Another demographic circumstance affecting racial residential patterning is the fact that many northern cities have had large influxes of Negro migrants. Because land is limited, and Negro residential areas are even more limited, incoming Negroes in northern cities have had either to crowd into existing densely settled Negro areas or to attempt to move into dwellings in predominantly white districts. As a result, many if not most Negro districts in northern cities consist of old and unattractive houses formerly occupied by whites. By contrast, southern cities have set aside new sections for Negroes from the beginning. Although change in racial homogeneity in northern cities is thus describable largely in terms of Negro movement into deteriorating white areas, in southern cities the areal separation of the races is fostered by new construction designed from the start for occupancy on a segregated basis. Consequently, whereas in northern cities Negroes and whites tend to respond similarly to economic differentiation of areas (high-status areas generally remain high in status, and whether or not they do decline is not primarily a question of racial tenancy), ecological districts in southern cities are defined far more by race and relatively little by socioeconomic status.

The contention that Negroes' moving into previously all-wh[ite] inevitably brings about a drop in property values is a tenacio[us] —but one to which many people respond by attitude and ac[tion.] fact, property values sometimes rise following invasion of an [area by] Negroes, for nonwhites frequently have to pay prices above [the] value because fewer residential choices are open to them; [in other] words, the supply of housing available to Negroes often fails [to meet] the demand, resulting in inflated prices. A comprehensive [study of] prices paid in middle-class neighborhoods undergoing [Negro] entry, in comparison to prices in control neighborhoods wit[h similar] properties but not experiencing nonwhite invasion, concluded [that re-] sulting price changes vary considerably from one situation to [another.] Depending on various circumstances, racial change may be [de-] pressing or stimulating—or neither—to real-estate prices. "[Weigh-] ing all of the evidence, the odds are about four to one th[at] prices in a neighborhood entered by non-whites will keep u[p with or] exceed prices in a comparable all-white area." [16]

The recent downfall of many legal barriers has stimulate[d recogni-] tion that residential segregation can accomplish in actual s[ociety] what can no longer be accomplished by law. Recognition of [the] relationship between residential segregation and numerous [other] social problems has brought both segregationists and egali[tarians] to view ecological patterning as one of the most important [of] our day. Despite the fact that Negroes have made substantia[l gains in] economic welfare in recent years, residential equality is n[ot in] sight. Continuing conflict over residential segregation appe[ars] inevitable, in large part because Negroes recognize that [spatial] discrimination is one of the most pertinacious obstruction[s to their] participation in American society.

Residential segregation occupies a key position in patter[ns of race] relations in the urban United States. It not only inhibits t[he develop-] ment of informal, neighborly relations between whites an[d Negroes] but ensures the segregation of a variety of public and privat[e facilities.] The clientele of schools, hospitals, libraries, parks, and stor[es is deter-] mined in large part by the racial composition of the neigh[borhoods in] which they are located.[17]

[16] Luigi Laurenti, *Property Values and Race* (Berkeley: University [of California] Press, 1960), p. 52.

[17] Taeuber and Taeuber, *op. cit.*, p. 2.

Public utilities must also match the requirements of each area to achieve fiscal efficiency; the equipment needed by fire stations, the optimal width of streets, and the requisite frequencies of postal deliveries, for example, are all functions of the density and types of activities conducted in the vicinity—single-family homes, tall apartment buildings, retail businesses, heavy industry, and so forth.

Practitioners of urban ecology need to know the manner in which metropolitan areas, cities, and neighborhoods are put together (the subject of Part Two of this book) before they can begin deciding on and effecting plans for rearranging or maintaining existing social, economic, and spatial patterns (the substance of Part Three). Also prerequisite to rational action is knowledge of the ways in which cities have grown through the centuries, supplemented by understanding of the basic properties of modern cities and their residents—topics discussed in the remainder of Part One.

chapter 2

HOW ECOLOGICAL FACTS ARE KNOWN

How ecologists collect and interpret data is of pivotal importance, for the validity and therefore the utility of research turn on methodological competence. Students of urban ecology have long since passed the point of uncritical belief in presumed facts; they impose rigorous standards before accepting data.

Thorough training of ecological and other sociological researchers requires years of graduate study and work experience. For this reason, the intent of this chapter is not to instruct the reader in how to do research but to acquaint him with the kinds of methodological and statistical operations common in ecological analysis. Since most such techniques are shared with sociology and especially demography, anyone desiring more information on this topic can profit by examination of books describing social statistics, methods of research, and demographic analysis.

○ *Ecological Explanation and Determinism*

Ecologists sometimes seem too materialistic or deterministic in their analyses of the forces that encourage men to live at high density in one place and low density in another or to cluster together in like types (for example, high-income persons or small businesses or heavy industry) in some areas and tolerate divergent types in other areas. They are accused of assuming that variables beyond man's control force him to locate in certain places and to live in certain ways. But, just because ecologists make use of nonsocial variables, it should not be assumed that they ignore human volition; indeed, one of the purposes of ecological analysis is to ascertain the manner and degree to which man asserts control over such physical and biological forces. The fact that a researcher uses such nonsocial variables as distance, water supply, transportation routes, and temperature does not mean that he believes that those variables are the sole or even the major influences on ecological distribution of people and activities.

Some forces do appear beyond man's control, and others are controllable only at great expense. For example, a large lake in the center of a city is a geographic fact that is difficult to eliminate, and it is a foolish sociologist indeed who disparages an ecologist for acknowledging the lake's existence. Anyone attempting to deny the effect of two sizable lakes on the ecological patterns of Madison, Wisconsin, is guilty of making a special effort to avoid one of the basic facts of Madison's life: The lakes influence commuting routes and times, location of upper-class residences, location of the city limits, the sites of public schools, the size and shape of the downtown business district, and the expansion of the University of Wisconsin campus, to name only the most obvious consequences. In any city, both social and nonsocial variables affect residential zones, business districts, and other patterns of land use and social groupings; either type of causal variable taken alone is so incomplete as to be of little use in explanation or prediction.

A thorough explanation therefore requires several variables of different types, although they may not always be needed at any one stage of analysis. For instance, we may explain certain ecological variations by distance from the center of the city, as in Schmid's study of crime cited in Chapter 1. But this factor is only the first step on the ladder of causation, for next we need to inquire why distance influences human behavior in this fashion. We then introduce additional factors—for example, cost of transportation and emotional attachment to certain locations—for it is largely through man's social values and activities that distance from the city center acquires ecological significance. Use of a nonsocial variable is thus seen to be merely an early link in the causal chain, to be succeeded by social variables.

The dichotomy between social variables amenable to human manipulation and nonsocial variables not subject to man's volition is thus less a fundamental distinction than a mere separation into the stages of ecological explanation. When the analysis is complete or nearly so, the initial appearance of a materialistic orientation is replaced by a view of ecology as explaining man's adaptation to space by means of social acts and preferences. Space is what people make of it. Walter Firey states the intent of ecology as the explanation of "the territorial arrangements that social activities assume." [1] Looking at the picture from a different angle, ecology is the study of the social behavior that serves the function, either manifestly or latently, of sustaining and orienting man in his adaptation to the physical and biological features of the space around him. The distribution of man and his institutions over space is mediated by cultural values and social norms.

Ecological inquiries may take either of two broad forms: They may be simply descriptive studies of the areal distribution of certain behavior (mental illness, crime, fertility, and so forth), or they may attempt to explain *why* spatial location is relevant to the etiology of mental disorders or the differentials in crime and birth rates. Both types of research—fact finding and causal explanation—are ecologically useful. The utility of descriptive information is immediately obvious: One thereby knows which sections of town have the highest crime rates, the lowest fertility, and so on. Sometimes description is just what the doctor ordered, but at other times we want to test theories by comparing theoretical statistics deduced from hypotheses with actual statistics observed in the community: for instance, the farther

[1] Walter Firey, *Land Use in Central Boston* (Cambridge, Mass.: Harvard University Press, 1947), p. 3.

from the city center, the lower the average number of years of schooling; and, the higher the social class, the higher the rate of mental illness (both hypotheses are false). Testing a theorized relationship among two or more variables enables us to learn causes of events in addition simply to measuring the events themselves, as in purely descriptive research. There is thus an intimate relationship between theory and research; findings from exploratory studies may suggest theoretical explanations, and theories can suggest further research. For this reason researchers need to have two seemingly disparate skills: familiarity with ideas related to the subject at hand and competence in techniques of research design and statistical analysis.

Subject matter and research methods interconnect in many ways. Anyone doing research has to know which factors are potentially causative (called "independent variables") and which are subject to determination by one or more other variables (called "dependent variables"). The distinction between the two varies according to the nature of each study, and one variable may sometimes be treated as independent and at other times as dependent. Social behavior cannot be fully understood simply by ascertaining that A causes B, for in reality there is a long chain in which A causes B, which in turn causes C, which then brings about D, which influences E, which has an impact on F, which makes possible G, and so on. Fortunately, the entire sequence (and its interplay with parallel and intersecting sequences) does not need to be examined in every study; Jones may analyze the relation between A and B, Smith may examine the connection of B with C, and so forth. Residential segregation provides an example: One scholar may test several hypotheses concerning the origins of biased attitudes of whites toward Negroes; another may hypothesize bias as causing ghettoization; and a third may note the consequences of such segregation on the school system. Residential segregation is thus used as an independent variable in one study (the third) and as dependent in another (the second). In the last few decades there has been an increasing tendency among sociologists to regard residential segregation as an independent rather than as a dependent variable: The fact that segregation of Negroes may cause other discriminatory phenomena is coming to be viewed as more significant (contrary to what was previously assumed) than its causation by such variables, including differences in occupation, education, marriage, income, and other relevant characteristics.

○ *Means of Obtaining Data*

Ecological data are collected in much the same manner as other sociological information—through either field or library research. Field research consists of interviewing persons about their knowledge and attitudes or observing the behavior of persons in given situations. In some studies, interviewing is the most appropriate method; in others, observation yields more valid results; and sometimes both are used.

Rather than securing his own data, a sociologist often is able to find relevant data that have already been collected by someone else, although generally for a different research objective. Libraries are storehouses of information gathered by academic researchers, and precollected data often may be secured from agencies and corporations—sometimes from a local utility company or welfare council but more frequently from the U.S. Bureau of the Census or the National Center for Health Statistics or their counterparts in other countries.

Modern censuses do more than merely count the number of inhabitants; they collect detailed information about the social and economic characteristics of the people, their housing, and their business activities or farm production. The 1960 U.S. Census, for example, included such items as year and place of birth, marital status, place of residence five years earlier, race, amount of schooling, number of children, place and type of work, income, means of transportation to work, size and age of living quarters, rent paid, estimated market value of house, and kind of bathroom and heating facilities. The Bureau of the Census also collects such nonpersonal information as the sizes of businesses and farms, value of equipment, and kinds of goods produced or services rendered. Acquiring such data every ten years is not sufficient, however, and between complete enumerations Federal data collectors secure up-to-date information about some of the mentioned items, unemployment statistics, intention of purchasing appliances and automobiles, major illnesses, disabilities and other chronic health conditions, births and deaths, marriages and divorces, and the like. Because these data are published, extreme care is taken not to expose any information that would identify individual persons or families; when tabulations show only a few persons in a given area or statistical category, that portion of the table is not reported in detail (persons so protected are included in over-all totals, however, to maintain the accuracy of the data). All modern nations have elaborate census and registration systems for obtaining such detailed information about their population and commercial and industrial establishments, but some underdeveloped countries are sadly lacking in these useful sources of knowledge. In such cases, resort may sometimes be made to privately conducted surveys.

National census and registration systems are particularly valuable sources of historical data about city populations, for until the last century or two there was very little collection of quantitative data by universities or other nongovernment organizations. All modern nations have vital registration and census systems that keep track of both urban and rural people and record those characteristics deemed most pertinent for social understanding and policy. Registration systems record such events as births, marriages, serious sicknesses, moves, deaths, and the like, whereas censuses are static counts of the population and its characteristics at a given time. Official enumerations have a long history, dating back to ancient times, and many of the most notable early censuses and registration systems were conducted in urban places—for example, pre-Christian Athens and Rome, Nuremberg in 1449, and Paris in the 1500s. However, complete and accurate counts at regular intervals awaited the innovations of Sweden in 1749 and the United States in 1790.

The large majority of the world's people are periodically enumerated, and more than 90 per cent of all city residents have been counted at some time since 1950, yielding a huge storehouse of data about urban populations. Yet world-wide information is still incomplete, for certain countries suffer major gaps in demographic and ecological knowledge. Probably the most serious deficiency is the quality of statistical data from China; although a census was conducted in 1953, it was only partially accurate, and the People's Republic appears to be not completely trustworthy in releasing population statistics. Scholars are therefore not entirely sure how many cities there are in China, let alone their sizes and the social and economic characteristics of their residents. Although most countries have taken censuses of their people within the past ten years, some have failed to do so—notably the new African nations, which frequently lack the financial and personnel resources to perform this huge task. Ethiopia, one of the older African nations, has never had a complete census. In addition, most Asian countries have only semireliable population statistics, and about half the Latin American countries are inadequately enumerated.

To avoid a false impression of accuracy, city populations and properties must be reported somewhat loosely. Fortunately for students of urban areas, however, cities are more fully and accurately covered than rural areas, and in general it is possible to make approximate statements about the size and distribution of their populations without fear of major misrepresentation. In some regions, knowledge is both extremely detailed and highly precise; it is these areas that are most fully described in this book, other parts of the world being regretfully neglected in the interest of accuracy.

Enumerators ordinarily go from door to door—an expensive process—but, in an effort to reduce costs, some census directors mail questionnaires. Another consequence of the heavy expense of interviewing all adult inhabitants is that sample surveys are coming into increasing use. For example, the United States decennial census is supplemented by the monthly Current Population Survey of about 35,000 households across the nation, which yields more up-to-date information at greatly reduced cost. Sampling is also used within censuses: In the 1960 U.S. Census only a few questions were asked of everyone, most items being directed to a 25 per cent sample.

Universities and private agencies use much the same techniques but are even more oriented toward sampling, largely for financial reasons. Often, however, the area under study is small enough to be covered completely. Much information about cities and their residents comes from nongovernmental researchers, especially when the knowledge sought concerns a sensitive subject (marital happiness or sexual behavior, for example).

○ *Techniques of Analyzing Data*

Once obtained, data are useless unless their implications can be read. To this end, five broad classes of skills are applied: general statistics, computers, mathematical simulation models, census tract-ing, and techniques associated with mapping. The first three are somewhat mathematical, the last two graphic.

Any set of data involving hundreds or thousands of people requires statistical operations like computing means, standard deviations, indexes, correlation coefficients, and significance tests. Although these statistical manipulations can be very complicated and demanding, they can also be surprisingly simple. The reasoning and arithmetic used in ecology differ little from any other application of statistics.

Like other statistics users, ecologists are now benefiting from modern computer technology. Digital computers are indispensable in processing the mountains of data collected in the more exhaustive enumerations and offer the advantages of lower costs, higher accuracy, earlier publication of results, and faster retrieval of stored information. As computer techniques now in their infancy are improved, ecological and other social research will continue to benefit.

One especially promising application of computers is in simulation —the preparation and analysis of hypothetical models imitating possible actual events and conditions. A researcher may put into a machine data on urban topography, land values, size and composition of population, and other relevant characteristics of a city or set of cities; the computer then analyzes the data using specified theoretical principles (like those discussed in Chapters 7 and 8) and yields the probabilities of specific kinds of city growth (for example, a new suburb of 5,000 on the west side or increased density immediately south of the city center). Because many variables are involved, and because we do not ordinarily know the magnitude of every variable for every plot of land, randomization generally is applied through Monte Carlo methods.[2] Prospects for adding to man's knowledge through simulation in the near future are even more promising than are the other benefits offered by computers.

[2] William L. Garrison, "Toward a Simulation Model of Urban Growth and Development," in Knut Norborg (ed.), *Proceedings of the 1960 International Geographical Congress Symposium in Urban Geography* (Lund, Sweden: 1962), pp. 91–108.

○ *Graphic Presentation*

Ecology also requires graphic and cartographic methods especially suited to analysis of spatial data. Mathematical models of various kinds are effective in analyzing the interplay among several relevant variables. The models are usually worked out in detail on a computer, but generally they are also presented graphically. Ecologists particularly need means for breaking up larger areas analytically into smaller ones such as blocks, enumeration districts, and census tracts. Many ecological theories are supported by information tabulated according to enumeration districts or census tracts.

For administrative convenience in taking the census, the U.S. Bureau of the Census divides the nation into enumeration districts, each of a size that one interviewer can cover. The average enumeration district contains about 1,000 residents and, in an urban area, usually consists of several adjacent blocks, varying in number and extent according to the density.

A census tract is a small area having fixed boundaries and embracing from 2,000 to 10,000 inhabitants. Tracts were created to provide a permanent, consistent set of areal groupings within city limits. Wards, precincts, and other political or administrative areas tend to have bizarre or whimsical boundaries and to change them frequently. Once tract boundaries are established, they change infrequently, thus ensuring comparability of, say, 1960 data to 1930 data concerning the number of preschool children in the area. If, through city growth, a tract becomes too large to yield narrowly localized information, it may be split into two or more parts, which taken together possess limits coinciding ·with the original single tract. Another advantage of census tracts is that their boundaries are not determined by historical accident or political expediency; where possible, boundary lines are deliberately placed so as to maximize homogeneity within each tract and heterogeneity among tracts (such homogeneity, however, tends to disappear with time). Although these objectives are not always achieved, census tracts remain, with enumeration districts and blocks, the most satisfactory areal units for urban research. Since their origination by Walter Laidlaw in New York City in 1906, tracts have gradually come to be used in nearly all large cities in the United States.

Spatial relationships are especially appropriate for graphic portrayal on maps and diagrams of various kinds. Particularly indispensable to ecological analysis are cross-hatched, shaded, colored, dot, point-symbol, diagrammatic, and isoline maps.[3] Cross-hatched, shaded, and colored maps convey information by the varying density and patterning of lines and spots. Dot maps are prepared by placing a mark at each point of occurrence of the phenomenon under study (for example, burglary or venereal disease); the areas of greatest incidence are readily identified by the darkened hue caused by clusters of dots. Like other pictograms, symbol maps are designed so that representational signs (men, houses, stacks of silver dollars, and so forth) compare quantities in a self-evident manner. Diagrammatic maps or cartograms are abstracted or schematic representations: examples are route maps showing the sequence of stops on trips; value-area maps, in which each area is in proportion to the magnitude of the given variable; and migration and traffic-flow maps, in which the volume of movement is portrayed by the thickness of the arrow connecting the points of origin and destination. On isoline maps (from the Greek *isos*, "equal"), lines are drawn connecting places having equal rentals, juvenile delinquency rates, travel time to the city center, travel cost, or the like. Time-consuming though their preparation may be, such maps and diagrams are worth their weight in words many times over, and ecological analysis would be severely hampered without them.

○ *Research Organizations and Personnel*

All this collection, analysis, and presentation of data must, of course, be performed by professionally trained researchers, some of whom work individually and others who team up in small or large organizations. Being enormously expensive and needing authoritative enforcement to ensure full coverage, complete enumerations and regis-

[3] See for example Calvin F. Schmid, *Handbook of Graphic Presentation* (New York: Ronald, 1954).

tration systems are possible only under the auspices of government agencies. Sample surveys, on the other hand, are conducted by numerous groups, both public and private. But, although data collecting is primarily the responsibility of governments, data analysis is performed largely in universities and other private organizations. Several foundations, notably the Ford Foundation, support research in many nations and graduate training in the United States, where the best educational facilities in ecology are found.

An increasing number of universities conduct ecological teaching and research in their sociology, economics, and geography departments and in their centers for demography. Among the most prominent research centers are the Office of Population Research at Princeton University, the Population Research and Training Center at the University of Chicago, the Population Studies Center at the University of Michigan, International Population and Urban Research at the University of California at Berkeley, and the Population Studies Center at the University of Pennsylvania. Clearly, data concerning cities form a part of demography, and much research on urban areas is done in population centers; for example, the study of crime in Seattle cited in the opening chapter was done at the Office of Population Research of the University of Washington. However, growing interest in urban matters is encouraging universities in all parts of the nation to set up centers specifically designed to promote and conduct research on urban places, people, activities, and problems. A prominent example is the Joint Center for Urban Studies of the Massachusetts Institute of Technology and Harvard University.

Urban ecological knowledge is achieved mainly through the efforts of scholars in two areas, sociology and demography. Although tabulations designed specifically to measure performance in urban ecology have not been made, such information is available for the most closely related specialty, demography. Two compilations of doctoral theses in demography over the years 1933 to 1963 show the dozen outstanding contributors among American universities to be, in rank order: Chicago, Michigan, Columbia, Washington, Princeton, Wisconsin, Harvard, North Carolina, Pennsylvania, New York, Northwestern, and Clark.[4] Demographers most often cited in eleven population books

---

[4] Glen V. Fuguitt, *Dissertations in Demography: 1933–1963* (Madison: University of Wisconsin, 1964); and Population Association of America Committee on the Recruitment and Training of Demographers, *Report* (1964).

published between 1953 and 1961 were associated with the London School of Economics, Princeton University, and Columbia University.[5] Similar tabulations for general sociology are too large in scope to be useful here, for most sociological research is only marginally relevant to the study of urban ecology. The University of Chicago, however, has an unequaled tradition of research activity in urban sociology extending over nearly half a century.

A few of the greatest individual contributors should be identified. John Graunt (1620–1674) deserves to be called the father of demography; although his major contribution was to the study of mortality, Graunt, like his sometime collaborator, William Petty, also analyzed and made predictions about the population growth of London and other large cities. Thomas Robert Malthus (1766–1834) was the first full-time professional demographer. Probably the greatest technical contributor was Alfred J. Lotka (1880–1949). Graunt and Malthus were both English, and Lotka, although born in Austria, spent most of his life in the United States. From its beginnings in European political economy, demography has transferred allegiance to American sociology, for the United States contains more demographers than any other nation, and most of them are sociologists. The world total of population experts is probably between 2,000 and 3,000, or fewer than one demographer per million people—a discouraging statistic unless one realizes that the number of demographers is increasing at a faster rate than the number of people.

The leading urban sociologists are more difficult to distinguish, partly because the field is less clearly defined than is demography and partly because the principal contributors are all of the twentieth century and hence cannot be viewed through the perspective of time. Certainly Robert E. Park and Ernest W. Burgess and their many graduate students at the University of Chicago were among the major pioneers in the 1920s and 1930s. Quite a bit of urban research was conducted in earlier centuries, but most of it was neither ecological nor sociological, and lack of skill in quantitative techniques limited its ultimate contribution. Perhaps the earliest usable work of a partially systematic nature dealing with urban areas was Giovanni Botero's 1589 treatise in Italian on the growth of cities—a book whose present appeal, however, resides more in its priority than in its profundity.

[5] Ralph Thomlinson, "A Note on the Most Frequently Cited Demographers," *Population Review*, 7 (July 1963), 81–3.

The best indicator of the extent of each individual's accomplishments in this field might well be the frequency of entries following his name in the indexes of this and similar books.

⬡ *Projections*

All the fact-discovering and analytical techniques described—censuses, statistics, diagrams, and so forth—may, according to the desire of their user, lead sooner or later to the preparation of more or less speculative prognostications about the future. Estimating city size is a technical endeavor not to be undertaken by the inexperienced or unwary; it is a questionable activity even for the expert. Although projections of national populations over short periods of time can be made with some accuracy, smaller areas and longer time spans present almost insurmountable obstacles to close prediction, especially in regions undergoing industrialization or other rapid social change. Installation of a single factory in a small town or a major variation in any one demographic factor may substantially affect either the growth or internal patterning of a city's population.

The difficulty of estimating the future effect of these forces is partially counteracted by the circumstance that certain urban conditions and events are under the control of the city government (though often requiring approval of the state or other local government). For example, by zoning predominantly for single-family homes a city can keep its density low, and by zoning for tall apartments it encourages a high density. A city's population and economy may also be deliberately directed by the manner of zoning for industry and business, subject to the qualification that stores and factories do not always conform to zoning ordinances. Another example is annexation, which obviously influences the growth of a city by taking in land, buildings, and people: Civic leaders may try to annex surrounding parcels of land, or they may oppose such a policy; in either case, of course, the potential annexees also have something to say in the matter. The point remains that cities do have some control over their destinies.

Social scientists usually specify conditions and qualifications on which their estimates are based. Although at first glance it may

seem merely a way of avoiding responsibility, a qualified statement is much more useful than one that is not qualified. If demographers say that, given certain conditions, the population of
a city will change in a specified fashion, legislators or other
policy makers can plan better because they are made aware of the
direction and extent of likely errors. Analogously, a parent may ad-
vise a teen-age son, "If you go too fast, you will go off the road at a
sharp turn"; less likely, he could improve on the prediction with the
statement, "Since your tires are somewhat worn and you are driving a
car with comfortably soft suspension and moderate understeer, if you
drive at sixty miles an hour around Hinkey's corner, then the odds are
three to one that you will spin off the road or roll over."

Published estimates of population usually contain several projections, each tracing the demographic consequences of certain stated
assumptions about economic and political conditions, leaving the
reader to use his own judgment as to which of the conditions is more
probable. Such multiple projections are superior to single unqualified
(and hence more emphatic-sounding) predictions, for three reasons.
First, they do not build up a false sense of accuracy, because a margin
of error is implicit. Second, by making the estimate in the deductive
form, "The population will be —— if ——," the statistician is recognizing that he cannot know the conditions that will prevail over the
period covered by his estimate. Third, as the assumptions are explicit,
poor or unrealistic projections can be sifted out and mediocre ones
revamped at a later date if the political, economic, or social conditions change.

If these remarks seem to imply that estimates of the population or
internal proportions of cities five or fifty years hence are weak from
the start, understanding is indeed being achieved. Any statement
about the future is uncertain, and ecologists join other scientists in
obeisance to the vagaries of technological inventions, economic fluctuations, and political catastrophes. Recognizing that, where the future
is concerned, the only certainty is uncertainty, social scientists have
learned to live with, take for granted, and even make explicit quantitative allowance for the inevitability of probability. Measurement
and calculation of uncertainty presuppose knowledge of the laws of
chance, which can be thoroughly comprehended only by using the
calculus and other basic mathematics. Without knowledge of the calculus one has little choice but to accept on faith the statistical fact

that virtually nothing is known absolutely, nearly all knowledge in all fields being probabilistic. Although these caveats may discourage the literal-minded from saying or accepting anything at all about the future, persons capable of subtlety can proceed nonetheless, acknowledging the constant presence of the Devil of Probabilistic Uncertainty. It is in this context that all responsible estimates are made, whether optimistic or pessimistic, enthusiastic or reluctant. Still, certain statements can be made with a high degree of confidence.

Without question, one projection on which all can agree is that urbanization will increase during the rest ot this century. And it is not unlikely that the following century will experience a massive urbanization reaching what some people may consider ominous dimensions. If that happens, rurality will virtually disappear and a new kind of urban existence, of a form not now completely specifiable, will emerge.

chapter 3

THE NATURE AND RISE OF CITIES

THAT CITIES AND CITY PEOPLE MUST BE DIFFERENT FROM RURAL AREAS and farmers seems obvious but, like other obvious beliefs, it must be documented lest it prove false. And as with so many other "obvious facts," it can be accepted too readily and generalized too far. Consider the smart, sophisticated talk to be heard in the world's largest metropolis:

"Well is it hot enough for you?" the driver said as we waited for a light.

"I'll say," I said.

"It was worse yesterday," he said.

"No kiddin'?" I said.

"Yeah, jeez it was awful," he said.

"It don't sound good," I said.

"I hope it don't get no worse," he said.

"I seen in the paper," I said, "where it was 101 down in Phoenix yesterday."

"Yeah, but that was more of a dry heat. That dry heat ain't nothing like this."

"It's the humidity does it," I said.

"You can say that again," he said.[1]

After this heady New York City cosmopolitanism, it is relaxing to turn to small-town talk, midwestern style:

"Was you to the dance last night out at the Royal?" says the waitress, talking through her nose.

"I was there, was you?" says a milk-truck driver likewise.

"Yeah, I was there, I never seen you though."

"That's funny, I was there."

"Well, I never seen you."

"Where was you at? I never seen you."

"Well, it's funny we never seen each other." [2]

Reading these two doses of conversation, one begins to wonder who the hicks are. Certainly not all urbanites are urbane (which both the second and third editions of Webster's unabridged dictionary naïvely define as "evincing the polish and suavity characteristic of social life in large cities"), nor are they necessarily less provincial than inhabitants of the backwoods (again the ingenuous Webster: "provincial" means "exhibiting the ways or manners of a province or rural district; not urbane; countrified").

Still, there are differences, the point of the above two conversations being that variables such as intelligence and education play parts in influencing a person's habits and values that may be fully as important as locale of residence. Without denying the impact of such variables, it nonetheless is incumbent upon urban sociologists to search for defining properties of cities.

Defining cities is as confusing as labeling them. Urban areas are referred to in various times and places by such words as "city," "town," "borough," "municipality," and "burg"; distinctions among these rough synonyms, although highly meaningful to residents of certain regions, are not sufficiently agreed upon to be useful in either academic research or practical application. Regarding certain distinctions, however, some agreement does exist: "Metropolis" clearly refers to a large city, and "village" and "hamlet" denote essentially

[1] Richard P. Bissell, *Say, Darling* (Boston: Little Brown, 1957), p. 6.

[2] Bissell, *7½ Cents* (Boston: Little Brown, 1953), p. 4.

rural communities. The word "community" constitutes the necessary generic label; it is a broad term that may refer to places that are either urban or rural or ambiguously classifiable.

○ *What Is a City?*

The initial observation pertinent to defining a city is that neither social scientists nor governing bodies in various countries agree among themselves on a definition. Disagreement often exists even within a nation, as in the United States, where the Bureau of the Census has had to set up a special category for urban places not classified as cities by the relevant state governments—a condition found in several states in the Northeast and a few in the rest of the nation. Although officials and scholars agree in defining a city in contrast to the surrounding countryside, this urban-rural comparison is made by means of many different criteria.[3]

A common approach is to specify a minimum number of inhabitants; above a certain number of residents, a community is called a city. Minimum population has been set by legislative and other bodies at 200 in Denmark; 300 in Iceland; 1,000 in Venezuela and New Zealand; 1,500 in Ireland; 2,000 in France, the Congo, Israel, and Argentina; 2,500 in the United States and Mexico; 5,000 in Belgium, India, Ghana, and the Netherlands; and 10,000 in Greece. In the nineteenth century, the United States favored 8,000. Some countries—Japan, for instance—define two or more "urban" categories with different minimum sizes. Therefore no one can fix an absolute figure that will meet with international unanimity. This definition possesses the further weakness that there are many areas larger than 2,500 (or 10,000) that do not seem urban in character, and smaller communities that we do regard as urban.

A second type of quantitative definition uses density as its criterion. Mark Jefferson said that a density of 10,000 people per square mile is indicative of a city. Other scholars have suggested smaller figures. Although not agreeing with Jefferson in other respects, Hope Tisdale Eldridge wrote that "urbanization is a process of population

[3] Georges Chabot, "Introduction," *Les villes* (Paris: Colin, 1948).

concentration." The same criticism applies here as to the first kind of definition: It does not always agree with our conception of what a city is.

Historical criteria are used in the third method: A community is a city insofar as its role in the past has conferred this title upon it. We thus refer to earlier times to decide what is a city. But it is just in this way that people accept a number of places as cities. The historical criterion takes us back to a time when city and country were much more distinct than they are today, thus ensuring a less arbitrary definition. Unfortunately, use of this criterion entails the risk of including many now-defunct cities. And how are we to treat newly founded communities?

A fourth kind of definition is based on administrative law: A city has privileges and obligations not possessed by unincorporated rural areas. In this case, a government decision is necessary to place an area on the list of cities. In the United States, state legislatures grant municipal charters, officially declaring that a place is a city, town, borough, or whatever else they choose to call it; this charter provides both rights and duties. In some European countries during the Middle Ages only a city had the right to open a market. To a lawyer a city may be a municipal corporation endowed with a legal existence that enables it to own property, to sue and be sued, and so forth. Juridical factors are central in this definition: A city possesses a charter guaranteeing it certain rights and privileges and imposing upon it certain obligations. But these legal distinctions are breaking down as suburbanization surrounds corporation limits with a juridical haze.

Fifth, the exterior aspect of a community is relevant, for it is by physical impressions that we recognize and classify places. An urban area is built up; a rural area is not. A city is a man-made landscape of buildings, streets, water mains, and other contrived appurtenances. Richard L. Meier defined a city as a place where "artifacts have accumulated to such an extent that they have extinguished most features of the natural environment." But some built-up places are essentially rural, the tall structures being grain elevators and the elongated ones being storage sheds for various agricultural products. Furthermore, say sociologists, cities should be defined in terms of people, not things. And some critics insist that the appearance is only the manifestation of a more profound reality—the way of life—and that phenomena should not be defined by symptoms.

The type of life then supplies a sixth criterion: modes of living and feeling. Some styles and attitudes are appropriate to the city and others to the country. When people contrast the city and the country-side, this difference is usually what they mean. A city is more than just the physical accompaniments of high density—busy streets, sky-scrapers, and crowded subways; it is also a style of living and a cul-turally different manner of regarding life. A stereotypical urbanite talks fast, keeps close track of time, lives in an apartment, and does not know his neighbors. In short, as Louis Wirth said, urbanism is a special way of life. But this way of life is not susceptible to precise definition, which makes it difficult to use as a principle of classifica-tion.

A seventh point of view is that the dominant factor determining urban or rural way of life is the occupations of the inhabitants. Stated simply, the urban habitat is made up of workers who do not cultivate the soil. The 1938 Congress of the International Statistical Institute recommended adoption of a definition based on the percentage of the population engaged in agriculture; in a city the most frequent means of subsistence are service, commercial, and industrial occupations. Also, the division of labor is more varied in cities. But by this defini-tion some large towns in Hungary and Bulgaria would have to be labeled "rural," yet a tiny cluster surrounding a railroad coaling stop in Kansas would be called "urban." This criterion also leads to diffi-culties and ambiguities in the case of mining areas: Extractive activi-ties are not farming, but they are not urban either.

The eighth criterion is insistence on commercial character as defin-ing a city, emphasizing the distributive function of the marketplace. The market element is paramount in Friedrich Ratzel's definition: A city is "a permanent collection of men and habitations which covers a large area and which is found at the crossing of large commercial routes." Arthur Smailes regarded a city as a place having banks and shops. This criterion appears too narrow, for business plays only an accessory part in the activities of many cities.

A ninth approach uses the industrial occupations as the sole crite-rion: A city is where factories are. But a few factories, or one large one, in a rural area do not constitute an urban enclave worthy of the designation "city." Both this definition and the objections to it are similar to those of the seventh and eighth approaches.

These last three criteria imply a tenth standard: the dependent or even parasitic nature of cities. Werner Sombart spoke of cities as "aggregations of men dependent on products of outside agricultural labor for their subsistence." The daily need to bring in food and other necessities places the city in the position of relying upon rural areas for its existence. Traditionalists often proclaim rural areas as the source of life and cities as parasitic, hypercivilized, and degenerating. In return, these decadent cities usually supply the luxuries of life to rural regions in exchange for foodstuffs, or they may simply exploit the surrounding countryside through military dominance. This view of urban-rural relations often brings forth such virulent criticism as Henri Bordier's "cities represent points of ossification of the social organism." In any case, definition by dependence is not fully satisfactory because, in modern countries, rural and urban areas are interdependent in their industrial, agricultural, military, educational, medical, and artistic needs.

Related to dependence is an eleventh basis for definition: A city is a central place for transportation. Anyone who has traveled the French railroad system knows that nearly all routes lead to Paris and that one often cannot go directly from A to B even though they are only 50 miles apart; rather, he must ride 150 miles to Paris, change trains, and ride 175 miles back out to reach city B. Similar conditions prevail in the hinterlands of New York City: To go from one place in metropolitan New Jersey to another late at night, it is sometimes advisable to cross the Hudson River into New York City, ride the subway, and then recross the Hudson to New Jersey. Rural areas are places that buses pass through; where they stop is usually a town. And if a community is too small to merit a bus station, it hardly deserves to be designated a city. Charles H. Cooley theorized that stops or breaks in transportation provide nuclei for the founding of cities. But, without denying the indispensability of transport to modern city functioning, it is not sufficiently central to urban existence to adopt as the primary defining criterion.

Commuting is becoming common enough to be regarded as the twelfth defining attribute of cities. Most city dwellers commute—but so do many farmers in various parts of the world. Jean Brunhes and Pierre Desfontaines used commuting to distinguish a city from a village: "A city has the majority of its inhabitants employed most of the time inside the agglomeration; a village has the majority of its inhabitants employed most of the time outside the community." Then is a suburb a city or a village—and is a village urban or rural? But this commuting phenomenon may be more closely related to the cost and rapidity of transportation than to the extent of urbanization and therefore is not a fully satisfactory test for urbanism.

A thirteenth criterion is government or religious functions: Cities are essentially church or political centers. In a few countries these two criteria are appropriate now, and in a large number of nations they once were excellent defining criteria. Henri Pirenne described medieval cities as "distinguished by gates, churches, and population density." But this kind of definition is no longer suitable, for religious and government activity are of slight importance in many modern urban communities.

A fourteenth approach is that a city has a central focal point, a place where "things happen." This nucleus, known in Chicago as The Loop and in many cities as Main Street or Downtown, is a markedly congested, massively built-up area in which no one lives but to which many persons come for work, shopping, and entertainment; consequently, the highest property values in the city are found there. Although a central business district is characteristic of many cities, quite a number of old ones have several such districts, and a few very new cities have remarkably little central concentration. The degree of downtown development appears to be largely a result of the type of transportation that prevailed during the formative years of a city's growth; cities that came of age in the automotive era often have highly dispersed businesses, shops, and entertainment facilities.

The fifteenth and final criterion is diversity: Cities are undoubtedly more complex and varied than are rural areas. The variety is evident in the appearances and functions of both buildings and people. Hans Dorries said: "A city is known by its more or less orderly form, closed, grouped around a nucleus which is easy to find; and by its very varied appearance, composed of the most diverse elements." This approach, though containing considerable truth, is not conducive to precise demarcation between urban and rural modes.

The most likely way out of this maze involves a sixteenth possibility: using several of the already-listed criteria. A modern city is

1. a large agglomeration of people living in a contiguously built up area,
2. who function to produce non-agricultural goods and services, and

more particularly, to distribute all manner of goods and services,
3. and who, as a result of carrying on such functions develop a way
of life characterized by anonymity, impersonal and segmentalized
contacts with other people, and secondary controls.[4]

Yet even this compromise approach is not without blemish, for it
more closely resembles a definition of a complex metropolitan area
than of a single city.

Although scholars have failed to agree upon a universal definition
of a city, largely because cities themselves differ in different culture
areas of the world, their points of disagreement have shed considerable light on the urban dweller and his habitat. Furthermore, a formal
definition is probably less valuable, albeit far more succinct, than is
this sixteen-part description of the fundamental properties of cities
and qualities of city living. A precise definition of the word "city"
that would be legitimate and useful in all regions of the world is not
possible, but we do know approximately what cities are like.

In sum, cities are built up of large quantities and varieties of edifices offering physical contrasts and requiring transportation facilities
to relieve congestion and permit flow of materials and people. Urban
centers are characterized by rapidity and fluidity of life, specialization
of activities, complex social organization, and intensification of opportunity. Compared with inhabitants of rural areas, city residents
are more heterogeneous, often anonymous, and given to impersonal
and secondary relationships as a result of their far more numerous
recurrent personal contacts.

○ *The Earliest Cities*

Cities came into being with man's emergence from a primitive to a
civilized state. This simultaneity was not a coincidence, for the first
cities provided seats of government, bastions of defense, altars of
worship, markets for exchange of goods, and meeting places for the

---

[4] Abram J. Jaffe, "Summary of the Proceedings of the University Seminar on
Population" (New York: Columbia University, 1951), mimeographed, p. 15.

interchange of ideas. Among the most commendable achievements of human history, the development of the city ranks with that of fire, agriculture, and printing.

Cities appeared first in the Mesopotamian basin, probably about 4000 B.C. Whether by diffusion or independent invention—archaeologists disagree on this matter—they were found in the Nile Valley by 3000 B.C., the Indus Valley by 2500 B.C., the Huang Ho Valley by 2000 B.C., and in Latin America by A.D. 500. The region now known as Iraq can thus claim to have housed the first known city, and Egypt, West Pakistan, China, Mexico, and Peru can stake legitimate claims to having exhibited a similar early capacity for urban ingenuity. Archaeological excavations and reconstructions of these ancient cities lend invaluable support to the few written records that have survived.

The Sumerians established their cities on the silted plains of the Tigris and Euphrates Rivers and extended their agricultural land by an intricate irrigation system. Although milestones in man's history, these cities were small by modern standards, having generally 5,000 to 20,000 inhabitants and reaching an estimated maximum of 34,000 in Ur early in the second millennium.[5] Heavily fortified walls protected the generally wealthy and privileged residents of these cities, and temples and palaces were the most prominent structures, with private residences scattered helter-skelter along narrow, twisted paths used for both pedestrian access and disposal of refuse.

The emergence of cities in Mesopotamia may possibly have stimulated city growth in the valleys of the Nile, Indus, and Huang Ho, but the sparsity of data makes this diffusionist inference questionable. Whatever their inspiration, urban centers did spring up along the lower Nile and in the delta at various times between 3000 and 2000 B.C., although even the largest communities were little more than shrines and market centers serving the rural hinterlands. Next came the urban settlements on the alluvial plain of the Indus Valley, where archaeological unearthing of Harappa and Mohenjo-daro gives evidence of their having been capitals of empires dominating scores of small towns and villages. The valley of the Huang Ho, or Yellow, River was the first host to cities in eastern Asia, but precise dating and accurate description await further excavation. The earliest New

[5] Leonard Woolley, *Excavations at Ur* (London: Benn, 1954), p. 193.

World cities were those of the Mayas in the Yucatan peninsula, followed by those of the Incas in what is now Peru; both cultures are insufficiently documented to establish dates with any certitude. Like the Sumerian cities, the Mayan and Incan urban centers were small, generally with populations of about 10,000.

Turning from the great cultural centers of the ancient Orient to the classical civilization of Greece would have seemed to the Syrians, Persians, Egyptians, Minoans, and other luxury-laden materialists of the time a lapse into barbarism. These sybarites, whose orientations were comparable with modern American standards, lost out both in power and in intellectual acclaim to the relatively ascetic tastes of Athens and Sparta, the most powerful of the Greek city-states.

The Greek *polis*, or city-state, was an autonomous and self-sufficient unit comprising a city and its hinterland, from which it drew sustenance. The term "city-state" is somewhat misleading, for the *polis* did not consist solely of a city, and the rural hinterland was fully as important to the Greeks as the city was. Except for a few merchants, most inhabitants of the city owned and operated farms. As Max Weber reminded us, "the full urbanite of antiquity was a semipeasant." [6] Topography greatly influenced the political system, for Greece is predominantly mountainous, and settlements were located in small valleys. Communication among the valleys was slow, hampering development of an integrated economy and fostering hundreds of small *poleis*, each fiercely protective of its independence. Emphatically contradictory in their temperate philosophy and their actual highly contentious behavior (both of which have contributed unquenchable legacies up to the present time), the Greek city-states provide vivid historical vignettes of urban dominance, a fact often obscured by their remarkable contributions to aesthetic, democratic, and intellectual endeavors. With a population that apparently never exceeded 300,000—of which half were slaves and aliens—the Athenians made ineradicable impressions upon world history.

Ancient urbanization reached its apogee under the Roman Empire, when a vast state controlling the destinies of more than 50 million people was concentrated at Rome. At the peak of its power, in the second century A.D., Rome may have housed as many as 1 million people, making it the largest city to exist prior to industrial times. But

---

[6] Max Weber, *The City* (1921), trans. by Don Martindale and Gertrud Neuwirth (New York: Free Press, 1958), p. 71.

thereafter its population diminished, dropping below 20,000 by the ninth century. No other city reached Rome's maximum population until London attained 1 million early in the 1800s.

○ *The Middle Ages in Europe*

From the fall of the Roman Empire to the sixteenth century, a Dark Age of cities prevailed. The few large cities dwindled drastically in size and function, and no new ones arose as replacements. Because western Europe sank into an essentially agrarian civilization for several centuries, there is a question whether or not any medieval community was a true city. Before the end of the first millennium, "burgs never consisted of more than a few hundred men," and "towns probably did not pass the figure of two or three thousand souls." [7] Greatly reduced in size, the few remaining cities consisted of mere clusters of dwellings grouped around a monastery or castle and serving mainly as administrative foci for religious, political, or military jurisdiction. Weekly markets were held, to which peasants from roundabout brought their produce, and there was an occasional annual fair. Otherwise, towns served the dictates of the bishops or military commandants. "Neither commerce nor industry was possible or even conceivable in such an environment." [8] These circumstances, and the fact that daily necessities generally needed to be within easy walking distance, ensured that few medieval towns extended more than half a mile from the center.[9] During the Renaissance, even towns of considerable prominence often housed only 10,000 to 30,000 persons, and lesser towns generally had fewer than 10,000.[10] Throughout the Middle Ages, only Paris, Florence, Venice, and Milan are conjectured (in the absence of reliable data) to have reached 100,000 population.[11]

[7] Henri Pirenne, *Medieval Cities* (Princeton: Princeton University Press, 1925), p. 77.

[8] *Ibid.*, p. 76.

[9] Lewis Mumford, *The City in History* (New York: Harcourt, 1961), p. 313.

[10] Frederick R. Hiorns, *Town-Building in History* (London: Harrap, 1956), p. 110.

[11] Pirenne, *Economic and Social History of Medieval Europe* (New York: Harcourt, 1936), p. 173.

As long as each region was broken up into numerous small fiefs held by feudal lords with their vassals and serfs, each suspicious of other fiefs and refusing to cooperate even when not waging intermittent wars, cities were not likely to spring up. For cities to prosper, peace and cooperation are necessary so that merchants and teamsters can bring in food and supplies and move out salable commodities. The breaking up of the feudal system thus facilitated the rise of cities initiated in the Renaissance and coming to fruition in modern times.

○ *Urbanizing the World*

Some city growth did occur after about A.D. 1000, and by 1400 many villages and a few cities were scattered across western and central Europe. But the appearance of a few cities does not denote true urbanization, by which is meant the change from a predominantly rural population to one living mostly in urban areas. Urbanization, as distinguished from the growth of cities, is measured by the percentage of the national or regional population residing in urban places. Urbanization is thus based on the relative growth of the urban and rural segments of the population; if the city and farm populations increase at the same rate, urbanization is not occurring. The first genuine urbanization occurred in northwestern Europe (England, France, and so on) in the early nineteenth century, for it was there that, for the first time, a substantial proportion of the population came to live in urban areas. During the last hundred years, most regions of the world have experienced increases both in the degree of urbanization and in the sizes and numbers of their cities.

In the 1600s, cities began to burgeon, and by 1800 not only London but also Paris had exceeded 500,000 population, and Vienna and St. Petersburg had reached 200,000. A century later, ten cities each contained more than 1 million people: London, Paris, Vienna, Moscow, St. Petersburg, Calcutta, Tokyo, Chicago, Philadelphia, and New York. In the first half of the twentieth century, urban growth was far more rapid—an estimated 875 cities throughout the world had reached 100,000 population by 1950, and nearly 100 had reached 1 million.

These larger urban agglomerations resulted from several forces: growing population in various world regions, improved control over the natural environment resulting from technological advances in agriculture and industry, more rapid and reliable means of communication and transportation, and more sophisticated economic and political mechanisms permitting efficient exchange of goods and money between urban and rural residents. Aided by extraordinary new sources of power, factories prospered, surplus farm products flowed into the cities in increasing quantities over railroad and canal systems, businesses enlarged, and capital accumulated in these new industrial cities of the nineteenth century. In the twentieth century still more power sources were added, and, of course, the automobile arrived; together with the railroad, it practically eliminated in many regions the need to live close to one's workplace, thereby permitting city men to encroach upon the once-rural fringes of the cities. So developed the metropolitan region, with its satellite communities surrounding the central core and supplying a diurnal flow of commuters to work and pleasure.

The results of these urbanizing forces can be seen in Figure 2. Of the world population of about 900 million in 1800, fewer than 2 per cent lived in cities of 100,000 or more, and only about 3 per cent lived in cities of 5,000 or more. By 1900, of 1.6 million people, the percentages had grown to nearly 6 and 14 respectively. And of the globe's 2.4 million population in 1950, the percentages were 13 and 30.[12] Between 1800 and 1950, the number of people living in cities of 5,000 or more was multiplied by twenty-five, and the population in cities of 100,000 grew twentyfold, whereas the total world population did not even triple. By 1950, a larger percentage of the world's people (and, of course, a far larger number of people) lived in cities having 1 million or more inhabitants than lived in places of 5,000 or more in 1800. Comparison of the mid-twentieth century with 1700 or 1600 would yield even more striking contrasts, but data are not sufficiently accurate for periods before 1800 to permit reliable quantitative comparison on a world basis.

[12] Kingsley Davis and Hilda Hertz, "The World Distribution of Urbanization," *Bulletin of the International Statistical Institute*, 37 (1954), 227–43.

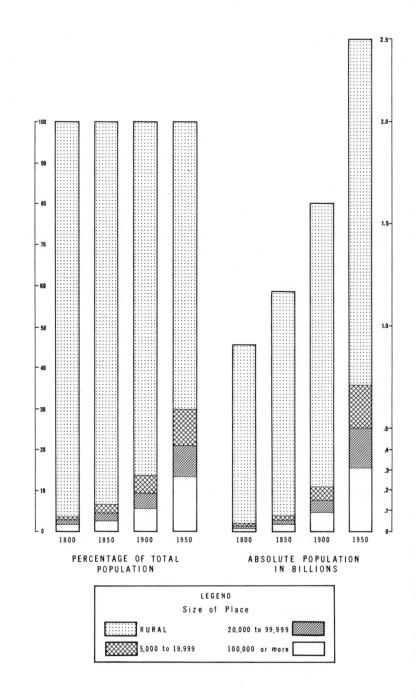

PERCENTAGE OF TOTAL
POPULATION

ABSOLUTE POPULATION
IN BILLIONS

LEGEND
Size of Place

RURAL

5,000 to 19,999

20,000 to 99,999

100,000 or more

○ Continental Variations

Although both small and great cities exist on all continents, the global distribution of urbanization is quite uneven. Nearly all cities lie in temperate zones; tropical cities are rare, and Arctic cities are virtually nonexistent. Europe, Anglo America, and Oceania are proportionately much more urban than are Asia and Africa, although Asia is so huge (larger in population than the other five continents combined) that it contains the largest share (one-third) of the world's urban inhabitants.

Asian urban-rural life is marked by sharp distinctions: Multitudinous rural villages contrast with a few huge metropolises, there being relatively few small-to-middling cities. In India, growth of the several largest centers was encouraged by the administrative and commercial activities of the English, followed after independence by nationalistic industrial efforts, with the effect that the fastest city growth in recent decades has been attributable principally to enlargement of factories. On the other hand, the rate of growth of small towns has declined slightly, thereby magnifying the disparities between large and small communities. A countryside full of peasants and a few giant cities are also characteristic of mainland China. Except in Israel and Japan, the peoples of Asia are predominantly peasants.

African urbanization is a new phenomenon, except for several cultures in West Africa where cities existed long before the arrival of European colonists. Pre-European West African cities generally were centers either of political and military authority or of trade and commerce. Industrialization played a negligible part in their growth until recent years. Differences between the indigenous and the intrusive cultures in Africa helped to generate a rural-versus-urban gap greater than on any other continent. When indigenous people do move to the cities in search of higher wages, they are generally segregated in peripheral locations characterized by much lower living levels than

FIGURE 2. Growth of World Urban and Rural Population: 1800–1950

Data from Kingsley Davis and Hilda Hertz, "The World Distribution of Urbanization," *Bulletin of the International Statistical Institute*, 37 (1954), 227–43.

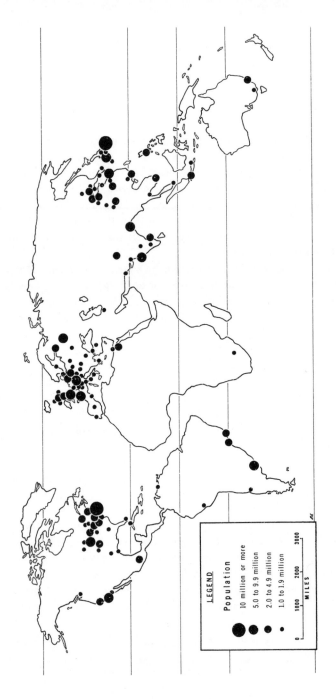

LEGEND

Population

10 million or more
5.0 to 9.9 million
2.0 to 4.9 million
1.0 to 1.9 million

MILES

0   1000   2000   3000

those of Europeans. The percentage of the African population living in cities of 20,000 or more in 1965 was the least of any continent: 9 per cent.

Latin America is intermediate in degree of urbanization. The urban centers established by the Mayans, Aztecs, and Incas were supplemented by those of the Spanish and Portuguese conquerors. Cities flourished as foci of wealth and power, dominated by administrative leaders and landowners and peopled largely by artisans, laborers, and a paltry middle class. Until recently the prevailing social and urban-rural structure consisted of an elite class and one large city, a large rural peasantry, and very few medium-sized cities or middle-class people; in other words, Latin America has a tradition of extremes in urbanization accompanied by similar extremes in social stratification. The population of most Latin American countries remains preponderantly rural—a condition that may be reversed within a few years as increasing quantities of people migrate to cities, alleviating problems of land hunger but grossly enlarging the impoverished and sometimes repulsive shantytowns that surround many of the cities.

Degree of urbanization is not related to population density; in fact, the rank-order correlation between over-all density and per cent urban for the six continents is -0.14. Some countries, like India, have high national densities and relatively little urbanization, and others, like Argentina, are highly urban but have low over-all density. Sparsely populated Australia has more than half its population living in cities.

The United States is among the most urban countries, having grown from 5 per cent urban in 1790 to 70 per cent in 1960. American urbanization continues unabated; during the decade 1950–1960, the rural population declined in number as well as percentage for the first time in the nation's history.

By 1960 two metropolitan areas had exceeded 10 million people (see Figure 3): New York, with 14 million, and Tokyo, with 11 mil-

FIGURE 3. Metropolitan Areas of 1 Million or More Residents in 1960

Data from Homer Hoyt, *World Urbanization*, Urban Land Institute Technical Bulletin No. 43 (Washington, D.C.: 1962), pp. 39–41; United Nations, *Demographic Yearbook* (1960), pp. 285–348, (1962), pp. 316–78, (1964), pp. 169–89; Morris B. Ullman, "Cities of Mainland China," *Current Population Reports*, Series P–95, No. 59, (August 1961); and International Urban Research, *The World's Metropolitan Areas* (Berkeley: University of California Press, 1959). The map is a homolosine equal-area projection, with oceans interrupted to minimize distortion of land areas.

lion. Metropolitan areas between 5 and 8 million were London, Moscow, Shanghai, Chicago, Los Angeles, Paris, Osaka, Buenos Aires, Calcutta, Bombay, and Essen (lack of comparability of international definitions prohibits a high degree of confidence in this rank order). As far as we can tell, a total of 111 cities attained populations of 1 million or more, of which 23 were in the United States, 15 in China, 8 in West Germany, 7 in India, 6 in the United Kingdom, and 5 in Japan. Every continent had at least two of these "million" or "millionaire" metropolises, as they are sometimes called. Figure 3 shows the manner in which these urban agglomerations are distributed throughout the world.

Such raw statistics must not be taken at face value in making international comparisons—or intranational contrasts either. Size is not necessarily correlated with importance to the same degree or in the same manner in all parts of the world. A city of 250,000 in eastern United States or western Europe may have relatively less to do with determining or reflecting the lives of the persons in that country than might a city of only 50,000 in many parts of Africa or Asia, where metropolitan centers occur less frequently. In some regions, a city of 200,000 population is a national dominant containing the capital and the financial and cultural centers for a large area. On the other hand, the 190,000 residents of Yonkers and the 344,000 of Long Beach are so lacking in dominance and independence as to be officially classified as only parts of the New York City and Los Angeles metropolitan areas, respectively. Geographic, economic, and social contexts—particularly the area, density, and use of the surrounding territory—affect the roles played by cities differently in different areas of the world.

chapter 4

WAYS OF LIFE IN CITIES

RELATED TO THE QUESTION "AT WHAT POINT IS A CLUSTER OF PEOPLE entitled to be called a city?" is the exploration of characteristic differences between urban dwellers and their rural counterparts. And related to the delineation of the historical growth and distribution of cities around the world are the questions of whether cities should, after all, exist—and what, if anything, they contribute to man's happiness or well-being. Not only the fact but also the legitimacy of man's increasing flocking to cities has provoked both calm analysis and fevered expostulation in many places and times.

○ *Attitudes Toward Cities*

For centuries men have considered agriculture the natural way of life; urban life has been regarded as unnatural and therefore inferior or even sinful. The Old Testament denigrated cities as places of depravity and evil, of luxury and wealth; in a religion especially suited for the downtrodden masses, these characteristics were clearly undesirable. According to Genesis (4:17), the first city was built by the villain Cain, and, when Noah's descendants built a city and a tower called Babel, "the Lord scattered them abroad from thence upon the face of all the earth; and they left off to build the city." (Genesis, 11:8) But cities are no more abnormal than agriculture, which has prevailed for only about 12,000 of man's vaguely 500,000 years of existence. The reasoning of the antiurbanites leads to the conclusion that every mode of existence is abnormal except extremely primitive life. "All civilization is 'unnatural'; to be purely 'natural' we must perch nude in trees." [1] What perturbs these people is that urbanites lose certain traditional moral values to which men have clung for lifetimes. The city has given rise to technological and moral change for many centuries; as most of us are hidebound in our resistance to change, we resent the innovations that force us to think and adapt to new ideas and values.

The religious and secular literature of ancient Persia, India, China, Japan, Greece, and Rome contains numerous attacks on urban occupations as unwholesome and mendacious. Sodom and Gomorrah were destroyed by "brimstone and fire from the Lord" (Genesis, 19:24), and Isaiah called the wrath of God on Babylon, which he blamed for the sins of mankind. Ibn Khaldoun, Machiavelli, Rousseau, and Thoreau complained of the city as a breeder of decay, vice, disorder, and social ills. Thomas Jefferson distrusted men who did not till the soil and, according to Arthur M. Schlesinger, "perceived good even in the yellow-fever epidemic as a means of discouraging the growth of great cities." [2] Oswald Spengler felt that rural life holds the key to basic human values; uncompromisingly hammering on the kettledrums of doom, he proclaimed that the megalopolis will inevitably be destroyed by its sins, carrying civilization down with it: "The birth of the city entails its death." [3]

Other writers have contented themselves with lauding rural life without deriding cities. Daniel Webster reminded us: "Never forget that the cultivation of the earth is the most important labor of man.

---

[1] Frank L. Lucas, "The Greatest Problem of To-day," *The Greatest Problem and Other Essays* (London: Cassell, 1960), p. 327.

[2] Arthur M. Schlesinger, "The City in American History," *Mississippi Valley Historical Review*, 27 (June 1940), 43–66.

[3] Oswald Spengler, *The Decline of the West*, II (New York: Knopf, 1924), 102.

When tillage begins, other arts follow. The farmers, therefore, are the founders of civilizations." Lewis Mumford campaigns against uncontrolled city growth, calling for cities that permit their residents to enjoy the beneficial effects of open stretches of grass and trees: "The home, the garden, the park, must be planned for lovers and for lovemaking: that is an essential aspect of an environment designed for human growth. Love-making and home-making, eroticism and domesticity, sexual delight and the assiduous nurture of children—these are among the highest human goals of genuine biotechnic planning." [4] In Mumford's view, we should try to keep the more appealing rural benefits, even though committed to increasing the number and size of cities.

From Mumford's learned tolerance, it is but a step—though a large one—to extolling cities. Thomas Aquinas called cities the natural state of man (an exceptional attitude in his day) and said that peasants live in the country for reasons of ignorance and incompetence. H. L. Mencken acclaimed New York as "the icing on the pie called civilization." That the Latin root *civis* ("citizen") is shared with the words "civility" and "civilization" suggests reference to the heights of man's achievement in cities as opposed to the uncouth and barbaric rural ways. Intellectual thought, art, and technology are said to rise to their loftiest pinnacles in cities, though not without retribution in the form of crowded slums and a cheapening of human life. Such writers evidently have never seen rural slums, some of which can equal those of any metropolis in poverty and misery. According to William Munro, man's triumph over environmental adversity as well as his understanding of his own nature are fostered maximally in the city: "In all ages and areas, from ancient Egypt to modern America, the highest development of human mentality, initiative, and achievement has been in urban communities." [5] Samuel Johnson provides the ultimate although slightly ambiguous compliment: "When a man is tired of London, he is tired of life; for there is in London all that life can afford." [6]

This conflict of values can be seen in a single source: Describing the attitudes of American intellectuals, Morton and Lucia White write

[4] Lewis Mumford, *The Culture of Cities* (New York: Harcourt, 1938), p. 433.
[5] William B. Munro, "City," *Encyclopaedia of the Social Sciences*, III (New York: Macmillan, 1930), 474.
[6] James Boswell, *Life of Johnson* (London: Oxford, 1953), p. 859.

with engaging ambiguity of cities as "too big, too noisy, too dusky, too dirty, too smelly, too commercial, too crowded, too full of immigrants, too full of Jews, too full of Irishmen, Italians, Poles, too industrial, too pushing, too mobile, too fast . . . too greedy, too capitalistic, too full of automobiles . . . too heartless, too intellectual, too scientific." [7] Perhaps one should adapt the French saying *Comprendre c'est pardonner* ("To understand [the city] is to forgive [its excesses]"). An extended version would be "To understand the multiphasic complexity called a city and the heterogeneity and polyglot character of city dwellers is to appreciate the vitality and excitement offered therein." Whether cities have more lovers or enemies is moot —and rather academic, for, whether we like them or not, cities have been around a long time and seem destined to remain. "The history of man can be written in large part as the history of cities and city life." [8]

○ *Rural-Urban Comparisons*

Considering the urbanization of almost one-third of the world's people, urban-rural distinctions around the world ought to be examined. Of course, lumping together all rural persons in their infinite variety in order to make comparisons with urbanites, who also constitute a far from homogeneous classification, results in omission of much detail and runs the risk of undue oversimplification. Another qualification of the following urban-versus-rural observations is that —as is the case for most social behavior of any type—persons as well as places form a continuum rather than a dichotomy, but a dichotomy must be assumed if the discussion is to be kept brief and clear.

To begin with the obvious, rural occupations are primarily agricultural, and urban employment tends to be industrial, commercial, or service. Let us use the United States as an example, remembering its

[7] Morton White and Lucia White, *The Intellectual Versus the City* (Cambridge, Mass.: Harvard University Press, 1962), p. 222.

[8] Paul K. Hatt and Albert J. Reiss, Jr., "The History of Urban Settlement," in Hatt and Reiss (eds.), *Cities and Society* (New York: Free Press, 1957), p. 175.

definition of a city as a community with 2,500 or more residents. In 1950, 71 per cent of rural employed persons in the United States worked in agriculture, as opposed to 1 per cent of the urban workers; 29 per cent of urban workers were employed in manufacturing, 26 per cent in trade and finance, and 25 per cent in services. The corresponding figures for rural residents were 9 per cent, 5 per cent, and 6 per cent. City dwellers generally work with people and man-made objects, whereas rural workers deal more directly with nature. And of course urban occupations are far more varied.

Another difference lies in the frequent independence of the urbanite from weather. Some New York residents hardly see the sun all winter except on weekends. They descend into the subway cavern before daylight, traverse underground passages connecting the subway with their places of employment, work in windowless air-conditioned buildings, climb back into the subway, and emerge after sunset. When the fierce snowstorm of 1947 struck the city, many New Yorkers could not believe that their lives would be affected; they had never known the transportation system to be disrupted by adverse weather conditions and were shocked to learn that it was possible.

Social interaction is greater in the city. Groups are more numerous, complex, and occasionally exotic. People come into contact with many more persons every day than they would on a farm. Urban contacts have a higher proportion of secondary or impersonal relationships in comparison with the generally primary or first-name, face-to-face relations of the farmer. A metropolitan resident may buy a paper every evening for twenty years at the same newsstand yet not know the vendor's name or such a simple fact as whether or not he is married; here is a secondary relation indeed. The city is a place of social and ethnic heterogeneity; inhabitants of big cities think nothing of hearing a strange language spoken on the next seat in a bus.

Personality differences seem to persist. City residents often appear to rural persons to be more impersonal, less sympathetic, more individualistic (and yet more subservient to time schedules and rules of behavior), more sophisticated, less religious, more tolerant of deviant behavior, freer to arrange their own lives, and more dependent on other persons—their services or products, that is, not their personalities. Rural and small-town residents sightseeing in big cities sometimes feel affronted by what they regard as insulting avoidance, when in fact the inhabitants are merely following their usual abstention from verbal contact with other persons. Urban dwellers can simulate aloneness even when closely pressed against other bus or subway riders, a degree of aloofness inconceivable to many residents of sparsely settled areas.

The interdependence of urban functions is an important fact of life that has far-reaching consequences for many spheres of activity. For example, a strike affecting a city's transportation system or newspapers can be crippling, partly because time and information are especially important in governing urban activities of all kinds. In fact, the viability of a city demands facile communication. Personal and other services that farmers or their families perform for themselves are contracted and paid for in urban shoe-shine parlors, lunch counters, laundries, and similar emporiums less frequented or nonexistent in villages and hamlets.

These attributes of urbanites add up to a colorful, richly complex, rapidly changing environment—a lively and fascinating yet tension-packed setting that has in recent years shown its ability to explode into active violence. The juxtaposition of luxury apartments and turgid slums from which there seems to be no escape provides the underprivileged poor with frequent reminders that the facts of life for successful stockbrokers are vastly different from those for permanent shipping clerks. And when such distinctions in living conditions are explained as consequences of racial discrimination, the fire of discontent burns brightly, encouraging such responses as the summer riots of 1967 and outspoken threats of more violence to come. Not only does it *seem* more peaceful on the farm; it actually *is*.

The traditional urban stereotype of the farmer as dull, plodding, inarticulate, frugal, stolid, innocent, and, in short, a "hick" is well known. The classic rural stereotype of the city slicker is also familiar: a smoothly dressed, fast-talking, opportunistic salesman of dubious products. Some of the more extreme images of the metropolis held by village residents in upstate New York were reported by Arthur J. Vidich and Joseph Bensman:

1. Cities breed corruption and have grown so big and impersonal that they are not able to solve the problems they create.
2. Cities are an unwholesome environment for children and families, and have had an unhealthy effect on family morals.

3. Urban politicians and labor leaders are corrupt and represent anti-democratic forces in American life.
4. Washington is a place overridden with bureaucrats and the sharp-deal, fast-buck operator, both of whom live like parasites off hard-working country folk.
5. Industrial workers are highly paid for doing little work. Their leaders foment trouble and work against the good of the country.
6. Cities are hotbeds of un-American sentiment, harbor the reds and are incapable of educating their youth to Christian values.
7. Big universities and city churches are centers of atheism and secularism and in spite of occasional exceptions have lost touch with the spiritual lesson taught by rural life.
8. Most of the problems of country life have their origins in the effects which urban life has on rural ways.[9]

Yet there are many similarities between rural and urban life styles, as peasant-agricultural societies are changing with industrialization. The traditionally great sociological difference between Manhattan, New York, and Manhattan, Kansas, is now diminishing rapidly, as unsophisticated villagers become urbanites by proxy through the expedients of modern communications and transportation. The gulf between city and country is far smaller in industrial countries than in underdeveloped nations.

Cities situated in underdeveloped areas with low levels of living are now going through the same type of urban transition as European cities did 200 years ago, experiencing unsanitary conditions, overcrowded housing, and so forth. Only recently have Western cities matched the life expectancy of the countryside; Oriental cities have not yet done so.

In modern countries, rural-urban differences are declining rapidly and threaten to vanish. The Mountain Williams of today regularly outsmart the city slickers. American farmers read urban newspapers and magazines, watch city-produced television shows and listen to urban radio stations, drive to the city to shop and to go to the movies, visit urban dentists and physicians, and buy factory-made shoes and blue jeans rather than making their own. Ohio farmers who in 1947

[9] Arthur J. Vidich and Joseph Bensman, *Small Town in Mass Society* (Garden City, N.Y.: Doubleday, 1958), p. 33.

did not know that there was such a thing as a professional actor outside the movies could discuss in 1967 who was appearing on Broadway, thanks to having seen a bit of the play on the Ed Sullivan Show.
Not only are overt behavior and knowledge changing, but attitudes
and values also are oriented increasingly toward urban themes—a
syndrome decried by traditionalists who fear the moral consequences
when the *Playboy* philosophy succeeds the plowboy philosophy as a
national social ethic. In sum, much of the world is gradually becoming urban in its behavior and beliefs, and in many countries, such as
the United States, farmers are in many respects more urban than
rural.

But there are rural survivals in this urban nexus. "Early to bed and
early to rise make a man healthy, wealthy, and wise." For a farmer,
certainly—but for an urbanite, not necessarily. Still, a large number
of urban people cling to the old belief that there is little restorative
value in the hours of sleep after dawn, and politicians often make a
point of presenting a public image of rising early. But why are eight
hours of work beginning at 8:00 A.M. better than eight hours of work
beginning at noon or 3:00 P.M.? Novelists wanting to portray an
upright character have traditionally made him an early riser; the villain or idler is easy to identify—he is still in bed at 10:00 A.M.

Clothing and neatness are also influenced by survivals. Franklin D.
Roosevelt redeemed his manhood lost in effete city living by wearing
"an incredibly battered and decrepit object which can only be described as a candidate's campaign hat." [10] His opponent Wendell
Willkie, unable to top the Roosevelt hat, devised a counterstroke: He
campaigned entirely hatless and with unruly crumpled hair—here was
a manly man indeed! Thomas E. Dewey, stigmatized as a city man,
had his hair rumpled accidentally one day while climbing the steps to
the speaker's platform. When asked by a supporter why he stopped to
comb it instead of leaving it disarranged, he replied that the voters
considered him a city slicker who never had rumpled hair and would
think that he had mussed it deliberately. This contrast was destroyed
in the late 1960s by the urban hippies, who have become famous for
the intentional disorder of their hair and the stylized disarray of their
clothing.

Wise politicians frequently deprecate urban values in favor of rural

[10] Adolph S. Tomars, "Rural Survivals in American Urban Life," *Rural Sociology*, 8 (December 1943), 378–86.

ones, and royalty and presidents do well to show some competence in farming. American presidential candidates try to identify themselves with farms, or at least small towns. In 1952 and 1956, Dwight Eisenhower and even the witty, urbane Adlai Stevenson made ostentatious trips to hamlets to give campaign speeches, visit their "folks," and remove the stigma of the big city. In the 1964 election, both Johnson and Goldwater played up their rural connections. During the 1940s anti-New Deal cartoonists caricatured Roosevelt as a mawkish figure using a cigarette holder; as Tomars pointed out, the more anti-Roosevelt the paper, the longer the holder. And in the 1953 Army-McCarthy hearings, elected public officials stressed repeatedly their unfamiliarity with a posh eating house that figured in the testimony.

○ Urban Social Stratification

Certain politicians and posh restaurants are often viewed not only as urban but also as "upper class." Although social stratification marks all communities, it is generally fragmented into more levels in urban areas. Cities have more social classes than farm districts have, although the differences between the upper and lower extremes are not necessarily greater. The stratification system is probably less rigid in cities, however, for there both upward and downward mobility are easier. As a consequence, many people move to cities, or to other sections of their city, to facilitate satisfying their status aspirations.

Except for Negroes and the far less visible old-line aristocracy, the United States has an open class system—movement from one rank to another is not difficult and in fact happens frequently. This system grew out of the stratification structure of the European nations from which most Americans are derived. While the states were still colonies, immigrants brought the Old World class structure with them, particularly the semiclosed system that existed in England. At first, under the prevailing rural conditions, Americans maintained a small aristocracy and a numerous lower class. But, as elsewhere, the rise of cities was accompanied by an enlargement of the middle class.

In the last few decades, sociologists have conducted studies of social class in dozens of American cities, the best known being W. Lloyd

Warner's research in Newburyport, Massachusetts.[11] Warner and his associates collected extensive data on the 17,000 residents of what they chose to call "Yankee City" and grouped them into six hierarchical classes. The elite or "upper-upper" class is a very small group of native-born, Harvard-educated, Episcopalian, hereditary aristocrats. In class two, the new aristocracy or "lower-upper," the same propensities exist but in lesser degree and without being hereditary; for the exceptionally successful person, it is possible to climb into the lower-upper in one generation. Class three, the "upper-middle" or professional group, is the most intellectual set, but its members' slight eminence is relatively recent and generally based on a combination of educational and occupational achievement. The fourth class, "lower-middle," consists of a large group of white-collar employees and skilled workers; they are the backbone of the fraternal orders and the community in general. The "upper-lower" or fifth class comprises self-respecting, reliable factory workers with little education, few social skills, and more than a little economic insecurity. Finally, the "lower-lower" class contains the unskilled laborers, the jobless, and the slum dwellers; here economic and familial security are low, and many are members of ill-regarded ethnic groups. The two upper classes are very small, and the two lower classes make up the majority of the population. Although the Yankee City study has been criticized extensively, the six-step outline of the class structure is not greatly dissimilar from the typologies used in other studies of social classes—except that in most cities there is no upper-upper class, and a few also lack a lower-upper class.

More recent stratification studies tend to report fewer classes, a common grouping consisting of upper, middle, working, and lower classes. Upper-class persons are the social leaders of the community, the middle class consists of white-collar workers, the working class is the skilled and semiskilled backbone of the city, and the lower class is made up of manual and uneducated laborers. Dependent wives and children are classified perforce in the same category as are the family wage earners, in accordance with the increasing tendency to equate social status with occupational level. In many cities the status hierarchy is divided into two separate parts, one white and one nonwhite, each having its own set of classes. Given the ultimate stratification cri-

11 W. Lloyd Warner and Paul S. Lunt, *Social Life of a Modern Community*, Yankee City Series, Vol. I (New Haven: Yale University Press, 1941).

terion of acceptability of a spouse for one's daughter, it is noteworthy that upper-class Negro parents have been known to frown upon marrage of their daughters to working-class white men.

Contrary to popular belief, the best indicator of social class is not simply money. Rather, it is a combination of the type of occupation (the usual rank order is: proprietary, professional, managerial, sales, clerical, skilled blue-collar, manual, and service) and the amount and kind of education (highest rank is accorded to liberal-arts graduates of Ivy League and related colleges, moderately high status to alumni of state universities or those holding technical degrees, medium status to high-school graduates, and lowest status to persons with only elementary or trade-school training). The amount of income is not only less important than occupation, education, and family and ethnic heritage but is also qualified by its source (status order is: inherited investments, earned profits, salary or fees, hourly or piece-work wages, gambling or other disreputable activities, and public assistance). This disparity between income and status—and also the related characteristic, power—is illustrated by the millionaire garbage collector in the movie *Born Yesterday*, who was certainly rich and who was able to dictate policy to a few congressmen, but whose poor English and manners made him too much of a boor to be acceptable socially in the homes of men he claimed he could "buy and sell."

Location of residence, which is both a determinant and a consequence of social class, is the manifestation of prestige most pertinent to urban ecology. Studies of stratification normally include the area in which one lives as an indicator; in Yankee City, seven ecological categories were identified and assigned points in status rating:[12]

1. the residential area of highest repute in the community;
2. better suburban and apartment-house areas, homes with large grounds;
3. preferred residential areas with adequate grounds, good apartment buildings;
4. residential neighborhoods with no deterioration, reputed to be average;
5. areas beginning to deteriorate, into which business or industry is entering;

[12] Warner, *Social Class in America* (New York: Harper, 1960), pp. 123, 153–4.

6. areas considerably deteriorated but not slums, depreciated reputation;
7. slum areas, neighborhood in bad repute.

If the origin of the middle class lies in the origin of the city, it is also true that continuing urbanization is resulting in a great increase in the number of middle-class people and concomitant adherence to middle-class values. The term "middle-class morality" has come into use to denote unremitting, ostentatious striving to comply with the standards set by one's middle-class peers—and, that unavailing, an almost equally ostentatious hypocrisy. Unlike the upper and lower classes, middle-class persons gain most of their status through the evaluation of their fellows—a circumstance conducive to maximization of conformist behavior. When this conformist impulse is superimposed on a prevailing neo-Calvinism, as is often the case in the United States, the result is a persistent stress on self-improvement and industry; in this view, man is placed on earth to fulfill obligations, not to enjoy himself. In its purest form, then, the middle class has its moral code, and the upper and lower classes have their fun.

○ *Kinds of Cities*

Differences among urbanities imply differences among cities, and one of the simplest ways to grasp variations in the characters of cities and their inhabitants is through assortment into types. Urban places may be classified according to size, shape, street pattern, density, land use, dependence, and function. These properties of cities and their parts are always fundamental, generally objective, and sometimes so obvious as to be overlooked—as in the case of population size, a variable that powerfully affects the range of activities in the city (small towns are incapable of having as much variation as big cities can have), the manner and degree of social control, and the variety of social behavior.

Silhouettes of cities vary from circular or rectangular shapes set off by old protective walls, to attenuated ribbons along a river or mountainside, and to octopus-shaped outlines with tentacles of road stretching out from the center. Urban outlines are affected by many forces, both natural (ocean or lake shores or irregular topographic contours) and man-made (highways, railroads, large building complexes), and, of course, time (an ancient walled city may have been engulfed by a larger medieval walled city, which in turn was enveloped within a modern city of indefinite boundary).

Streets may wander irregularly, radiate from a center like the spokes of a wheel, parallel and intersect one another in right-angle plats, ring the city in a series of concentric inner and outer belts, follow an elaborate curving layout, or combine two or more of these themes. Such internal patterns may or may not be adapted to conditions of the site. The practical utility of the gridiron plan is so apparent that many cities have been laid out in this repetitious street design, for, as a city grows, it is necessary only to add a few more rectangles on one edge or another. Nearly all of Manhattan is covered by such a grid, and the gridiron reached a ridiculous climax in San Francisco, where unimaginative insistence on right-angle intersections and straight-line roads on the city's graceful hills created inharmonious and needlessly steep thoroughfares.

Density of habitation varies from semirural scatterings of single-family houses on acre lots to closely spaced detached homes and row houses, two- and three-family converted dwellings, garden-type apartments, multifamily high-rise apartment buildings, and congested tenements with little light, air, or privacy. Social problems as well as benefits are affected by variations in density from section to section and from city to city, as has been demonstrated on numerous occasions since the abortive construction of mankind's first "high-rise" building—the Tower of Babel.

Land use is classified into four broad categories—residential, commercial, industrial, and public—and many subcategories. Residential uses range from single-family (at various densities) to multifamily units. Commercial uses may be retail, wholesale, office, financial, or service. Manufacturing may be light or heavy, inconspicuous or obnoxious, large or small. In the public and semipublic category are streets and parking lots, transportation facilities, government buildings, parks, churches, and educational institutions. Among the main purposes and problems of city governments is how and to what end to direct these specialized activities so that the city can function and evolve most efficiently, economically, and comfortably.

Regarding independence, scholars distinguish four major types: independent cities, central cities, satellite cities, and suburbs. The independent city is isolated and more or less sufficient unto itself; it is not a part of a metropolitan complex. A central city is the principal city in a metropolitan cluster. A satellite can stand partly on its own feet but remains under the influence of a metropolitan center; overshadowed by its big brother, it nonetheless has enough industrial or commercial establishments to provide employment for most of its residents and some from neighboring suburbs. Most suburbs are essentially dormitories; they are generally small and within commuting distance of the central city. Examples of these four types may be seen in Massachusetts (Fall River, Boston, Cambridge, and Brookline), New York (Canton, New York City, Yonkers, and Hastings-on-Hudson), Illinois (Rockford, Chicago, Evanston, and Kenilworth), and Arizona (Winslow, Phoenix, Tempe, and Scottsdale).

○ *Functional Types*

Several economists and geographers have formulated functional typologies, notably Grace M. Kneedler[13] and Chauncy D. Harris[14] for American cities and Marcel Aurousseau[15] for European cities. These typologies, however, are based largely on the proportion of persons in each occupational category, an overstress on a single variable that sociologists tend to find objectionable. Instead, the composite classification by sociologist E. E. Bergel, from which the following outline is freely derived, supplies a more widely based portrayal of the role each city plays in the activities of the nation.[16] Like other functional typologies, this outline is intended to identify the basic force pervading each city: its reason for existence, the one activity that, more than any

[13] Grace M. Kneedler, "Functional Types of Cities," *Public Management*, 27 (July 1945), 197–203.

[14] Chauncy D. Harris, "A Functional Classification of Cities in the United States," *Geographical Review*, 33 (January 1943), 86–99.

[15] Marcel Aurousseau, "The Distribution of Population: A Constructive Problem," *Geographical Review*, 11 (October 1921), 563–92.

[16] Egon Ernest Bergel, *Urban Sociology* (New York: McGraw-Hill, 1955), pp. 150–2.

other, makes the city tick and differentiates it from other urban communities. What urban function underlies the spirit of each cluster of people? What flavor is given to people's lives as a result of living in a particular community? What does most to form the personality of the city? What generates the city's metabolism and weaves its texture? Rigidly exclusive categories are not necessary for such a typology; in fact, they are minor hindrances. Consequently, the following types contain overlapping classes.

I. Economic
  A. Extractive
    1. Fishing (Gloucester, Mass.)
    2. Mining (Butte, Mont.)
    3. Oil (Tulsa)
    4. Farming (numerous small towns)
  B. Manufacturing
    1. Large-scale industry (Bethlehem, Pa.)
    2. Medium-scale industry (Milwaukee)
    3. Small industry (New Bedford, Mass.)
  C. Trade
    1. World (New York, London, Tokyo, Amsterdam)
    2. National (Brussels, Stockholm)
    3. Regional (Chicago, Caen, Liverpool)
    4. Local (most small towns)
  D. Transportation
    1. Ports (San Francisco, Marseilles, Southampton, Bremen)
    2. Inland cities (St. Louis, Kansas City)
    3. Vehicle manufacture (Detroit, Wolfsburg, Coventry)
  E. Service
    1. Financial (Salt Lake City)
    2. Insurance (Hartford)
    3. Advertising (New York)
    4. Storage and distribution (most cities)
II. Political
  A. Civil
    1. World (New York, Geneva, London, Paris)
    2. National (Washington, Moscow, Ottawa, Canberra)
    3. Regional (Chicago, Toronto, Quebec)
    4. Local (Jefferson City, Mo.; Augusta, Me.)

B. Military
1. Fortresses (Gibraltar, Singapore)
2. Bases and training centers (Brest, Toulon, San Diego, Norfolk)

III. Religious
A. Authority and leadership (Salt Lake City, all bishoprics)
B. Pilgrimage (Lourdes, Mecca, Benares)
C. Symbols (Jerusalem, Bethlehem)

IV. Educational
A. Higher learning or research (Oxford, Princeton, Ann Arbor, Amherst)
B. Communications media (London, Tokyo, New York, Los Angeles)
C. Museums (Rome, Florence)
D. Historic shrines (Stratford-on-Avon, Athens, Boston, Philadelphia)

V. Entertainment
A. Summer recreation (Nice, Monte Carlo)
B. Winter recreation (Colorado Springs, Sun Valley)
C. Showplaces (Venice, Williamsburg, Virginia City)

VI. Health
A. Medical care (Rochester, Minn.)
B. Convalescence resorts (Vichy, Atlantic City)

VII. Residential
A. Dormitory suburbs (Scarscale, N.Y.; Montclair, N.J.; Beverly Hills, Calif.)
B. Retirement cities (St. Petersburg, Fla.; a number of California and Arizona towns)

The almost inevitable return of this classification scheme to the defining properties that opened Chapter 3 is a reminder both of the diversity within and between cities and of their tendency to grow into the metropolitan complexes discussed in the following chapter. And the more complicated they are, the more excitement is generated.

◯ *Exotic Diversity and Personal Freedom*

To a real city man, any place having fewer than half a million residents is suspected of being a hick town—and if the lights go out at 11:00 and nothing is open at 3:00 A.M., his suspicions are verified. As the Broadway gambler-hero of *Guys and Dolls* (based on a short story by Damon Runyon) sang:

My time of day is the dark time, a couple of deals before dawn
When the street belongs to the cop and the janitor with the mop
And the grocery clerks are all gone;
When the smell of the rain-washed pavement comes up clean and
fresh and cold
And the street lamp light fills the gutter with gold;
That's my time of day—my time of day.[17]

Not all big-city denizens share this romantic attachment to the night; in fact, the large majority go to bed before midnight so that they can rise the next morning in time to down a cup of coffee and reach the office by 9:00. Still the opportunity is there—and some eagerly grab it. Partly this difference is a statistical one: If, for example, one-tenth of 1 per cent of the residents of any community enjoy the midnight hours, a village of 3,000 persons would have only three night owls—hardly enough for a wild party—whereas a metropolis of 3 million would have 3,000 potential revelers. The three villagers might go to sleep anyway out of boredom and lack of nocturnal inspiration, but at least a few of the 3,000 urbanites should be able to find one another or something to do; no business will remain open for three customers, but 3,000 are another matter.

As with being awake at 2:00 A.M., so with other practices. Because people with exotic tastes tend to seek the metropolis, that is where there are the most people with divergent preferences. Anyone with a fondness for some exotic avocation or occupation, whether it be atonal chamber music or Lotus grand-prix cars, is most likely to find confreres in a metropolis.

[17] "My Time of Day" by Frank Loesser. © 1950 Frank Loesser. Used by permission.

Added to this life-enriching variety is the freedom permitted to the urban dweller. Among the greatest advantages offered by the large city is the ability to change jobs without having to move one's home (and the converse), thus providing breadth of choice for workers, employers, and consumers. But even more important than this freedom is the liberty of being able to move. Ecologically and socially, freedom almost inevitably implies mobility. Rejection of proximity or propinquity as a prominent, if not the foremost, determinant of one's friendships, marital choice, and kind of work is a major achievement of modern urban civilization—a power that rural dwellers rarely ever had. Nonmobile societies offer their members little choice of activities and little knowledge of the world beyond their limited circle of movement. The intimate conjunction of freedom and mobility is exemplified in the "underground railroad" to the North used by escaping Negro slaves from the South. Slaves and peasants may be kept down in part by the shackles of immobility, for "mobility is always the weapon of the underdog." [18] If we don't like it, we can leave—and, if the oppressor knows it, he may tread more gently, for fear that his underlings may find work or life better "there" than "here." In this way, the areal dispersion and demographic magnitude of the city offer many alternative opportunities to the individual and, in consequence, a maximum freedom of choice.

[18] Harvey Cox, *The Secular City* (New York: Macmillan, 1965), p. 52.

chapter 5

METROPOLITAN REGIONS

CARRYING THE DEFINING PROPERTIES OF CITIES IN CHAPTER 3 AND
their social characteristics in Chapter 4 one step further brings us to
the metropolis, which is a city, but more so. Compared with an ordinary city, a metropolis is usually larger, denser, more powerful, taller,
less agricultural, more commercial and industrial, more parasitic,
more packed with commuters, and more varied. Difficult as defining a
city is, even more difficult is determining whether or not a given large
city is a metropolis and, if it is, where its outer limits are located.

○ *Defining and Bounding Regions*

The most obvious procedure for defining and delimiting a metropolis is to set a minimum size (such as 100,000 persons) and to accept
the official city limits. But this approach neglects the bond uniting the

central city with its commuting suburbanites who spend five days a
week working downtown, not to mention attending occasional Sunday
afternoon ball games and Saturday evening shows. This functional
unification of several contiguous legal cities often reaches the point
where they are in social (but not political) fact a single entity. Politicians, however, may recognize this unity: President Johnson's "Message to Congress" of March 2, 1965, included a footnote defining a
city as "the entire urban area—the central city and its suburbs."

A complex web of sociological and economic relationships binds
the small peripheral settlements to the center—and for that matter, it
to them, for how could the central city get along without its commuting workers and shoppers? Thus, structurally and spatially, the parent and its surrounding offspring cling together to form a single metropolitan area or region. This interdependence is manifested in many
ways. The suburbanite may subscribe to a metropolitan newspaper,
go to plays or concerts in the central city, or seek a better job in
another incorporated place in the region; in fact, whether he be a
grocery clerk, a policeman, or a realtor, the suburban resident has his
life geared to events and conditions in neighboring parts of the metropolitan community. For these reasons, the most useful sociological
definition of the metropolis includes all of these integrated subordinate and superordinate municipalities, the better to correspond to the
actual operating metropolitan milieu.[1]

With increasing urbanization and the growing tendency of people
to settle in the rural-urban fringe whether or not they commute to the
central city, the metropolitan region has become the basic functional
urban unit. The old rural-urban dichotomy has broken down; sociologists today assume an urban-rural continuum of varying degrees of
urbanization. The automobile especially has made it difficult to specify definitive rural and urban categories. But, although gradients of
urbanization surround the center of a large city, boundary lines are
still valuable for distinguishing the various zones of the continuum.

The question then arises: Which of the surrounding municipalities
are sufficiently integrated with the central city to be included as a part
of the metropolitan region? And which of them are metropolitan in
character? Because interaction of each community with the center

---

[1] Guillaume Wunsch, "Niveau et tendance de l'urbanisation: quelques prob-
lèmes de mesure," *La Revue Belge de Géographie*, 19 (1966), 75–85.

tends to diminish gradually as distance from the center increases, just how far out along this weakening gradient is the borderline of the metropolitan zone? In other words, how do we identify the marginal mile, inside of which lies the metropolis but beyond which the area is either nonmetropolitan or part of another metropolitan region? In the latter case, the ecologist must decide toward which of two or even three metropolitan centers the area is oriented—a much easier task than deciding whether or not the area is metropolitan at all.

In practice it is rarely necessary to delimit such a boundary definitively, desirable though that might be for statistical purposes. Indeed, there are so many varied uses for metropolitan regional data that ecologists often prepare maps showing several boundaries—one for each criterion—and the user may select the boundary most relevant to his subject of study. The illustration in Figure 4 is taken from a classic study of Salt Lake City and environs. Both Salt Lake City and the example in Figure 5—Mobile, Alabama—demonstrate the possible variation in boundaries. At some points the various criteria set the same bounds, sometimes they cross one another, but often they diverge considerably.

Donald Bogue has suggested that each metropolis has at least two regional limits: one delimiting daily contact and the other outlining a broader area of dependence. Indexes for areas of daily interaction are:

1. Circulation of daily newpapers.
2. Express or other special bus, train, or streetcar service at commuters' hours.
3. Number of passengers arriving inside the central city between the hours of 7:30 A.M.–9:30 A.M. from each outlying area in proportion to the total labor force of the outlying area.
4. Department store delivery areas.
5. Distribution of checking accounts in city banks and their branches.
6. Traffic surveys showing commuting distances.
7. Home addresses of workers in a few of the largest firms in the city.[2]

---

[2] Donald J. Bogue (ed.), *Needed Urban and Metropolitan Research* (Chicago: University of Chicago Population Research and Training Center, 1953), p. 17.

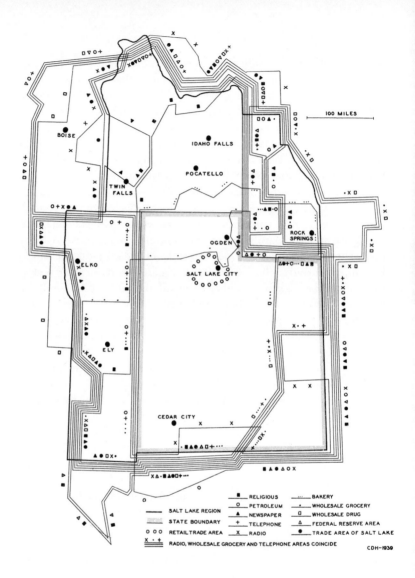

100 MILES

BOISE

IDAHO FALLS

POCATELLO

TWIN FALLS

ROCK SPRINGS

ELKO

OGDEN

SALT LAKE CITY

ELY

CEDAR CITY

■	RELIGIOUS	⋯⋯	BAKERY
O	PETROLEUM	·	WHOLESALE GROCERY
▲	NEWSPAPER	▢	WHOLESALE DRUG
+	TELEPHONE	△	FEDERAL RESERVE AREA
X	RADIO	●	TRADE AREA OF SALT LAKE

——— SALT LAKE REGION
▨▨▨ STATE BOUNDARY
O O O RETAIL TRADE AREA
≣≣≣ RADIO, WHOLESALE GROCERY AND TELEPHONE AREAS COINCIDE

CDH-1939

FIGURE 4. Tributary Areas of Salt Lake City, Utah

Reprinted by permission of Chauncy D. Harris from *Salt Lake City: A Regional Capital* (Chicago: University of Chicago Libraries, 1940), Figure 10.

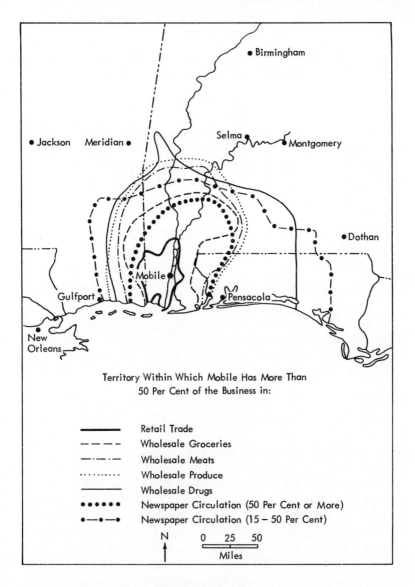

Territory Within Which Mobile Has More Than
50 Per Cent of the Business in:

—————— Retail Trade

— — — — Wholesale Groceries

—·—·— Wholesale Meats

··········· Wholesale Produce

—————— Wholesale Drugs

••••••• Newspaper Circulation (50 Per Cent or More)

•—•—• Newspaper Circulation (15 – 50 Per Cent)

N

0   25   50
Miles

FIGURE 5. Service Areas of Mobile, Alabama

Reprinted by permission of Edward L. Ullman from *Mobile: Industrial Seaport and Trade Center* (Ph.D. dissertation, University of Chicago Department of Geography, 1943), Figure 7.

A comparable set of indexes to determine if an area lies inside or outside the influence of a metropolitan region includes:

1. Centers where farmers sell truckload lots of farm produce.
2. Sunday newspaper circulation.
3. Center to which most residents travel to purchase specialized goods.
4. Ratio of department store charge accounts to population.
5. Migration of high school graduates to look for work.
6. Wholesale trade areas.
7. Farm machinery service areas.
8. Frequency of bus travel to alternate metropolitan areas.
9. Volume of long distance telephone calls to particular metropolitan areas.[3]

Other criteria used to define metropolitan areas include trucking zones, radio listening areas, livestock-supply areas, regional banking areas, milk-supply areas, and such demographic variables as fertility, age composition, and sex ratio. Perhaps the greatest emphasis has been given to newspaper circulation, which has been used by Robert E. Park, Stuart A. Queen, and Roderick D. McKenzie, among others.

○ *Standard Metropolitan Statistical Areas*

For some years the U.S. Bureau of the Census has worked with the notion of metropolitan regions. Metropolitan Districts were first reported in the 1910 census; at that time Metropolitan District data were also compiled retroactively for 1900. No previous effort had been made because the metropolitan concept was not deemed of sufficient significance in the nineteenth century. Metropolitan Districts continued to be used in revised form with each succeeding census, the number of districts rising from 44 in 1910 to 58 in 1920, 96 in 1930, and 140 in 1940, by then incorporating 48 per cent of the national population. The 1950 census altered the terminology to Standard Metropolitan Statistical Area (reflecting a revised definition), of which

[3] *Ibid.*

there were 168, and the 1960 census disclosed 212 SMSAs (Standard Metropolitan Statistical Areas). An SMSA consists of a central city (or a pair of "twin cities") of 50,000 or more residents, plus the county containing the city and those contiguous counties that are demonstrably metropolitan in character and socially and economically integrated with the central city. (Because historical events have led to the administrative unimportance of counties in New England, towns are used instead of counties.)

In 1950–1960 the SMSAs grew by 24 million people, or 87 per cent of the total national population increase, leaving only 13 per cent divided among smaller urban places, rural settlements, and isolated areas. Four areas accounted for one-fourth of this metropolitan increase, and eighteen areas contributed 51 per cent. Although net migration contributed 8 million new metropolitan residents, two-thirds of the metropolitan growth resulted from natural increase—the excess of births over deaths—thus refuting the widespread popular notion that, without migrants from rural areas, metropolises would die because of their low fertility. It is true that metropolitan birth rates are lower than rural birth rates, but in both metropolitan and rural areas the death rates are lower still. Components of population change in the eighteen areas accounting for one-half of all metropolitan increases are given in Table 1. The list is dominated by large and long-established metropolitan areas, but it also contains several that only recently emerged to prominence, in California, Texas, and Arizona.

The inconsistency of the sources of growth makes generalization hazardous: Los Angeles grew by 1.6 million from net migration and a relatively small 0.8 million by natural increase, whereas New York gained only 0.4 million from migration but 1.5 million by natural increase (even so, New York was second only to Los Angeles in volume of net migration). Some other metropolitan areas show proportionately larger divergences, although the numbers are smaller. The largest and oldest areas tend to have a large growth momentum from natural increase. In newer areas the increase is mainly attributable to their ability to attract migrants.

By 1965 almost 70 per cent of the people of the United States lived in the 219 SMSAs. About half of these metropolitanites resided in the central cities and about half in the adjoining hinterlands—proportions that are changing as the suburban peripheries grow more rapidly than the central cities. The largest SMSA, New York, had a July

TABLE 1. Components of Population Growth in Selected Metropolitan Areas: United States, 1950–1960

Metropolitan Area	Net Change, 1950–1960 (in millions)	Natural Increase, 1950–1960 (in millions)	Net Migration, 1950–1960 (in millions)	Population in 1960	Rank in 1960	Percentage Change (mid-decade population)
All areas	23.6	15.4	8.3	112,885,000	—	23.3
Los Angeles, Calif.	2.4	0.8	1.6	6,732,000	2	42.8
New York, N.Y.	1.8	1.5	0.4	10,695,000	1	13.3
Chicago, Ill.	1.2	0.9	0.3	6,221,000	3	19.5
Detroit, Mich.	0.7	0.7	0.1	3,762,000	5	22.0
Philadelphia, Pa.	0.7	0.5	0.2	4,343,000	4	16.8
San Francisco, Calif.	0.5	0.3	0.2	2,783,000	6	21.6
Washington, D.C.	0.5	0.3	0.2	2,002,000	10	31.0
San Diego, Calif.	0.5	0.2	0.3	1,033,000	23	59.9
Miami, Fla.	0.4	0.1	0.3	935,000	25	61.5

Houston, Tex.	0.4	0.2	0.2	1,243,000	16	42.5
Tampa, Fla.	0.4	0.1	0.3	772,000	31	61.4
San Bernardino, Calif.	0.4	0.1	0.3	810,000	30	56.8
San Jose, Calif.	0.4	0.1	0.3	642,000	39	75.5
St. Louis, Mo.	0.3	0.3	0.0	2,060,000	9	18.0
Dallas, Tex.	0.3	0.2	0.2	1,084,000	20	37.2
Phoenix, Ariz.	0.3	0.1	0.2	664,000	37	66.7
Cleveland, Ohio	0.3	0.2	0.1	1,797,000	11	20.3
Minneapolis, Minn.	0.3	0.2	0.1	1,482,000	14	25.1
Remaining areas	11.6	8.6	3.0	—	—	21.6

Adapted from Amos H. Hawley, Beverly Duncan, and David Goldberg, "Some Observations of Changes in Metropolitan Population in the United States," *Demography*, I (1964), 151–2; U.S. Bureau of the Census, "Number of Inhabitants: United States Summary," *U.S. Census of Population: 1960* (Washington, D.C.: Government Printing Office, 1961), p. 117.

1, 1965, population of 11 million, and twenty-eight others exceeded 1 million. Table 2 shows the estimated sizes and ranks of all SMSAs that were larger than 500,000 in 1965, beside indicating their relative growth during 1960–1965. Of the twenty-nine million-plus areas, five are centered in California and no more than two each in any other state. The most salient point is that the nation has one gigantic and two very large metropolitan areas, one in the Northeast, one in the Middle West, and one in the Far West, each serving as a focal point for many satellite communities and even whole states.

These metropolitan giants frequently extend their influence over smaller metropolitan areas in their vicinity, as New York does over Paterson, New Jersey, and Los Angeles does over Anaheim, California, thereby creating supercities (see Table 2). In the future it seems likely that New York and Los Angeles will be the giants of the nation, extending their built-up areas north and south along the ocean fronts for several hundred miles affording hardly a view of cows or corn-

TABLE 2. Population of Standard Metropolitan Statistical Areas of 500,000 or More in 1960 and 1965

STANDARD METROPOLITAN STATISTICAL AREA	POPULATION		RANK	
	July 1, 1965 (*estimate*)	*April 1, 1960* (*census*)	*1965*	*1960*
New York, N.Y.	11,348,000	10,694,633	1	1
Los Angeles–Long Beach, Calif.	6,776,000	6,038,771	2	3
Chicago, Ill.	6,636,000	6,220,913	3	2
Philadelphia, Pa.–N.J.	4,667,000	4,342,897	4	4
Detroit, Mich.	3,972,000	3,762,360	5	5
Boston, Mass.	3,199,000	3,109,158	6	6
San Francisco–Oakland, Calif.	2,935,000	2,648,762	7	7
Washington, D.C.–Md.–Va.	2,413,000	1,989,377	8	10
Pittsburgh, Pa.	2,367,000	2,405,435	9	8
St. Louis, Mo.–Ill.	2,239,000	2,104,669	10	9
Cleveland, Ohio	1,971,000	1,909,483	11	11
Baltimore, Md.	1,857,000	1,727,023	12	12
Newark, N.J.	1,827,000	1,689,420	13	13
Houston, Tex.	1,695,000	1,418,323	14	15
Minneapolis–St. Paul, Minn.	1,602,000	1,482,030	15	14
Cincinnati, Ohio–Ky.–Ind.	1,329,000	1,268,479	16	17
Buffalo, N.Y.	1,322,000	1,306,957	17	16

Dallas, Tex.	1,289,000	1,083,601	18	22
Paterson–Clifton–Passaic, N.J.	1,288,000	1,186,873	19	19
Milwaukee, Wis.	1,269,000	1,232,731	20	18
Atlanta, Ga.	1,205,000	1,017,188	21	24
Seattle–Everett, Wash.	1,187,000	1,107,213	22	20
Kansas City, Mo.–Kans.	1,179,000	1,092,545	23	21
San Diego, Calif.	1,145,000	1,033,011	24	23
Anaheim–Santa Ana–Garden Grove, Calif.	1,111,000	703,925	25	38
Denver, Colo.	1,091,000	929,383	26	26
Miami, Fla.	1,064,000	935,047	27	25
San Bernardino–Riverside– Ontario, Calif.	1,033,000	809,782	28	30
New Orleans, La.	1,026,000	907,123	29	28
Indianapolis, Ind.	986,000	916,932	30	27
Portland, Ore.–Wash.	889,000	821,897	31	29
San Jose, Calif.	887,000	642,315	32	43
Tampa–St. Petersburg, Fla.	874,000	772,453	33	31
Phoenix, Ariz.	837,000	663,510	34	41
Columbus, Ohio	828,000	754,924	35	32
San Antonio, Tex.	807,000	716,168	36	37
Rochester, N.Y.	802,000	732,588	37	33
Louisville, Ky.–Ind.	777,000	725,139	38	35
Dayton, Ohio	776,000	727,121	39	34
Hartford, Conn.	761,000	689,555	40	39
Sacramento, Calif.	742,000	625,503	41	46
Memphis, Tenn.–Ark.	741,000	674,583	42	40
Providence–Pawtucket–Warwick, R.I.	739,000	718,543	43	36
Albany–Schenectady–Troy, N.Y.	688,000	657,503	44	42
Toledo, Ohio–Mich.	647,000	630,647	45	45
Norfolk–Portsmouth, Va.	645,000	578,507	46	49
Birmingham, Ala.	644,000	634,864	47	44
Akron, Ohio	634,000	605,367	48	48
Fort Worth, Tex.	627,000	573,215	49	51
Jersey City, N.J.	611,000	610,734	50	47
Syracuse, N.Y.	597,000	563,781	51	52
Gary–Hammond–East Chicago, Ind.	594,000	573,548	52	50
Oklahoma City, Okla.	587,000	511,833	53	53
Honolulu, Hawaii	573,000	500,409	54	55
Youngstown–Warren, Ohio	511,000	509,006	55	54

From "Provisional Estimates of the Population of the Largest Metropolitan Areas: July 1 1965," *Current Population Reports*, Series P-25, No. 347 (August 31, 1966), p. 9.

fields. In this way the oft-decried problems of urban congestion, slums, and commuting inefficiency may be spread farther and farther and affect more and more people. A California citizen group even coined the word "slurb" to update the labeling of suburbs, which are now, it says, becoming "sloppy, sleazy, slovenly, slipshod semi-cities."

◯ *Central Cities and Tributaries*

For each metropolitan center there are adjacent tributary areas (see Figure 6). These economically and socially subordinate territories include semi-independent satellite cities of sometimes consider-

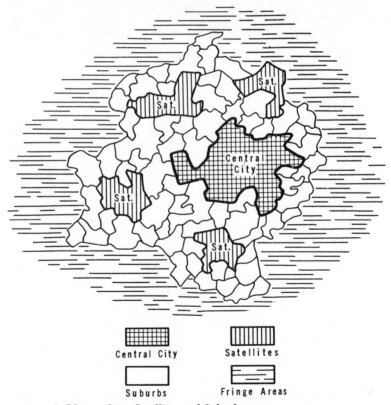

FIGURE 6. Metropolitan Satellites and Suburbs

able size, small bedroom suburbs virtually completely dependent upon the central city for income and services, and combinations of the two types, called "balanced" or "employing" suburbs. In this fashion each metropolitan area can be divided into two parts: inside and outside the central city.

The flocking to metropolitan areas characteristic of the twentieth century has not been uniformly distributed between these two parts. In the early decades both central cities and suburbs grew rapidly. The middle third of the century was marked by a relatively greater growth of suburbs—a tendency now beginning to lose its momentum. In the 1960s this established contrast between heavy population buildup in outlying areas and slow growth or even loss of population in central cities began to show signs of yielding to a more uniform rate of growth between the two metropolitan parts.

During the decade 1940–1950 population in the nation's central cities increased by 15 per cent, and the outlying areas grew 36 per cent. In 1950–1960 the corresponding percentages grew wider apart: 11 and 49. The tendency of central cities to enlarge slightly and of outer areas to increase greatly has been both decisive and persistent. Furthermore, several central cities have lost population: During the 1950s Boston lost 13 per cent, while its outer areas gained 18 per cent; Providence lost 13 per cent, and its outlying areas grew by 23 per cent; New York lost 1 per cent, as contrasted with 75 per cent growth in outer areas; Pittsburgh lost 11 per cent, as opposed to a 17 per cent gain in peripheral areas; Cleveland lost 4 per cent, as against a 67 per cent suburban growth; St. Louis decreased by 12 per cent, and its suburbs grew 52 per cent; and San Francisco declined by 4 per cent, whereas its periphery gained 55 per cent.[4]

Racial ecology is being affected. Between 1950 and 1960 the white population grew by 5 per cent in central cities, 49 per cent in the outer parts of SMSAs, and 9 per cent outside SMSAs; increases in the Negro population were 50 per cent in central cities, 31 per cent elsewhere in SMSAs, and not at all (to be precise, − 0.3 per cent) beyond SMSAs.[5] In that decade the central cities of the twelve largest

[4] U.S. Bureau of the Census, "Number of Inhabitants: United States Summary," *U.S. Census of Population: 1960* (Washington, D.C.: Government Printing Office, 1961), pp. 108–11.

[5] Irene B. Taeuber, "Population Trends in the United States, 1900 to 1960," U.S. Bureau of the Census Technical Paper No. 10 (1964), Table 2.

metropolitan areas lost a total of 2 million white residents and gained 1 million nonwhite residents. Outside the central cities the population remained more than 90 per cent white—a proportion essentially unaltered since 1930, when the percentage of white persons began to decline in the central cities. Explanation probably lies in the migration of Negroes from the rural South to metropolitan centers and in the movement of whites toward the suburbs. Soon the central cities of many major metropolitan areas (Los Angeles, for example) will acquire Negro majorities (Washington, D. C., has already done so) — and lower-class ones at that. This change may reach other cities earlier than we expect; in 1966 a majority of the school children of Chicago were Negro. "Many central cities of the great metropolitan areas of the United States are fast becoming lower class, largely Negro slums." [6]

Nationally, about nine-tenths of the total 2.9 million increase in the nonwhite population between 1960 and 1966 occurred in the central cities of SMSAs. As a result of this continued concentration of nonwhite growth in central cities, well over half the national nonwhite population in 1966 was living in central cities of metropolitan areas. In contrast, the white population of the central cities declined by 1 per cent between 1960 and 1966 and increased by 21 per cent in the outer parts of SMSAs. Continuing white suburbanization is indicated by the fact that additions to the outlying parts of SMSAs accounted for seven-eights of the national gain in the white population over the six-year period. In 1966, 27 per cent of whites lived in central cities, 37 per cent in metropolitan areas but outside central cities, and 36 per cent in nonmetropolitan locations. Corresponding nonwhite percentages were 55, 13, and 32—a notable change from the 1960 proportions of 42, 13, and 45.[7]

A crude comparison of metropolitan and nonmetropolitan populations can be made by arrangement into tiers. Around an SMSA is a first ring consisting of all contiguous counties, a second ring of counties bordering the first ring, and a final encircling area con-

[6] Morton, Grodzins, *The Metropolitan Area As a Racial Problem* (Pittsburgh: University of Pittsburgh Press, 1958), p. 1.

[7] "Population of the United States by Metropolitan and Nonmetropolitan Residence: April 1966 and 1960," *Current Population Reports*, Series P-20, No. 163 (March 27, 1967), pp. 1–2.

sisting of all remaining counties in the nation. On the average, the perimeter of the first ring is 40–50 miles from the central city and that of the second ring 60–70 miles. Table 3 shows the redistribution of population among the tiers. In 1900 more than 40 per cent of the national population was located beyond the second ring; by 1960 the proportion had been cut to less than 10 per cent. In every decade the SMSAs exhibited the fastest rate of growth, but, whereas the second fastest increase was in the residual population during the first three decades, since 1930 the first ring has been growing second fastest. Since 1940 the rank order of growth has correlated directly with degree of centrality, tier by tier outward from the metropolitan center, as the regions beyond the second tier continued their tendency to grow at a decreasing rate, thereby lagging more and more with each passing decade.

TABLE 3. Population, Growth, and Density of Metropolitan-Nonmetropolitan Tiers: United States, 1900–1960

Tier	1900	1910	1920	1930	1940	1950	1960
Population (in millions)							
SMSAs	23.9	34.5	46.1	62.1	67.9	85.6	113.1
First ring	10.6	13.9	16.9	19.9	21.7	25.3	29.3
Second ring	9.9	12.1	14.7	17.3	18.9	20.2	20.3
Remainder	31.6	31.5	28.0	23.5	23.2	19.6	15.8
Growth Rates Over Preceding Decade (percentage)							
SMSAs	—	31.4	24.6	26.8	8.1	21.2	25.2
First ring	—	15.1	8.1	8.2	6.6	12.8	17.5
Second ring	—	7.6	5.7	5.8	6.2	4.6	6.3
Remainder	—	19.3	10.8	8.9	6.3	4.2	2.4
Density (in persons per square mile)							
SMSAs	346	378	395	405	399	400	367
First ring	35	38	37	37	36	37	35
Second ring	24	24	25	26	26	25	22
Remainder	14	16	16	15	16	16	17

Adapted from Amos H. Hawley, Beverly Duncan, and David Goldberg, "Some Observations of Changes in Metropolitan Population in the United States," *Demography*, I (1964), 153–4.

These trends are encouraged by more rapid and inexpensive transportation, which has increased the accessibility of metropolitan centers to nonmetropolitan residents. In contrast to the massive redistribution of population, the intensity of land settlement within each tier has remained approximately constant throughout the century, hovering at densities of about 390, 36, 24, and 16 persons per square mile moving outward through the tiers. The nonmetropolitan densities do not differ much ring from ring, the major difference being between metropolitan and nonmetropolitan densities, the greater accessibility of the first ring to the metropolis apparently having relatively little effect on density.

○ *Suburban Living*

Within the SMSA itself, the suburbs catch much attention from commentators, both scholarly and journalistic. Suburbs also attract misunderstandings, the foremost of which is the impression that a suburb is half urban and half rural, at best combining the benefits of each in a single package and at worst offering the less pleasant attributes of either or both. But in fact a suburb does not represent an equal balance of rural and urban properties; rather, it is the result of a city overflowing into the surrounding countryside, converting a rural area into a basically urban one. A suburb is intrinsically a part of urban civilization, having few of the attributes of rural life. There are community forms that partake, by a compromise of equals, of both rural and urban social norms and organization—for example, some country towns surrounded by farms, or true garden cities (of which there are remarkably few)—but suburbs are not among them. As Harlan P. Douglass said almost half a century ago, the suburb "makes physical compromises with country ways, but few compromises of the spirit. It is the city trying to escape the consequences of being a city and still remaining a city." [8]

In order to justify calling a suburb half rural, suburban residents would have to think and act in considerable part as rural dwellers—

[8] Harlan P. Douglass, *The Suburban Trend* (New York: Century, 1925), p. 4.

which is generally far from both their desire and their capability. To paraphrase an old rural folk saying, "You can take the man out of the city, but you can't take the city out of the man"—especially when the man continues to work in the metropolitan center and his wife makes forays downtown to pillage department stores and eat at Schrafft's. Because it is the essentially urban character of suburban inhabitants that is responsible for the predominantly urban quality of suburbs, it behooves us to examine these people.

Such an examination is not a simple task. Generalization about suburbanites and suburbs is difficult because, like the metropolitan centers to which they are tied, they vary greatly one from another. Nonetheless, some common properties have been observed.

In the early years of suburb formation, suburbanites generally fitted the stereotype of young, middle-class married couples with children. Today they take on the properties of the population at large. Nuclear families are adding relatives to their households, and the classic middle-class suburbanites are being supplemented by newcomers of lower-class position (which raises the politically serious question whether and to what extent the traditionally Republican suburbs are changing toward Democratic affiliations).

The classic suburb was clearly and defiantly matriarchal and even filiarchical. Because the men were away all day earning the money to meet mortgage payments, the sidewalks of suburban tracts were dominated by women and children, to the extent that a man who answered the doorbell or stepped into the street to buy a dozen doughnuts from the bread truck was enough to arouse suspicion: Was he sick, recently fired, or a suspicious character? Psychiatrists complained that children grew up too much in the company of women, knowing men only as night visitors and weekend guests, and lamented that such sexual segregation, uniform socioeconomic level, and monotonic subculture unduly limited the experience of the growing child. The matriarchal stereotype is becoming obsolete, however, as fathers work fewer hours and often are free on certain weekdays.

Another familiar feature of early suburban life was the stress on conformity: Lawns had to be kept mowed, and people had to be kept in line. One could safely neither fall behind nor get too far ahead of the Joneses. This deifying of conformity is still caricatured by stand-up comedians; Thoreau's "different drummer" did not stand a chance. As this pervasive emphasis on conformity articulates poorly with the old American value of individualism, it is perhaps for the best that this property is weakening. It is even permissible now for a suburbanite to indulge in the conspicuous consumption about which Thorstein Veblen wrote—though one must not overdo it.

Consistent with conformist, matriarchal, and middle-class traits is another stereotype: Suburbanites go to church, especially those of the most respected Protestant denominations. But in reality the church does not fare so well. Many suburbanites do not go, and those who do are likely to shift denominations as they move, often giving their allegiance to the denomination in the new town most suited to their actual or intended social class. Church attendance may thus be based as much upon ecology and social class as upon denomination or doctrine.

Claims are made that suburban living lowers moral standards. Commuting, coupled with a shift from nonagricultural occupations, is said to have promoted the office romance and the spectacle of the suburban wife's pondering whether or not her husband is really working late at the office. This claim, like its fellows in the preceding paragraphs, is largely overstated. In fact, suburban men and women seem as subservient to received moral standards as are their downtown counterparts.

This congeries of traits, which for a time seemed on the way to becoming the dominant pattern of life in America, fascinated and still fascinates psychoanalysts and poets who, with the late T. S. Eliot, do not like to see people measure out their lives in coffee spoons. But with the maturing of suburbs has come a loss of their once distinctive properties, as they increasingly take on the qualities of the mainstream of society; indeed, as their numbers grow, they are coming almost to constitute the mainstream. Whatever the characteristics of suburban dwellers, they can no longer be attributed solely or even primarily to the fact of living in commuting tracts. The United States has now reached the point where suburbs and suburbanites are so common as to be only minimally distinguishable from other habitats and habitants.

In their efforts to find fresh air, sunshine, elbow room, and similar purported desiderata, metropolites have abandoned their high-rise cliff dwellings and migrated to ranch homes in such droves that the crowded suburbs have sometimes become cities in their own right, attracting factories and offices to their peripheral locations (with the ironic consequence that suburbanites commuting downtown each morning see residents of the central city hustling to their jobs in the suburbs). The ultimate result of this chaotic situation may well be a city without any discernible central area—a metropolitan region within which workers commute in approximately equal numbers in every direction and where housing density varies hardly at all. Perhaps one day we may even reach the point at which central-city apartments and suburban bungalows will be regarded equally as "good places to bring up children."

○ *The Rural-Urban Fringe*

Those who insist on sharing the virtues of rural life must move out beyond the suburbs to the truly half-rural, half-urban fringe of the metropolis. Some of the fringe lies inside the limits (as formally defined) of an SMSA, and some lies outside. This inconsistency of statistical treatment is caused by using counties as the basic component. Another metropolitan grouping, the urbanized area (a central city of 50,000 plus the built-up surrounding area—therefore similar to but smaller than an SMSA), is more nearly complementary to the fringe; a few sociologists define the fringe as the difference between the urbanized area and the SMSA.[9] A better basis for distinction, however, is that suburban communities are definitely urban in character whereas fringe communities are mixed. As the words imply, "suburban" means subordinately urban and a "fringe" is the border or outer edge and therefore semiurban at most. As suburbs are urban (albeit "sub" or minor), they are usually legally incorporated as cities; fringe areas, not being truly urban, are nearly always unincorporated.

The rural-urban fringe is what some suburbanites claim suburbs to be: an approximately even mixture of urban and rural ways of life and territorial settlement. There the inhabitants sometimes work in the city and sometimes on farms; houses sometimes are urban in style

9 Stuart A. Queen and David B. Carpenter, "The Sociological Significance of the Rural-Urban Fringe from the Urban Point of View," *Rural Sociology*, 18 (June 1953), 102–8.

and sometimes modernized farm dwellings; social relations sometimes follow city patterns and sometimes rural ones. In sum, the fringe area and its residents are very mixed in degree of urbanization, and the suburb certainly is not.

Consider as an example a side road leading from a highway near a city of 200,000 persons. Driving out from the city center on the highway, one first passes apartments and homes within the city, succeeded by suburban tracts, and then an unincorporated area extending several miles beyond the last suburb. Open fields are dotted with sheep or an occasional cow. Houses are left behind, and the last gas station is two miles back. Then, on the left, is Seven Springs Road, a rural-seeming paved strip dividing a pasture from a cornfield. Turning off the highway is easy, as there is little traffic, for the area offers no coin-operated laundries or frozen-custard drive-ins. But around a bend a mile from the highway are five houses, each surrounded by four or five acres of land. In an ordinary frame house lives a farmer turned truck driver who supplements his income by keeping sheep; a modernistic work of architecture houses a writer and his family; in a two-living-room, four-bath structure reside a lawyer and his coupon-clipping wife; the fourth home is rented by a young college professor; and the fifth house shelters a farm family that once owned the land now occupied by the writer, the lawyer, and the professor.

Unlike suburbanites commuting to their jobs in the city, these people are mixed in more respects than just urbanity of occupation. The lawyer and professor both commute to the city, but their dogs chase rabbits across the yard. The truck driver is often gone, but not always to the city. The farmer tills his remaining fields and makes disparaging remarks to his wife about the liquor consumption of his neighbors who moved out to the country to avoid wearing ties. The writer stays away from the city as much as possible but retains the values and attitudes of the urban slum in which he was reared.

This group of houses is part of exurbia, profitably caricatured in contemporary novels, whose characters work seventy-hour weeks to earn $40,000 a year to pay for wild, sexually transgressive weekend parties and spend $45,000 a year, which drives them deeper into debt and onto psychiatrists' couches. Of course, their rural neighbors who sold them the land for their quasi-Frank Lloyd Wright split-levels, with or without barns having original hardware, look on with disdain,

envy, often avarice, and more often a smug feeling that this phenomenon too will pass.

But this picture is overdrawn, for only a few exurbanites are fit
subjects for novels fixated on unfulfilled wives and their harried
mates. Some are simply people who live farther out than suburbanites
do. Until mid-century, most decentralized families remained within
fairly easy access to their jobs and near to such urban amenities as
water, electricity, gas, sewer lines, neighborhood stores, and bus
routes. Although release from the dirty, congested city was desirable,
sacrifice of modern conveniences for pastoral exurbia was too high a
price; hence the suburban compromise, which so often turned out to
be not really a compromise but simply longer commuting and more
weekend chores.

Since World War II, however, residential expansion has spread to
more distant fields. This centrifugal movement was made possible by
a high standard of living that permitted some people to live long distances from their work, perhaps driving 80 miles each way or riding a
train for 120 miles; often exurban residence was made possible because the man did not have to go to an office every day. This march
beyond the suburbs into what has previously been identified as "ring
one" (past the limits of the SMSA) was facilitated by fast automobiles and all-weather roads, electric water pumps and septic tanks,
bottled gas and telephone lines, a yearning to avoid the artificiality of
city living and return to nature, and sociopsychological impulses that
are still being researched. This movement is essentially an American
phenomenon and has few or no counterparts elsewhere, a circumstance attributable to differences in level of living and images of the
urban "rat race" versus the "wide-open spaces."

Fringe residents have to learn to live with relatively few of the
services normally available in urban areas and to bear up under occasionally prolonged stoppages of water, heat, and toilets. Since exur-
bias are unincorporated, there are few zoning regulations and less
help from the gas and electric companies. Whether former urbanites
or farmers, fringe residents must expect from time to time to be
forced to go it alone. In the absence of community services, informal
assistance may spring up: When the lawyer's water pump fails, his
children may go to the writer's house to use the bathroom.

In one way, the fringe resembles the old-fashioned city extolled by

Jane Jacobs:[10] An amazing variety of people may be intermingled without apparent rhyme of reason; there are ample places for odd bedfellows in a fully matured city neighborhood or a growing rural-urban fringe. Fringe residents drive tractors, old station wagons, and new Jaguars; farmers' wives buy processed, insipid bread, and television executives' wives learn to bake their own coarse loaves. Land use also varies: Farms, roadhouses, trailer courts, cemeteries, factories, and hot-dog stands are interspersed among fashionable estates and middle-class cottages. Culturally and psychologically, some fringe residents are urban, some are rural, and some are quite literally both. Financial and intellectual variations are extreme as once-hick exurbia has been invaded by N.B.C. executives and *New Yorker* writers. Although some of these divergent types get along surprisingly well together, others are not neighbors socially but merely etymological nigh-dwellers. The fringe lies beyond the normal boundaries of the metropolis' area of daily interaction, but it is coming to be a part of the metropolis and a contributor to its life and problems.

○ *Megalopolis and Conurbation*

Whether or not the city of the future will be a monotonic expanse of suburbia and fringe, there is little doubt (assuming no nuclear destruction) that the twenty-first century will contain huge urban complexes each made up of several component cities. Such combining of two or more urban places into a single complex agglomeration, as illustrated in Figure 7, is known as a "conurbation" ("urbanizing together"), and a giant metropolis is called a "megalopolis" (Greek "great city").

As has so often been the case, the ancient Greeks foreshadowed modern times by planning a magnificent city-state named Megalopolis in the Peloponnesus, which was intended to become the largest in Greece. Founded in 370 B.C. by Epaminondas, the city never reached its potential, and its ruins now remain as the nucleus of a small town of no consequence ("Look on my works, ye Mighty, and

---

[10] Jane Jacobs, *The Death and Life of Great American Cities* (New York: Random House, 1961).

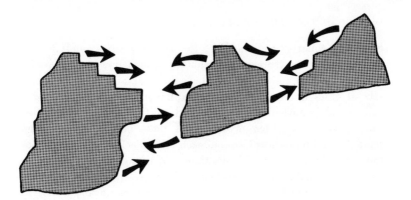

FIGURE 7. A Conurbation

despair!" [11]). More recently the word "megalopolis" has been used to denote a very large metropolis.

The idea, though not the name, of conurbation appeared in the writings of H. G. Wells, who in 1901 prophetically visualized the cities of England as "urban regions" or "town provinces": "Practically . . . the whole of Great Britain south of the highlands seems destined to become such an urban region, laced all together." [12] The word "conurbation" was coined in 1915 by Patrick Geddes[13] to designate a formless, undifferentiated urban mass extending for dozens or hundreds of miles of high but relatively even density. Lacking truly meaningful centers because of the flexibility of route provided by the automobile, this new urban form of the industrial era is being encountered more and more throughout the world. Both "megalopolis" and "conurbation" are sometimes used pejoratively, but they are also used simply as descriptions and without deprecatory intention.

Both labels are appropriate for the supercities of present-day United States and Western Europe, and conurbations especially may become increasingly suited to urban patterns now developing elsewhere in the world. In India, for instance, greater Calcutta is now an

11 Percy Bysshe Shelley, "Ozymandias," 1818.

12 Herbert George Wells, *Anticipations of the Reaction of Mechanical and Scientific Progress upon Human Life and Thought* (New York: Harper, 1901), p. 68.

13 Patrick Geddes, *Cities in Evolution* (London: Williams & Norgate, 1915), p. 34.

elongated conurbation straddling the Hooghly River, and Bombay may soon become the center of another conurbation curling around Bombay Harbor and extending along the Arabian Sea. Several clusters of cities in Japan and China exhibit every symptom of being full-fledged conurbations. By the end of this century the United States may contain ten or twelve of these massive urban dominants, extending outward around such combinations of cities as Boston–New York–Philadelphia–Baltimore–Washington, Miami–Tampa, Pittsburgh–Cleveland, Detroit–Toledo, Chicago–Milwaukee, St. Louis–Kansas City, Houston–Dallas, Seattle–Portland, San Francisco–Sacramento, and San Diego–Los Angeles–Santa Barbara.

The first-mentioned conurbation is the only one already in existence in the United States. Extending 600 miles along the Altantic coast from Virginia to Maine in a sprawling agglomeration—housing one-fifth of the nation's population in a land area comprising only 3 per cent of the national total—it includes four metropolitan areas of more than 2 million people each. In this unique concentration, the largest urban cluster in the world, reside the richest, most educated, healthiest, most luxury-supplied, and most pampered set of people found in any region of comparable population or areal extent. If the ancient Greek dream has reached fruition anywhere in any time, it is along the northeastern seaboard of the United States.

If that dream is to come true in a second place, the most likely spot is along the southern Pacific coast. Although New Yorkers may declare their megalopolitan superiority out of habit—and, it must be conceded, considerable merit—their primacy is about to be challenged by the upstart Los Angeles, which has grown so recently and, some say, so ill-advisedly, from 1,610 residents in 1850 to become in 1962 the second-largest metropolitan area in the country. The third city is Chicago, a metropolitan area destined to maintain its rank largely because the fourth-largest metropolis—Philadelphia—is part of the New York conurbation.

There are thus three megalopolises in the United States. New York is clearly the largest and most powerful, but Los Angeles is growing rapidly and offering so high a level of living as to constitute a threat to the long-standing supremacy of New York. Because the nation is large enough in extent and population to support more than one such supercity, because New York seems to be choking itself to death with congested transportation arteries, and because Los Angeles is relatively unclogged (however overcrowded it may seem to its impatient freeway riders) and therefore freer to grow, it is possible that the California parvenu may one day soon join the New York conurbation as an equally powerful force affecting American culture.

chapter 6

URBAN GROWTH AND SETTLEMENT

THE MOST IMPORTANT ELEMENT OF A CITY IS ITS RESIDENTS, AS HAS been recognized by Sophocles ("The city is people"), Shakespeare ("What is the city but people?" [1]), and, of course, modern sociologists. And, because cities are composed of people, urban increments—whether enlarging the number of cities or the number of residents in each city—consist intrinsically of accretions of urban people. A newly formed city results from recognition that a semirural village has grown large enough to take on the characteristics of a city. Such reclassification, however, has only a slight influence on the rate of urbanization in comparison to the enlargement of existing cities, which may be caused by any or all of three phenomena: Adjacent territory and people may be annexed to the city, persons may move into cities from rural areas or from other cities, or babies may be born in urban areas. In the last case, of course, no net addition of population takes place unless gains from births exceed losses from

[1] William Shakespeare, *Coriolanus*, Act III, Scene i, line 198 (*c.* 1609).

deaths; the difference between the number of births and the number of deaths is known as "natural increase."

The vital processes of birth and death are fundamental to growth or decline of human populations, whether world, national, or community. Although nearly all nations draw their population increments largely from natural increase rather than from migration (including the greatest immigrant-receiving country in the history of the world— the United States[2]), cities are quite varied in this respect, some growing by virtue of their large natural increase and others by net inward migration.

○ *Fertility Differentials*

After religious affiliation and social class, the variable most strongly affecting fertility is place of residence. Urban-rural fertility differences have been observed for more than 200 years in Sweden and other parts of western Europe, where rural residents were discovered to have higher birth rates than did city inhabitants. Urban-rural differences in natality probably existed in the United States in the eighteenth century, although documentation was not available until the early 1800s, when statistics showed that urban women had about one-third fewer children than rural women had. These differences are narrowing in the twentieth century, although rural fertility remains somewhat higher. A larger percentage of rural women marry, they tend to marry younger, and often there are fewer financial penalties (for additional food, housing, and so forth) to rural families with children.

Urban birth rates tend to vary inversely with city size; they are lowest in metropolitan centers and highest in small towns. This traditional difference, however, may be on its way to eradication. Superficially a part of, but in fact causally different from, this generalization is the central city-suburb contrast: Natality is higher in suburban areas than in the central city, not because suburbs partake of some of the qualities of rural areas but for other reasons, one of which is the

[2] Ralph Thomlinson, *Demographic Problems* (Belmont, Calif.: Dickenson, 1967), pp. 37-8, 79.

tendency of young married couples to move to the suburbs to bear and rear their offspring. (Nonwhite intrametropolitan variations do not follow this pattern: For example, nonwhites in the outlying areas of Chicago had a slightly lower fertility in 1960 than did nonwhite residents in the central city.[3]) A study of the demographic correlates of urbanism in China disclosed a similar intrametropolitan variation, the number of children per family increasing with distance from the city center, from the city proper through the suburbs into the close rural-urban fringe and finally the distant rural areas.[4] Differences also persist among neighborhoods within a city, especially in cities characterized by considerable ecological differentiation. If high-fertility racial, religious, nationality, or socioeconomic groups live in separate districts, their neighborhoods tend to have higher birth rates. Conversely, ethnic and other social groups having low fertility tend to depress natality rates in areas they inhabit.

Some—perhaps most—of these differentials are deliberate, for both family-size preferences and use of birth control tend to vary in similar fashion between farms and cities as well as among urban areas of varying sizes and properties. The negative correlation between fertility and the use of birth control is, however, not as high as might be supposed. Adoption of family-planning techniques appears to be proportionally highest in suburbs of large cities (where fertility is moderate), lowest in farm areas (where fertility is high), and intermediate elsewhere (where fertility is sometimes moderate but sometimes lower than in the suburbs). But such induced differentials may vanish as the spreading espousal of urban values and norms throughout rural districts erases these and other variations. It is even possible, although not very probable, that ultimately there will be no intercommunity size differences regarding preferred number of children and acceptance of birth-control methods.

[3] Evelyn M. Kitagawa and Philip M. Hauser, "Trends in Differential Fertility and Mortality in a Metropolis—Chicago," in Ernest W. Burgess and Donald J. Bogue (eds.), *Contributions to Urban Sociology* (Chicago: University of Chicago Press, 1964), p. 69.

[4] Ernest Ni, "A Study of Urbanism and Population Structure in a Metropolitan Community in China," in Burgess and Bogue, *op. cit.*, p. 426.

◯ *Mortality Differentials*

City growth is also affected by mortality. Had it not been for high rates of fertility and in-migration, preindustrial cities would hardly have survived, let alone prospered, for they often had appreciably higher death rates than did their surrounding rural areas. The reasons for this difference were three: Because urban dwellers met more people in the course of their daily activities, they were more likely to contract contagious diseases; sanitation and cleanliness were appalling everywhere, but their consequences were not so mortal in rural areas, where lower densities produced fewer organic and inorganic effluvia; and finally, recurring food shortages affected city dwellers more severely, because they had restricted access to food sources. The leading physician of colonial America, Benjamin Rush, declared that cities presented physical dangers akin to "abscesses on the human body," being "reservoirs of all the impurities."

Descriptions of New York in the mid-nineteenth century indicated no improvement. This exemplar of progress in America was represented by ex-mayor Philip Hone in 1832 as "one huge pigsty" but one into which a prudent farmer might avoid putting his pigs for fear they might not survive. In 1844 the editor of *The New World* wrote: "Our streets . . . are too foul to serve as the sties for the hogs which perambulate them . . . the offal and filth, of which there are loads thrown from the houses . . . is scraped up with the usual deposits of mud and manure into big heaps and left for weeks together on the sides of the street." Not until 1866 were the bands of scavenging hogs eliminated from the city's streets. In 1857, two-thirds of the city lacked sewers, leaving waste matter to soak into the soil or, if placed in receptacles, to be hauled away from time to time. It is little wonder that contagious diseases flourished; outbreaks of typhoid, dysentery, and typhus were continual, and cholera struck periodically as a result of contaminated water. Yellow fever ravaged the population intermittently, and malaria and consumption killed thousands. Other major cities were in similar distress, partly because most cities continued to use private cesspools until about 1880.[5]

[5] Charles N. Glaab and A. Theodore Brown, *A History of Urban America* (New York: Macmillan, 1967), pp. 86–9, 164–6.

Excessive urban mortality also characterized other nations. In Great Britain, one of the most advanced countries in the world, the life expectancy at birth in 1841 was about thirty-six years in London and twenty-six in Manchester, markedly below the forty-one that prevailed in England and Wales as a whole. Even as late as the first decade of the twentieth century, the urban counties in England and Wales had a death rate one-third higher than the rural counties (rates were standardized by age—a statistical method of holding age constant—to improve comparability).

Today community mortality differentials are relatively slight. Large cities generally have more medical personnel and facilities— even on a per capita basis—but there appear to be larger numbers of dangerous phenomena in large communities. Differences within metropolitan areas are social rather than areal, and the major difference between rural and urban death rates can be discerned in causes of death: Urbanites tend to die of diseases that modern medical science has not yet learned to control, whereas farmers more often die of ailments conquerable by modern diagnostic and curative techniques.

Because urban-rural and inter- and intra-urban mortality differences within a nation are small, it is mainly the variations in fertility that create differentials in natural increase. In this respect urban and rural communities resemble nations; since control over mortality became fairly widespread, incompletely controlled fertility has become in modern times (although it was not so in former times) the dominant force.

○ *Annexation*

Cities also add to the number of their inhabitants by annexing surrounding territory. Areas lying just outside a city or metropolitan area may be transferred legally from a rural to an urban classification by incorporation into the city or a suburb. Along with this addition of territory to the city's jurisdiction, the people living in these areas change, without moving, from rural to urban residence. Such reclassification of land and inhabitants is frequent in certain places and times, accounting in some instances for as much as one-fifth of the annual national growth of urban population. Of course, some annexations to large cities consist of extension of boundaries to include small, previously politically independent communities; in this case, urban-rural proportions are not affected.

Annexation is often a political issue, fought with great bitterness by opposing factions. Citizens doubtful of receiving services commensurate with anticipated increases in local taxes may resist annexation to the city; others favor urban classification because, for example, they believe that their children will benefit from the city's superior school facilities. What may happen to property taxes is perhaps the most influential motivation in the minds of potential annexees.

An inevitable feature of the annexation of rural land to an urban area is the correlative decrease in rural persons and acreage. That annexation adds to urban area and population is obvious, but that it subtracts from rural totals is often overlooked. Similarly, annexation of small cities to larger ones decreases the number of small towns and their total resident population, while simultaneously increasing the population—although rarely the number—of large cities. Important though annexation is, in the long run it is a less significant contributor to urban growth than either natural increase or migration.

○ *Migration Into and Between Cities*

Although urban areas grow by addition of newborn babies, so do rural areas; the more rapid increase in urban places as compared with farms is attributable primarily, and in many instances solely, to the migration of rural persons to urban centers. It is rural-to-urban migration rather than annexation, high urban fertility, or low urban mortality that causes cities to enlarge at more rapid rates than rural hinterlands. Also, movement from one city to another contributes substantially to the growth of certain communities, particularly the satellites and suburbs ringing metropolitan centers. Both demographic and spatial enlargements of cities are forwarded by an excess of in-migrants over out-migrants.

In the United States, as in most countries, the rural-to-urban flow of persons is far greater than the urban-to-rural stream. Indeed, heavy movement from farms to cities is characteristic of industrializing and industrial nations throughout the world. Movement from one city to another is also large and, in fact, increasing by leaps and bounds as suburbs expand and more and more people come to have automobiles or incomes sufficient to pay public carriers.

Because large numbers of people make such moves and because moves are most often made by persons between the ages of eighteen and twenty-five (who therefore have many years of biological and occupational productivity ahead of them), leaders of many communities are becoming greatly concerned. The largest single local tax expenditure is for public schools, and communities suffering this outward movement of twenty-year-olds are faced with paying for twelve years of education of youths who leave before they are old enough to contribute tax support for the next generation's education. On the other hand, communities experiencing net inward migration are in the fortunate position of taxing these newcomers, yet never having had to foot the bill for their education.

Another circumstance of social and economic significance associated with migration is the tendency of new arrivals, especially non-whites and foreigners, to congregate in the poorest and most dilapidated sections of a city—an ecological phenomenon that has been visible in both the United States and Europe for many years. Writing of Philadelphia in the 1890s, W. E. B. Du Bois pointed out that "new immigrants usually settle in pretty well-defined localities in or near the slums, and thus get the worst possible introduction to city life." [6] More recently, a study of 1935–1940 migration into Chicago disclosed that Negro migrants from the Deep South were highly concentrated in low-status areas; however, Negro migrants from the North and West did not cluster exclusively in the black ghetto. [7]

[6] W. E. B. Du Bois, *The Philadelphia Negro* (Philadelphia: University of Pennsylvania Press, 1899), p. 81.

[7] Ronald Freedman, *Recent Migration to Chicago* (Chicago: University of Chicago Press, 1950), p. 202.

○ *Explanation of Migration*

Both the study of migration and urban ecology are accompanying other branches of sociology in the continual thrust toward greater logical and quantitative rigor. One current in this methodological stream is the use of mathematical models to analyze the migratory movements providing the human raw materials that build cities.

Intercity and rural-to-urban migrations have been examined quantitatively by many scholars, from E. G. Ravenstein's attempt to set up laws in the 1880s[8] to recent efforts at simulation models. Many of these models were borrowed from physics and astronomy, as demographers attempted to chart analogies between size and distance as variables affecting the attractiveness of migration. Foremost among proponents of these gravitational models have been John Q. Stewart,[9] G. K. Zipf,[10] and Samuel A. Stouffer.[11] Stewart and Zipf attempted to estimate migration by assuming that the number of migrants is directly proportional to the sizes of the areas of origin and destination and inversely proportional to the distance (or the square of the distance) between them. Stouffer substituted the notion of "intervening opportunities" as a resistive force to replace the purely spatial variable, distance, on the assumption that "there is no necessary relationship between mobility and distance." [12] Although many sociologists welcome this substitution of a social variable (intervening opportunities) for a physical variable (distance), Stouffer's thesis, in common with other neogravitational models, has received mixed evaluations despite a quarter-century of empirical support.[13] This ambiguous re-

[8] E. G. Ravenstein, "The Laws of Migration," *Journal of the Royal Statistical Society*, 48 (June 1885), 167–235; and 52 (June 1889), 241–305.

[9] John Q. Stewart, "The 'Gravitation' or Geographic Drawing Power of a College," *Bulletin of the American Association of University Professors*, 27 (February 1941), 70–5.

[10] G. K. Zipf, "The P_1P_2/D Hypothesis: On the Intercity Movement of Persons," *American Sociological Review*, 11 (December 1946), 677–85.

[11] Samuel A. Stouffer, "Intervening Opportunities: A Theory Relating Mobility and Distance," *American Sociological Review*, 5 (December 1940), 845–67.

[12] *Ibid.*, p. 846.

[13] William R. Catton, Jr., *From Animistic to Naturalistic Sociology* (New York: McGraw-Hill, 1966), pp. 165–81, 241–301.

ception is partly attributable to the fact that the intervening-opportunities hypothesis was designed to be susceptible to varying definition: To men of working age, it may be a job; to retired men, good fishing; to males in general, girl watching; to mothers, a pleasant place to rear children.

Although more recent models have increased in complexity, explanatory and predictive effectiveness has not always been increased thereby. Demographers have utilized such spatial variables as the size of area of origin, size of area of destination, shape of area of origin, shape of area of destination, distribution of population within area of origin, distribution of population within area of destination, and distance moved.[14]

Also computed are origin-destination cross-tabulations indicating the probability of movement from any one area to any other given area; such matrices show, for example, the sizes of the various migration streams between regions of the United States.[15] Simple or first-order matrices describe the probability that a resident of area A resided in area B at the end of a specified time period (for example, 1960–1965); higher-order matrices cover more than one time period. From these matrices, statisticians can prepare series of projections by repeatedly multiplying the initial population in each area by the probability of movement from each area to each other area.[16] These probability models are known as Markov chains, after the Russian mathematician Andrei Andreevich Markov, who initiated the concept in 1907. A Markov chain is a special type of stochastic process—a semirandom series of states through which events proceed in time and in which the change from one state to another is not completely determined but is instead probabilistic. The increasing use of these processes by mathematically trained social scientists is one of many responses to the recognition that social behavior is in fact probabilistic and not describable either by absolute determinism or by the total rejection of determinism known as free will.

[14] Thomlinson, "A Model for Migration Analysis," *Journal of the American Statistical Association*, 56 (September 1961), 675–86.

[15] James D. Tarver and William R. Gurley, "A Stochastic Analysis of Geographic Mobility and Population Projections of the Census Divisions in the United States," *Demography*, II (1965), 134–9; and Thomlinson, *A Mathematical Model for Migration* (Ann Arbor: University Microfilms, 1960), pp. 88–93.

[16] Thomlinson, "Methodological Needs in Migration Research," *Population Review*, 6 (January 1962), 59–64.

One rather curious property of stochastic processes is their ability to avoid the one element ordinarily considered indispensable to analysis of causal sequences: independent variables. The familiar causal chains so beloved among social researchers may be linked together into a series of Markov states with a remarkable disregard for the seemingly essential ingredient of potentially causal variables, thereby implying that knowledge of the metal that forms the links is not a requisite part of the analysis of the causal chain. In migration research, the models frequently take no account of any variable impelling the migrant to change his residence, and projection of future migration currents is managed not by the customary meticulous examination of pertinent economic, psychological, political, geographic, sociological, and transportation variables but rather by merely extrapolating recent trends as recorded in the cells of the transition matrix—a contradiction of the old scientific saw that causation must be understood before prediction or alteration of events is possible. Not that independent variables are disruptive or contradictory to Markovian analysis or extrapolation; they are simply unnecessary in this context.

○ *Origins of Urban Migrants*

Attention to both the sending and receiving areas respects both the "push" from the previously tenanted area and the "pull" exerted by the new area. The sixth son of a farmer may be pushed off the farm because it is not large enough to support six brothers. On the other hand, a resident of an Iowa farm or Indiana city may be pulled to New York or Los Angeles by its occupational or recreational attractions. People who are pushed out of their old areas generally differ somewhat in both motivation and conduct from migrants who move because of the lure of the new area. Persons pushed out have already decided to move—the question then becomes "Where to go?" "Pulled" persons must decide whether or not to move at all. No matter which of the two forces in this simplified picture of migration is more compelling, both push and pull motives probably combine in encouraging most moves, and the migrants themselves would be hard put to compare accurately the propulsion to leave the farm as against the lure of the city. Since both push and pull stimuli operate—and since responses appear to be identical—differentiation of motive is difficult. The farm youth may learn of the greater occupational opportunity in the city, his sister may hear about the more comfortable standard of living, and both may yearn to escape the social restraints of the rural community. That there may be unemployment in the city, that the newcomers may have to settle in a slum, and that expectations of greater social freedom may turn out to be chimerical are irrelevant to the move, for people decide whether and where to migrate on the basis of received information and personal beliefs, which may or may not be consistent with facts. Numerous rural migrants in many nations respond to these motivations expressive of the relative desirability of one place of residence vis-à-vis another. Migrants who cross international boundaries may be impelled by additional forces—and faced with greater problems in adjusting to their new environments. Finally, some persons are "floaters" who drift from one city to another.

Which persons choose to move and which elect to stay put are questions that must be regarded as more meaningful than answerable. Inconclusive evidence limits the confidence that can be placed in this generalization, but there is some indication that rural-to-urban migrants tend to be young adults with better than average education and occupational skills. Although some scholars credit migrants with superior intelligence, physical condition, and ambition, definitive data are lacking on these points. Nonetheless, it does appear that, on the whole, cities gain desirable citizens by migration.

Sometimes, however, migrants are said to exert a disorganizing influence on the areas they enter. Evidence is also conflicting on this subject, but migrants do not seem more prone to deviant behavior than nonmigrants, nor does the act of migrating have a criminogenic effect on the migrant. Some migrant-receiving areas are disorganized, and for some persons the act of migrating is personally disruptive, but opposite conditions also hold in many instances. In short, sometimes disorganization is associated with migration and sometimes not. Assuredly, mobility is not likely to be psychologically or ecologically disturbing to a population accustomed to a mobile way of life. And when disruption does occur, it is most likely to strike certain susceptible types of persons or areas; but neither the disorganization-prone person nor the area can be predicted from present knowledge.

This conclusion regarding disorganization has a counterpart for the more desirable traits and influences of migrants: there is too much individual and areal variation to permit valid inference. Each city, subarea, group, and person seems almost a special case, and until elaborately detailed studies using controlled comparisons are completed, ecologists are confined to the weak generalizations reported in these paragraphs.

Whatever their provenance, properties, and plans, migrants carry to the city the habits and mores learned in their previous residences. Sometimes these norms agree with those in the areas of destination. But sometimes disparities occur, amounting generally to minor matters of protocol but occasionally—especially among international migrants—leading to sufficiently fundamental differences to induce what has been called "cultural shock" in reaction to major unanticipated divergences. Conceptions of familial and other obligations, acceptance of situational constraints, and definitions of tolerable behavior may differ greatly. Even in the more adaptive migrants, enthusiastic adjustment to the new culture is tinged with hard-to-eradicate overlays of familiar customs. Adherence to old norms is zealously upheld among the more inflexible new settlers, although a patina is gradually superimposed through exposure to the new urban culture.

Which of the old norms to uphold and which to reject is a difficult decision for any migrant, for cultural detachment and rearrangement are enervating processes—so much so that some migrants refuse the new culture, remaining in but not of the city. And if a newcomer can find other recalcitrant compatriots by the familiar procedure of "seeking out his own kind," he may separate himself from the life of the city by living and working in his own ethnic enclave or quarter, populated almost entirely by people of shared traditions and values that differ from those of the majority of the city. When this clustering occurs among a large percentage of the urban residents, the result is segmentation into urban subareas, each retaining strong village characteristics, as is so frequently found in cities of the Near and Far East. In Cairo, for instance, more than one-third of the residents were born outside the city, usually in rural Egypt. As a consequence of their numbers and their tendency to settle in their own sections of the city, their way of life continues to be rural or small-town; they live in rural-type dwellings and have lower literacy rates and higher fertility than do residents of other parts of the city. From these facts, Janet Abu-Lughod concluded that a "ruralization of cities" is occurring simultaneously with urbanization.[17]

Survival of these rural transplants with minimal assimilation is a familiar phenomenon in urban areas, especially in underdeveloped regions. Although their presence may be decried, the refractory migrants do serve the function of insulating the new arrival against an unfamiliar cultural environment until he has had time to adjust to it, thereby diminishing the incidence and severity of cultural shock or malaise. And to persons fortunate enough to be immune to this conflict, coexistence of old and new values of divergent origins lends to the city a variety that constitutes for many of us the spice of urban life.

○ *Assimilation of Immigrants*

Cities located along seaboards tend to have high proportions of foreign-born residents. The 1960 U.S. Census reported that four cities of 50,000 population or more had at least one-fifth of their inhabitants born outside the country: Miami Beach, Florida, 33 per cent; Passaic, New Jersey, 23 per cent; East Los Angeles, California, 20 per cent; and New York City, 20 per cent. By contrast, some inland cities, especially those in the South, contained fewer than 1 per cent foreign-born residents. Nationally, urban areas averaged 7 per cent and rural areas 2 per cent foreign-born.

The term "foreign stock" is used to designate persons who either were foreign-born or have at least one foreign-born parent—that is, first- or second-generation residents. Percentages of foreign stock are generally highest in coastal cities and lowest in southern cities and rural regions: Miami Beach, 66 per cent; New York City, 49 per cent; all urban places, 23 per cent; all rural areas, 10 per cent; Gadsden, Alabama (population 58,000), 1 per cent; Massachusetts, Rhode Island, Connecticut, New York, and Hawaii, 38 to 40 per cent; and Georgia, Arkansas, Alabama, South Carolina, Tennessee, North Caro-

[17] Janet Abu-Lughod, "Migrant Adjustment to City Life: The Egyptian Case," *American Journal of Sociology*, 57 (July 1961), 22–32.

lina, and Mississippi, less than 2 per cent. The most likely places to meet people of foreign stock are the large cities of the Northeast, whereas the southern states (including all of Florida except metropolitan Miami) contain very few residents of recent foreign heritage.

Cultural diversity is thus more often found in major cities, especially those near national borders. The early immigrants were nation builders, contributing manpower to factories as well as customs and artifacts that have done much to enrich American cultural life. Relatively few cities in other nations have experienced comparably large influxes, and, for that matter, the annual inflow of migrants to the United States has declined to less than one-third that of the peak years of 1907–1914. Whatever their numbers, immigrants to any country tend to settle in cities, sometimes by necessity but often by choice, especially when they come from groups—like the Jews—that possess little tradition of land ownership or—like Irish and Sicilian peasants —that have different rural traditions. Most immigrants spend the rest of their lives in the central cities, but their offspring may further Americanize by moving out of their parents' immigrant ghettos to ranch-style houses in the suburbs.

The move away from an ethnically segregated residential area is more than merely symbolic, for isolation of immigrants in separate sections generally hinders their assimilation. The propensity of immigrants to settle in ghettos practically ensures subordinate status, whereas movement out of these areas lowers their ethnic visibility, decreases the tendency to cling to their traditional culture, and contributes significantly to assimilation into the dominant culture; in fact, residential dispersion is almost a prerequisite for assimilation. Far from being a subsocial variable of little consequence, territorial distribution powerfully influences the rapidity of learning the new language, the likelihood of becoming a citizen, intermarriage with natives or other foreigners, and the ability to move up in the occupation hierarchy.[18] Ecological patterns are thus valuable indicators of ethnic assimilation in cities of many nations.[19]

[18] Stanley Lieberson, "Residential Segregation and Ethnic Assimilation," *Social Forces*, 40 (October 1961), 52–7.

[19] See for example Robert Gessain and Madeleine Doré, "Facteurs comparés d'assimilation chez des Russes et des Arméniens," *Population*, 1 (January-March 1946), 99–116; and Leo Kuper, Hilstan Watts, and Ronald Davies, *Durban: A Study in Racial Ecology* (London: Cape, 1958).

○ *Commuting and Routinization*

The typical manifestation of city growth in the United States has been peripheral: New residential developments spring up on the fringes, and both rural transplants and central-city residents are attracted in large numbers, sometimes to the extent of inducing population decreases in central areas. Because the central cities are already built up, because land on the outskirts is far cheaper, because modern transportation permits commuting from homes well removed from the place of employment, and because many downtown residents hunger for the "wide-open spaces" of suburbia, new growth increasingly occurs beyond the city limits. A trend toward suburbanization is discernible in all industrial nations and in some underdeveloped regions, although the pace is not always up to that of the United States. For that matter, American suburbanization proceeds at different rates in different regions and years, in response to various phenomena, including especially fluctuations in the economy.

Population movement out of the central city does not draw in equal proportions from all socioeconomic levels but consists mainly of high- and medium-status whites, leaving the central area increasingly to members of the lower strata. The socioeconomic constitution of metropolitan areas thus changes as people redistribute themselves according to income level, housing availability, racial prejudice, and personal preference. One consequence is a widening of the gap in social and economic characteristics between central cities and suburbs. Another consequence is that the centrally located apartments vacated by upward-mobile working-class families may subsequently be rented by newly arrived rural migrants, who in turn enter the daily commuting grind.

This daily movement of people back and forth every morning and evening has been given the label "routinization." The ebb and flow are sufficiently regular so that experienced residents can predict accurately how much longer it will take them to get somewhere during the rush hour. Seasonal movements may also be routine: for instance, the frenzied exodus of college students the day a vacation begins.

Commodities as well as people are routinized, especially when daily deliveries are required. Trucks carrying milk, fresh vegetables, and gasoline arrive on regular schedules to supply urban vendors while opposite traffic lanes convey outward-bound vehicles transporting the day's production of pleated blouses or extruded widgets. Opening and closing times of stores, factories, schools, and churches each supply an impetus to customers, workers, students, and worshipers to leave home or work at a certain time in order to reach their destination at the designated hour.

Routinization differs from city to city, a fact of life soon learned by New Yorkers moving to the Midwest and finding that the morning traffic jam begins an hour earlier than they expected. Cross-cultural variations are greater, resulting from differences in the mix of land use, the amount of commuting, and the type and quality of transportation facilities. Nonetheless, similarities can be discerned, the commonest being that most employees in any city go to work in the morning and quit in the afternoon. Yet in certain countries, notably Spain and Latin America, the work day is divided into two segments— morning and evening—separated by a midday siesta of two or three hours. Consequently, commuting is altered both in time and frequency, and the customary dinner hour is 10:00 P.M. In some areas of the Old World, the old and new sections of a city may operate on different daily time schedules according to the prevailing subcultures. Throughout the world, rural migrants to urban areas soon learn that the daily schedule of activities is no longer set by the rising and setting of the sun but is directed instead by various economic and social dispositions and proclivities.

○ *Mass and Private Transit*

Cities are associated with movement: People migrate to reach them and, once there, move about daily. No longer does settlement signify immobility, for, thanks to modern transportation, urban people—unlike their forebears in the era of foot and hoof—are not confined to a circle whose diameter is the distance they can walk in a few hours. Instead, they pile into streetcars, buses, and family cars, moving about the city with speed and frequency despite aggrieved outcries of traffic obstruction. In fact, it is difficult to say whether city growth in the nineteenth century forced the creation of public transit or whether mass transit made possible the rapid enlargement of cities; certainly the two went hand in hand. The horse-drawn coaches of the beginning of the century were superseded in turn by suburban steam railroads, horse-drawn trolleys on steel rails, electric trolleys, elevated railways, and, at the end of the century, the first underground subways. These railed commuter lines became extremely popular; in 1860 Philadelphia contained 148 miles of street railway for horse-drawn cars, and by 1895 electric trolleys were operating in 850 American cities. New York City alone supported nearly 700 miles of trolley track. Because these railed vehicles, whether single trolleys or trains of several cars, were confined to tracks, strip or ribbon suburban development resulted. Stores and homes were built along the rail lines, and relatively little construction took place beyond walking distance from the tracks.

Further outward dispersal of population (though not necessarily resulting in decreased densities in downtown residential districts) was facilitated by the advent of the gasoline-driven automobile, which rose to great popularity in the 1920s. Buses offered flexibility of routing, as they were not confined to rails and power lines, and the private car offered even greater flexibility for the individual able to purchase and maintain one. After World War II ownership of automobiles zoomed, particularly in the United States but also elsewhere, marking a switch back to private transportation, as had prevailed in earlier times. Streetcars and interurban rail lines fell into disuse, and rights of ways were given over to streets and highways, frequently bounded by ugly strings of filling stations and other conveniences to serve the motorist. Open countryside previously vacant because inaccessible by rapid-transit lines began to fill with housing tracts, and the perimeter of the city was pushed farther outward.

Because driving is more convenient, far more ego-satisfying, often less time-consuming, and sometimes cheaper than public transit, trolleys and buses suffered from the competition of private automobiles, which rising income levels were permitting nearly every family to own and, in three years, even to pay for. A survey by *Fortune* in 1957 disclosed that in the United States there were two metropolises in which most commuters traveled by car for every one in which the majority used public transit. And in small cities the automobile is even more frequently used. New York remains one of the few cities in the nation in which mass transit is the overwhelming norm; urbanites in all other parts of the country do most of their moving about by private car. Suburbanites especially drive to work and to other activities, forcing communities to build costly and space-consuming roads to meet the volume of traffic.

The strengths and weaknesses of private-car transportation have counterparts in the trucking that carries products out of suburban factories and into suburban department stores, for the trend in both industries and retail businesses is to move away from the central cities. But still the downtown areas live or die by transportation, to the extent that some—Los Angeles being only the best-known case—allocate more land to freeways, interchanges, streets, parking lots, and multitiered garages than to the business and entertainment facilities that the traffic facilities are intended to serve. So which is the master and which the servant?

Life in the city is thus arranged according to the will of men, not of nature; life patterns in cities are created, modified, and discarded by the individual and group efforts of fallible human beings. It therefore seems worthwhile to discover what the prevalent patterns of activity are (see Part Two of this book) and to evaluate recommendations regarding how these patterns might be altered or improved (see Part Three).

part two

HOW URBAN AREAS ARE ARRANGED

chapter 7

NETWORKS OF CITIES

URBAN ECOLOGY INVOLVES THREE LEVELS OF AGGREGATION, AS WAS
pointed out in Chapter 1: the nation or region, the metropolitan area,
and the neighborhood. This chapter is concerned with the largest scale,
the network of cities distributed throughout a region or nation. Chapters 8 and 9 will discuss the spatial patterning of human activity inside metropolitan areas, and Chapter 10 will analyze neighborhoods
and other subareas within cities. Part Two thus covers the three orders of magnitude of urban ecological analysis, beginning with the
largest and concluding with the smallest.

On the highest of the three levels, social scientists begin by recognizing the interrelatedness of cities in modern economic, political, and
social life. Today each urban area tends to specialize in those economic activities through which it can most effectively meet the competition of other cities and hinterlands. Such reciprocal efforts among
cities are not confined either to modern times or to single countries;
rather, they have existed for many centuries, extending in former

times and even more so today across national boundaries and often to other continents.

⋁ Each city is a nodal point in an intricate web of interrelationships; between these nodes and, of course, occupying by far the larger proportion of the territory are rural areas that supply the cities with food and raw materials and are in turn supplied by the cities with manufactured commodities. Because cities act as collection and distribution centers for farmed, extracted, and manufactured goods, they are usually strategically located to facilitate distribution. Not that these urban activities are confined to commodities, for cities have from their inception been suppliers of government, religious, and military services and surveillance. For all of these functions, location is important.

○ *Location and Growth Factors*

In earlier times, when defense was paramount, cities were located on hilltops, islands, or other protected sites, and, if nature did not supply enough protection, walls and moats were constructed around city-castles. Church centers too favored hilltop locations on which to construct their tall spires. Later, capitals of nations or empires were consolidated with centers of commerce along major transportation routes, often at the mouths of navigable rivers. Although hilltop sites are still preferred (generally today for aesthetic rather than practical reasons) and large bodies of water still provide the least expensive means of transport, the most important siting factors in the twentieth century are those associated with the production, distribution, and sale of goods.

A detailed examination of the variables influencing the location of manufacturing and hence of many modern cities is offered by C. Langdon White, Edwin J. Foscue, and Tom L. McKnight.[1] The major variables are, first, proximity to market—the most vital factor, especially for those industries that make products that are bulkier than

---

[1] C. Langdon White, Edwin J. Foscue, and Tom L. McKnight, *Regional Geography of Anglo-America* (Englewood Cliffs, N.J.: Prentice-Hall, 1964), pp. 23–9.

their raw materials (like agricultural implements, pianos, barrels), fragile or perishable products, rapidly changing technological devices, and whimsical products (like women's millinery); second, proximity to raw materials, especially for industries that process perishables (canning, dairy products, sugar milling) and those that involve considerable loss of weight in manufacturing (cement making, smelting); third, proximity to power, as with aluminum plants near hydroelectric power and textile mills near waterfalls; fourth, proximity to skilled manpower, which tends to perpetuate concentration of a particular industry in one area (although when an industrial process is automated to the point where semiskilled or unskilled labor can be used, dispersion occurs—besides, labor is becoming highly mobile these days); fifth, transportation—a "zone of minimum transportation cost" is determined by the weight of the raw materials, the value and weight of the final product, the distance to be covered, the type of transit medium, the character of the region, and the perishability and other character of the goods; sixth, climate—humidity is important in the textile industry, and labor becomes inefficient in very cold or hot weather (however, man is increasingly making his own climate with central heating and air conditioning); seventh, water supply, as water is critical for many such industries as iron and steel, rubber, chemicals, pulp and paper; eighth, capital, which can go anywhere but shows some hesitancy to cross certain international barriers or to enter regions of political disruption or social unrest; ninth, availability and cost of land (some expanding companies migrate rather than buy expensive nearby land—often making large profits from the sale of their old land when they move out of the city); tenth, the "human factor"—the "great man" at the head of the company may decide to move to San Diego in order to enjoy the beach at La Jolla; eleventh, taxation—industries may move to districts with lower tax rates; twelfth, the cost of living, which has a direct causative influence on wages (labor tends to be cheaper in smaller cities because the cost of living is lower, and vice versa); and thirteenth, disposal of waste (rivers are very convenient, but pollution alienates the inhabitants, especially if it interferes with fishing).

Consider the operation of these and other locational factors in one city in each of the four major regions of the country: Gary, Indiana; Mobile, Alabama; New York City; and Los Angeles. Geographers distinguish between general position factors and specific site factors, which determine the exact location in the general area already chosen.

The general factors for Gary are its location in the midst of a tremendous steel market, easy access via the Great Lakes to all raw materials, a crossroads position where the cheapest direct route between coal and iron-ore regions is crossed by the industrially important Atlantic seaboard and Chicago rail lines, proximity to Chicago enabling management to transact business conveniently, a stimulating climate and a lake, and a densely populated surrounding area providing a large labor supply. Specific site factors are a fairly level and uniform topography, room for expansion, placement at the extreme end of the Great Lakes water route (an advantage over Chicago and Milwaukee), an unlimited water supply from adjacent Lake Michigan, an unproductive sandy soil obviating the need to pay high prices for first-class agricultural land, enough distance from Chicago to avoid high taxes and urban land prices, and less stringent laws affecting industry than those in Illinois.[2]

Edward L. Ullman's case study of Mobile has as its primary purpose "to ascertain why a city of the size and character of Mobile has developed at its present location and to explain the relations between the city and the surrounding and distant areas."[3] Mobile was settled in 1702 because of its harbor in Mobile Bay; location near the juncture of the Mobile, Tombigbee, and Alabama Rivers; a fertile countryside; a trade area of friendly Indians; timber resources; accessibility to the Mississippi River via the Gulf of Mexico; and its value as a fort guarding the French frontier against the English. The advent of the steamboat stimulated a sudden growth after 1820, followed by a decline as the coming of the railroad swung the advantage to the interior cities. By 1900 the city had become important for paper mills and saw mills and as an ocean port servicing the hinterland of Alabama and neighboring states. Mobile is the closest ocean port to large sections of the South and Midwest—Louisville and St. Louis, for example. But New Orleans and the Mississippi waterway provide strenuous competition as commercial gateways to the area.

New York City has the least obstructed access to the Midwest of any Atlantic port. The "water-level route" for overland transport from New York does not have to cross the Appalachians; the city is

---

[2] *Ibid.*, p. 30.

[3] Edward L. Ullman, *Mobile: Industrial Seaport and Trade Center* (Ph.D. dissertation, University of Chicago Department of Geography, 1943), p. 6.

closer to most interior areas than Boston is; and it has a better harbor than Philadelphia. A port city needs a large and productive hinterland with easy access (New York's hinterland extends to the Great Lakes, whereas Boston has a small hinterland because of a mountain barrier); a good harbor deep enough to accomodate large vessels (forty to fifty feet), large enough to prevent delay, and ice free; a tidal range large enough to prevent piling up of silt but not large enough to cause docking difficulties (six to eight feet is best); and port facilities for loading, unloading, and outfitting quickly (New York's harbor operations have been called the most inefficient in the world per foot of dock space—facilities are obsolete, labor difficulties are chronic, and theft is excessive). New York's general locational advantage for serving the huge central hinterland as an entrepôt to transship goods is so great that shippers are willing to face the tremendous local transportation problems created by the attenuated shape of Manhattan and the necessity of crossing rivers and bays. One wonders what will be the ultimate effect of the St. Lawrence Seaway upon New York's regional dominance: Because water transport is so much cheaper than any other form, the city located at the inner terminus of the water route has a distinct advantage over its competitors. Until now this city was New York, but, with the completion of the new seaway, those commodities whose shipping cost is more important than time or convenience may be shipped through cities along the Great Lakes.

Los Angeles is a puzzle to location analysts. Before it created its own, the city had no populated hinterland, no suitable harbor, and little else besides a few oil wells to form the basis for a huge city. The oil base provided an initial source of fuel for industry, and the existing tiny port and mountain pass routes to the central valley of California and the Imperial Valley did give it some locational advantages. Also, the area possessed level land suitable for agriculture. Still, its real growth into a metropolis had to await the automobile age. Today its climate, aircraft industries, movie and television studios, ocean port, economic well-being, and booster-type advertising attract a growing market and labor supply. Citrus groves and sheep pastures have been replaced by so many suburban tracts in the last few decades that the water supply is threatened. While the first three illustrations of variables promoting city location and growth seem based in considerable part on geographic traits of the areas, the blossoming of Los Angeles demonstrates the ability of man to overcome geographic obstacles—motivated in this instance partly by climate, it is true, but also by proselytizing of real estate salesmen and seekers after the good life of patio living and mechanical gadgets purchasable under the prevailing high level of wages.

In response to changes in men's desires and ability to manipulate the forces of nature, each of the four cities changed through the years in its importance relative to other cities. Far from being destined to a certain location and size by natural conditions, cities are sited and matured in large part as men direct. Gary's placement and growth have been affected by both natural and man-made circumstances. Mobile waxed and waned in competition with New Orleans and other Deep South cities as new transportation means and new markets gave the advantage first to one, then to another, then to a third, and then back to the first. On the eastern seaboard, New York has been in fairly direct competition since Colonial times with Boston, Philadelphia, Baltimore, Washington, and Charleston. Its victory over these competitors is due in part to the excellence of its physical site and its accessibility to a large service area (the Midwest), but its pre-eminence was not automatic, having to await, for one thing, settlement of the service area. Los Angeles offers the briefest history, the fastest growth, and the most convincing evidence of man's ability to overcome negative spatial influences. One might have predicted that cities would arise at the southern end of Lake Michigan, on Mobile Bay, and at the mouth of the Hudson, but who could have anticipated the sudden rise of Los Angeles?

It is no coincidence that the youngest city of the four examples is also the least influenced by topography and other physical forces. For nearly all of his history, man had to locate his settlements in places favored by nature with a water supply, reasonably level land, suitable soil and climate for growing food, and access to land or water routes for moving people and goods in and out. Not until the middle of the twentieth century did men learn how to control their environment: They heat buildings and vehicles in winter, cool them in summer, fly over the most forbidding terrain, preserve and ship food long distances, pipe water from afar, and even transport bulky building materials thousands of miles. For the first time in history, men have the technological skill to put cities wherever they choose—in the midst of deserts (as in southwestern United States) or in the polar regions (the military installation at Ultima Thule). Not that many cities could be situated in such places, for men are not yet and perhaps never will be released from dependence on certain physical features to support technological and economic attainment. Consequently, we cannot locate more than a few specially contrived cities without regard for water, transportation routes, markets for products, and so forth. Still, the more favored nations have the power to locate a million-person city practically anywhere on the face of the earth; the immediate stumbling blocks today are the prohibitive transport costs and unpleasantness of living in the less hospitable locales—circumstances that surely will deter us from flocking to Florida's Big Cypress Swamp or the North Pole in the foreseeable future. And to the extent that we still settle in cities founded in the days when men were in large part at the mercy of their physical environment, we continue to respond to the traditional environmental forces.

○ *The Urban Economic Base*

Income brought into a city from outside is the bulwark of its economic life, not the circulation of money within the city. Nonlocal activities of the city—that is, the production and export of goods and services to other communities in exchange for money—form its economic base. The best examples are factories that sell their products outside the city.

Nonbasic activities supply goods and services that are consumed locally and therefore do not bring in money from the outside. They sell to basic enterprises, employees in basic industries, and other nonbasic activities and their employees. Examples are such maintenance enterprises as neighborhood grocery stores, bowling alleys and lawnmower repair shops.

It is the basic activities that build cities. A decline in basic employment may be disastrous, as in the case of the city whose factories produced mainly silk yard goods: When rayon began to replace silk, the city's products came to be less in demand, causing considerable unemployment in the city, and the subsequent popularity of nylon resulted in the closing of several factories that had been mainstays of the local economy. When the factories closed, employees who were laid off were unable to meet mortgage payments and grocery bills, which brought hardship to banks, markets, and other nonbasic enterprises. The city went into a depression, but, having other resources, it did not reach the extreme of becoming a ghost town, as has happened to mining communities when the ore was depleted.

Not that community life is impossible without basic enterprises; many villages exist on a subsistence level in underdeveloped areas. Subsistence agriculture, in which each family supplies its own needs with little or nothing left over to sell, can keep rural hamlets going indefinitely. Exclusively nonbasic work cannot, however, lead to a high level of living, for basic work is necessary to bring in the money needed to purchase those goods not produced locally—automobiles, refrigerators, and transistor radios, for example.

This dichotomy was first expressed by Marcel Aurousseau in 1921:

> It is well known that towns have an extraordinary power of growth. This appears to be due to the relationship between the primary occupations and the secondary occupations of the townsfolk. The primary occupations are those directly concerned with the functions of the town. The secondary occupations are those concerned with the maintenance of the well-being of the people engaged in those of primary nature.[4]

In the 1927 regional plan for New York and environs, Frederick L. Olmsted is quoted as distinguishing between primary and ancillary occupations.[5] The first attempt to calculate the proportion of basic to nonbasic workers was by Richard Hartshorne in a study of Minneapolis–St. Paul in 1932.[6]

Since the 1930s, Homer Hoyt and several other economic geographers have computed the basic-nonbasic ratios of a large number of cities. John W. Alexander reported six nonbasic employees for every

---

[4] Marcel Aurousseau, "The Distribution of Population: A Constructive Problem," *Geographical Review*, 11 (1921), 563–92.

[5] Committee on Regional Plan of New York and Its Environs, *Regional Survey of New York and Its Environs*, I: Robert M. Haig and Roswell C. McCrea, *Major Economic Factors in Metropolitan Growth and Arrangement* (New York: Regional Plan Association, 1927), 43.

[6] Richard Hartshorne, "Twin City District: A Unique Form of Urban Landscape," *Geographical Review*, 22 (July 1932), 431–42.

ten basic ones in Oshkosh, Wisconsin, and eight nonbasic for every ten basic in Madison.[7] Although this preponderance of basic workers is common in small cities, metropolitan areas usually have more nonbasic than basic workers—for example, 21 to 10 in New York, 12 to 10 in Detroit, and 17 to 10 in Cincinnati. Oshkosh and New York represent approximate limits to the ratio; there are rarely fewer than five or more than twenty nonbasic employees for every ten basic workers. The nonbasic component tends to vary with size of city, being largest in very large cities, which provide services (elevator operation, umbrella repair shops, and so forth) that are rarely found in smaller cities. Also, nonbasic functions seem to increase more than basic ones as a city ages.

It is conceivable that this tendency of nonbasic workers to increase proportionately with increasing city size may place an ultimate limit on city size: If a city reached the point of having, for example, forty-five nonbasic workers for every ten basic ones, its productive efficiency would be lower than that of smaller cities, and further growth in a competitive economy might be inhibited. Analogous to the concept of diminishing returns for large industrial enterprises (note also Parkinson's law), this force might keep cities from becoming inefficiently large. Such assumptions, however, are at best conjectural and may be entirely illusory.

Some feeling exists that basic workers contribute more to the economy because they create something, whereas the nonbasic workers only keep things going. By analogy with the home, such nonbasic activities as lawn mowing and tooth brushing seem less valuable than the basic activities of having and rearing children; in the latter case, something now exists that did not exist before, an accomplishment that offers much greater satisfaction than merely keeping the grass from getting too long. On this subjective basis, a high proportion of nonbasic workers in a city is regarded as undesirable, and the fact that the highest proportions are found in the largest cities becomes an argument for cutting down metropolitan growth. On this reasoning, New York would be better off if it were broken up into several smaller cities: if the 21-to-10 ratio were thereby changed to 15 to 10, a few of these marginal six nonbasic workers would be employed in basic activities, thus making more important contributions to the economy

[7] John W. Alexander, "The Basic-Nonbasic Concept of Urban Economic Functions," *Economic Geography*, 30 (July 1954), 246–61.

than they do operating shoe-shine machines or clerking in soda fountains. Less efficiency-minded persons retort that nonbasic functions are essential and that therefore there is little to be accomplished by their reduction.

Although this city-building versus city-serving antithesis has been criticized severely, it has survived and is widely used in ecological analysis. One of its foremost supporters, Homer Hoyt, has written of the important contribution of economic base theory to "furnishing a sound method of analyzing the economic structure of an urban region." [8]

The economic base is also closely intertwined with other ecological considerations, including the location and growth of cities. Cooley's "break in transportation" theory postulates that where transit is interrupted, certain basic functions such as loading, packing, repairing, refueling, and purchasing are performed. In turn, the people engaged in these basic activities need personal maintenance services: food, clothing, shelter, entertainment, and so on. Together, these basic and secondary functions form the nucleus of a city.[9] Notice also the prominence of basic elements in city formation and growth of Gary, Mobile, New York, and Los Angeles in contrast to the incidental or subordinate roles played by nonbasic functions.

Differentiation of productive activity into primary and secondary categories is also useful in establishing typologies of cities (being implicit, for example, in the classification scheme near the end of Chapter 4), for its basic activities give a city its distinctive flavor, as opposed to the bland irrelevance of the nonbasic activities, which tend to be more or less the same everywhere.

It is the city's basic functions that justify its existence in the eyes of residents of rural areas and other cities. The nonbasic functions generally mean nothing to outsiders, but a city's basic production offers something of value to the rest of the world. The extreme case is that of a city with no basic activity, contributing no products or services to other areas; if it were suddenly to disappear completely, it would hardly be missed (as a city, that is—its residents might well be

[8] Homer Hoyt, "The Utility of the Economic Base Method in Calculating Urban Growth," *Land Economics*, 37 (1961), 58.

[9] Charles Horton Cooley, "A Theory of Transportation," *Publications of the American Economic Association*, 9 (May 1894), 1–148; reprinted in Cooley, *Sociological Theory and Research* (New York: Holt, 1930), pp. 17–118.

missed). In sum, knowledge of the economic base teaches ecologists something about the interrelations of a city with other areas, rural and urban.

○ *Geometric Patterns*

Sociologists and economists have expended considerable energy and thought toward uncovering a latent system of interurban relationships that will explain the ways in which cities locate, prosper, and wane, each in relation to its neighbors. Travelers driving through the Midwest on nonturnpike highways pass frequent small towns; unlike tourists driving through the Far West or Rocky Mountain states, these vacationers can anticipate encountering towns at fairly regular intervals—a circumstance that diminishes fears of running out of gas but encourages sensations of monotony. But, just when boredom seems to be setting in for good, there appears a larger city offering almost as many motion-picture theaters as the small towns have gas stations. The question arises whether or not these occasional large cities and frequent towns are spaced with sufficient regularity to form a meaningful pattern; several scholars have responded by constructing theoretical systems hypothesizing the spacing of urban centers of varying sizes and distances from one another.

The classic model for the distribution of urban places was advanced by Walter Christaller in 1933.[10] This German scholar evolved an intricate and aesthetically appealing geometric system of hexagonal city-city and urban-rural networks with specified interstitial distances, the distance varying according to the position of the city in the urban hierarchy of function and size. The fundamental assumptions are that a rural area supports a town, which in turn services the rural area, and that there is a strong correlation between town size and area served (small town, small area; large town, large area). Table 4 shows the hierarchical arrangement of the "Seven Cities of Christaller" and their market areas and Figure 8 the correlative hexagonal pattern. Christaller never claimed that his system exactly reproduced an existing urban network, advancing it instead as a theoretical model de-

[10] Walter Christaller, *Central Places in Southern Germany* (1933), trans. by Carlisle W. Baskin (Englewood Cliffs, N.J.: Prentice-Hall, 1966).

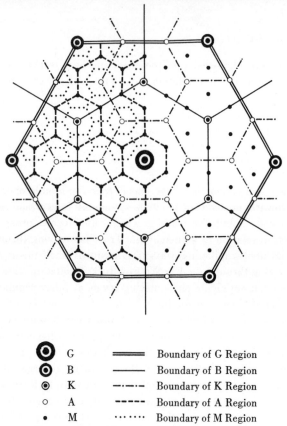

◉	G	═══ Boundary of G Region
◉	B	─── Boundary of B Region
⊙	K	─·─·─ Boundary of K Region
○	A	─ ─ ─ Boundary of A Region
•	M	······· Boundary of M Region

For meanings of letters see **Table 4**

FIGURE 8. Christaller's Hexagonal Network of Urban Places

TABLE 4. Christaller's Distribution of Cities and Tributary Areas

Community (region)	Population	Miles Apart	Tributary Population	Service Area (in square miles)
Market town (M)	1,000	5	3,500	17
Township center (A)	2,000	9	11,000	50
County seat (K)	4,000	15	35,000	160
District city (B)	10,000	25	100,000	470
State capital (G)	30,000	45	350,000	1,500
Provincial head city	100,000	75	1,000,000	4,200
Capital city	500,000	135	3,500,000	13,000

Adapted from Walter Christaller, *Die Zentralen Orte in Suddeutschland* (Stuttgart: Fischer, 1933), p. 72.

signed to explain location of cities of various sizes on a regular—although not completely featureless—plain.

Although Christaller's theory has many critics, it does help to explain the distribution of urban centers in regions where topography is relatively uniform. Christaller claimed that his hexagonal scheme fit southern Germany, and research indicates that the scheme is not too different from the existing urban networks in many of the American Midwest and Great Plains states. On the other hand, it is not well suited to coastal areas with river-mouth sites or to mountainous sectors (where there are relatively few cities anyway). Complaints are based largely on the rigidity of the system, and certainly it is not flexible enough to adapt to a region of elaborately varied topography. Another telling criticism is that there is in reality no discrete hierarchy of cities but rather a continuum. Abundant empirical evidence from every continent tends to confirm the existence of a continuum (or set of related continua) of central places, but the disagreement is merely with Christaller's choice of seven levels of communities, leaving his basic reasoning intact and even indirectly supporting it. The theory continues to be discussed, applied, and derided, and ambiguous evidence continues to be supplied by scholarly research; for example, a recent study of the administrative and marketing systems of cities in China.[11]

Christaller's theory assumes a free enterprise system: If economically motivated men "do what comes naturally," the stated patterns will result. To illustrate, everyone wants to be able to buy a quart of milk or loaf of bread nearby, and if there is not a grocery store within easy access of the inhabitants of an area, then some enterprising individual or grocery chain will open a store to meet this demand. In general, when services are sought by people willing and able to pay for them, these services will be supplied nearby. And if several services are supplied in any one location, a small community is born. Following the same reasoning, prospective purchasers of major items required less frequently (washing machines or winter coats) are willing to travel longer distances; therefore, larger towns supplying products not needed every day or week do not have to be located so close to home. And when the farmer's wife wants a fur coat after twelve or

[11] G. William Skinner, "Marketing and Social Structure in Rural China," *Journal of Asian Studies*, 24 (November 1964), 3–42; 24 (February 1965), 195–228; 24 (May 1965), 363–99.

twenty years, she is quite prepared to go to a distant metropolis. In this fashion, immediate demands are met in frequent nearby small towns, goods needed monthly or annually may be purchased in more widely spaced medium-size cities, and long-term or once-in-a-lifetime items are bought in the region's metropolis. This comfortable scheme, however, may break up if the government or other powerful force decides on a different urban pattern; for example, Copenhagen's deliberately planned urban fingers stretching out from the city, with intervening wedges of open country, systematically violate Christaller's hexagonal network.

Another German economist, August Losch, modified Christaller's theory into what has come to be known as a "Losch system"—market areas of various sizes, each encircling a market center of corresponding population. To Losch, the patterning of urban centers and population density was a part of an economic nexus made up of price gradients, division of labor, trade areas, and other factors contributing to regional equilibrium. "As towns are essentially agglomerations of locations of economic activities, the system of town locations is defined simultaneously by the general equations of location and the geometry of economic regions." [12] Losch avoided Christaller's assumptions that there are a certain number of cities of each size, that they are evenly spaced, and that the tributary regions for all cities of given size have the same area and shape. Losch did assume a network of cities classifiable by size and area of hinterland, but he preferred not to presuppose a certain set of distances and populations; rather, he examined each area carefully to ascertain the actual distances and population sizes in each case. Christaller's theory is a priori, whereas Losch's system is a posteriori. The fact that a Losch system does not necessarily exhibit the rigid geometrical pattern proposed by his earlier compatriot has resulted in greater acceptance of Losch's hierarchical network. Losch did, however, verify the hexagonally shaped complementary region as the most accurate pattern where purchasing power is uniformly distributed.

An American, Walter Isard, continued the work of Losch in attempting to set up a theory interrelating industrial location, market areas, land use, trade, and urban structure. "An urban-metropolitan

---

[12] August Losch, *The Economics of Location*, trans. by W. H. Woglom and W. F. Stolper (New Haven: Yale University Press, 1954), p. 84.

region comes to comprise a hierarchy of strategic nodal sites, classifiable by order and degree of dominance." [13] A founder of the Regional Science Association, Isard conceived the theory of location as "embracing the total spatial array of economic activities, with attention paid to the geographic distribution of inputs and outputs and the geographic variations in prices and costs." [14] Demand curves comparing the desirability of each commodity (as measured by the amount purchasers are willing to pay) in relation to the cost of transportation from the city or other place of production determine the salability of each product and, by product summation, the centrality of each urban place.

Isard, Losch, and Christaller all imply the notion that city development is intimately associated with the type of culture. Allied with the contentions of N. S. B. Gras and other scholars that technological and urban development go hand in hand,[15] modern ecologists expect each culture type to exhibit a different regularity of ecological patterning; that is, city sizes, intervening distances, and areas and populations serviced vary according to the prevailing economic and social system. Isard and Losch inspect the prospective flows of commodities or capital from each territorial-economic unit to every other one—a highly convoluted web of quantitative relations demanding intricate arithmetic and preferably a digital computer. A simplified diagram of a hypothetical region is provided in Figure 9a, in which each focal point of a natural or man-made resource is connected to every other such point.

○ *Central-Place Theory*

Such a large number of interconnections tends to create confusion and waste. Telephone and typing bills alone would compel businesses to seek a more efficient way to communicate with their fellows, and in

---

[13] Walter Isard, *Location and Space-Economy* (Cambridge, Mass., and New York: Technology Press and Wiley, 1956), p. 11.

[14] *Ibid.*, p. 53.

[15] N. S. B. Gras, *An Introduction to Economic History* (New York: Harper, 1922).

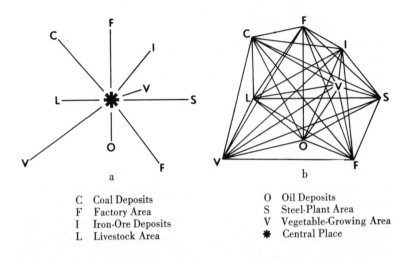

C	Coal Deposits	O	Oil Deposits
F	Factory Area	S	Steel-Plant Area
I	Iron-Ore Deposits	V	Vegetable-Growing Area
L	Livestock Area	✳	Central Place

FIGURE 9. Transportation Connections Between Resource Areas With and Without a Central Place

those cases where goods need to be transported, the trucking or railroad expense furthers the motivation. In such a situation, a center arises to handle commercial transactions, move goods in and out, store materials, and generally expedite the complex activities of modern industrial society. The center contains banks, warehouses, railroad and truck terminals, and so forth. In other words, a city arises, located close to the various productive enterprises it serves (C, I, O, L, V, F, or S in Figure 9), sometimes taking as its site one of these points and sometimes occupying an intermediate site. Comparison of Figure 9a with Figure 9b demonstrates the greater simplicity and probable economy of this arrangement; there are, however, partially compensating disadvantages, like the rise of middlemen and the probable increase in bookkeeping. Study of the forces affecting the location and growth of these nodal points is known as "central-place theory"—an attempt to ascertain how cities come to be located where they are as a consequence of the functions they perform for the surrounding areas and populations.

A central place has the fundamental property of being a source of goods and services for an area larger than itself—a marketplace through which flow commodities originating throughout its hinterland and in scattered other areas. Centrality is not synonymous with bigness, for some small cities are much more important as central places than larger ones. A suburban community of 40,000 people may serve hardly at all as a central place, being largely a dormitory for a nearby metropolis, whereas a city of half that population in a thinly settled farming or grazing district may be a distribution and financial center for thousands of square miles of surrounding territory. Smallness was not a deterrent to centrality in the Middle Ages in Europe, nor is it today in Africa. It is the function of the community that counts in this context; although size is relevant, it is only weakly correlated with centrality.

Although the relevance of size to centrality is moderated strongly by the cultural and regional context, within any one region size is one of the most important determinants of centrality. Reilly's "law of retail gravitation" states that two cities attract and divide retail trade from any smaller intermediate town approximately in direct proportion to the populations of the two cities and in inverse proportion to the squares of the distances of the cities from the intermediate town. Putting this relationship into a formula enables economists to locate the breaking point between the areas of dominance of the two cities— the point of equal influence.[16] Connecting breaking points in all directions around a city establishes a line delimiting the city's retail trade area, an element in the bounding of the metropolitan region.

Christaller developed a measure of the centrality of an urban place based on the assumption that the number of telephones is the best single indicator of the number of relationships between two places. Centrality (the functions performed over and above the needs of the city's inhabitants) equals $T_z - E_z \ (T_g/E_g)$, in which T_z is the number of telephones in the place, E_z the number of residents, T_g the number of telephones in the surrounding hexagonal region, E_g the number of residents in the region, and T_g/E_g the telephone density of the whole area.[17] The first term in this binomial is the actual importance of the center, the second term is what the importance theoretically should be (or the number of telephones it ought to have), and the difference is the degree of centrality. Christaller's use of telephones as an index has been extensively criticized and occasionally used. A superior index would be based on the relative number of calls, but this more subtle variable can be used only where a record of each

16 William J. Reilly, *The Law of Retail Gravitation* (New York: Knickerbocker, 1931).

17 Christaller, *op. cit.*, p. 147.

call is kept, as by phone companies in the United States. Curiously, the number of telephones makes nearly as poor an index in the United States (because the large majority of families have telephones, there is insufficient difference between the number of telephones and the number of people) as in those underdeveloped nations where telephones are rare. Because use of only this one variable tends to limit both validity and applicability, it would be wise to consider the addition or substitution of other variables; the basic reasoning, nonetheless, is consistent with the accepted conception of centrality.

Four English geographers have built upon Christaller's work on centrality. Arthur E. Smailes developed a hierarchical classification of centrality based on counting the number of banks, Woolworth stores, secondary schools, hospitals, movie theaters, and newspapers.[18] A few years later, F. H. W. Green and W. I. Carruthers, working independently, used bus travel as a criterion. Studying bus timetables, they rated each town according to the number of lines serving only places smaller than itself adjusted by the total number of bus journeys into or through the town.[19] Complete analysis of transportation as an index of centrality would, of course, require investigation into other means of transport: train, private automobile, airplane, streetcar, boat, bicycle, and walking. Which modes are most relevant, however, depends on the particular situation. Dissatisfied with Smailes' simple counting of shops and services as a measure of centrality, H. E. Bracey compiled indexes from questionnaires asking residents where they went for fifteen commodities and services: clothing, hardware, dentistry, banking, and so forth.[20] All four of these typologies form ordinal scales; that is, they result in sets of ranked categories. Eventually scholars may learn enough to set up interval scales to rate the degree of centrality of each community from 0 (a remote farmhouse) to 100 (the most central city in the region). At present, however, techniques are not adequate to such precise discrimination.

[18] Arthur E. Smailes, "The Urban Hierarchy in England and Wales," *Geography*, 29 (1944), 41–51.

[19] F. H. W. Green, "Urban Hinterlands in England and Wales: An Analysis of Bus Services," *Geographical Journal*, 116 (1950), 64; and W. I. Carruthers, "A Classification of Service Centres in England and Wales," *Geographical Journal*, 122 (1957), 371–85.

[20] H. E. Bracey, "Towns as Rural Service Centers: An Index of Centrality with Special Reference to Somerset," *Transactions and Papers of the Institute of British Geographers*, Publication No. 19 (1953), 95–105.

In the United States, John H. Kolb studied the distribution of service centers in agricultural counties in Wisconsin,[21] and other rural sociologists have made similar studies of town-country relations in Connecticut, New York, Minnesota, Louisiana, South Dakota, Washington, and other states. C. J. Galpin analyzed the functions of the agricultural village for the surrounding area and noted a decline through the years in the importance of these village centers. His graphic portrayal of the boundaries of rural service centers foreshadowed the metropolitan boundary determination discussed in Chapter 5.

> Take the village as the community center; start out from here on any road into the open country. You come to a home, and the deep wear of the wheels out of the yard toward the village indicates that the inhabitants of this home go to this village for trade, doctor, post office, church, lodge, entertainment, high school. The next road is the same, and the next and the next. Along each road, the houses show the same tendency. But by and by you come to a farm-house where the ruts run the other way and grass grows a little perhaps in the turn toward the first village, and you find that the residents of this home go to an adjoining town for their major associations. Between these two homes is the bounding line of the community.[22]

Galpin also predated one element of Christaller's hexagonal network by postulating that hinterlands of rural villages would take the form of overlapping circles (which reduce to hexagons) if all the pertinent conditions surrounding farms and trade centers were uniform.[23]

At the opposite extreme from these small village centers is the national center, which, when it overshadows in centrality all other cities in the country, is known as a "primate city." In the words of Mark Jefferson, the originator of this designation, a primate city is pre-eminent "not merely in size, but in national influence." [24] Heinrich

[21] John H. Kolb and R. A. Polson, *Trends in Town-Country Relations,* Research Bulletin No. 117 (Madison: University of Wisconsin Agricultural Experiment Station, 1933).

[22] C. J. Galpin, "Social Agencies in a Rural Community," First Wisconsin Country Life Conference, Madison, 1911.

[23] Galpin, *The Social Anatomy of an Agricultural Community,* Research Bulletin No. 34 (Madison: University of Wisconsin Agricultural Experiment Station, 1915).

[24] Mark Jefferson, "The Law of the Primate City," *Geographical Review,* 29 (1939), 226–32.

Heine put the idea poetically: "France is like a garden where all the most beautiful flowers have been picked in order to collect them into a bouquet—and this bouquet is Paris." To be a primate city, a metropolis must be several times more powerful a force in national events as the second most influential city. Not all countries have primate cities, but many do; examples are London, Paris, Buenos Aires, Montevideo, Singapore, Rangoon, Athens, and Moscow. Boosters of Chicago, Los Angeles, Washington, and other communities challenge New York's right to be called a primate city, but there is quite a bit of evidence in Gotham's favor.

Although the usual frame of reference is the nation, it is possible to evaluate the primacy of cities for regions and counties. For example, the United States is frequently regarded as divided into four regions —East, Midwest, South, and Far West—three of which have their own primate cities: New York, Chicago, and Los Angeles. That the South lacks a primate city is cause for lengthy discussion of sectional history and economics. Whether or not such a regional frame of reference is intellectually acceptable turns on the question of whether or not the regions themselves are meaningful functional entities; if so, then regionally primate cities are a legitimate conception.

Whereas many large countries are subdivided into regions, small nations may be merely parts of international regions—for example, Uruguay is one section of what might be called the "pampas region" of Latin America, of which Buenos Aires is the primate city. And, as is the case with countries, not all regions contain primate cities.

○ *Rank-Size Relations*

Beginning with the largest city, the frequency of communities increases as their size decreases; obviously, small towns are more numerous than medium-size ones, which in turn exceed the number of large ones. On a mathematically rigorous level, arranging towns in order of size exposes an interesting relationship: Rank times size tends to be constant.

This empirical rule was first recognized by Felix Auerbach in a

1913 study of German cities[25] and later restated by Alfred J. Lotka for American cities.[26] In 1936 H. W. Singer adapted Vilfredo Pareto's inverse exponential law of income distribution to the disposition of cities by size: $yx^a = 10^A$, where x is the number of inhabitants, y is the number of towns with x or more inhabitants, and A and a are parameters (necessary because the relationship is not always unitary; in fact, Lotka found an exponent of .93).[27] In choosing to begin with Pareto's curve of income, Singer assumed that underlying economic forces eventuate in the same relationship in the location and growth of cities as in individual earnings: according to Singer, there are a few huge cities, some medium towns, and numerous small hamlets; according to Pareto, few people have high incomes, some have medium incomes, and many have low incomes. Both are close to the truth.

The chief publicizer of the rank-size rule was G. K. Zipf, who tried to incorporate this relationship in his general theory of human behavior.[28] Also attempting quantitative explanations of urban rank-size regularities were Nicholas Rashevsky[29] and Herbert Simon,[30] both of whom deduced city-size formulas from general theories intended (like Zipf's) to explain a wide variety of biological, social, and economic phenomena.

Zipf preferred the formula $M = RS$, in which M is the population of the largest city in the nation, R the rank of each city, and S the population of the given city; thus the second-ranked city should be one-half as large as the biggest, the third-ranked city one-third as large, the fortieth-ranked city one-fortieth as large, and so on. One cannot always start with the largest city, however, as some are primate cities, which violate this rank-order regularity; in fact a strictly demographic definition of a primate city is that it is considerably

[25] Felix Auerbach, "Das Gesetz der Bevölkerungskonzentration," *Petermann's Geographische Mitteilungen*, 59 (1913), 74–6.

[26] Alfred J. Lotka, *Elements of Physical Biology* (Baltimore: Williams & Wilkins, 1925), pp. 306–7.

[27] H. W. Singer, "The 'Courbe des Populations': A Parallel to Pareto's Law," *The Economic Journal*, 46 (June 1936), 254–63.

[28] George Kingsley Zipf, *Human Behavior and the Principle of Least Effort* (Reading, Mass.: Addison-Wesley, 1949), pp. 374–6.

[29] Nicholas Rashevsky, *Mathematical Theory of Human Relations* (Bloomington, Ill.: Principia, 1947).

[30] Herbert A. Simon, *Models of Man* (New York: Wiley, 1957), pp. 145–64.

more than twice as large as the second largest in its nation. Plotting Zipf's curve for United States cities since 1800 demonstrates the marked stability of this rank-size ordering (see Figure 10). This regular urban hierarchy was believed by Zipf to be characteristic of industrial economies, and he regarded deviations from the curve as indications either of economic immaturity of the nation or of improper balance in the urbanization pattern.

Plotting Zipf's curve against curves representing the rank-size facts in 1960 for legal cities and Standard Metropolitan Statistical Areas reveals the SMSA curve entirely above Zipf's curve and the incorpo-

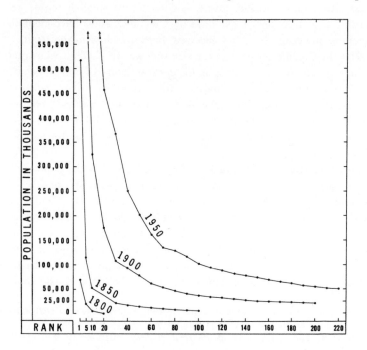

FIGURE 10. Rank-Size Relations of United States Cities: 1800–1950

Data from U.S. Bureau of the Census, *The Seventh Census of the United States: 1850* (Washington, D.C.: Public Printer, 1853), Tables 34 and 35, pp. lii–liv; *A Century of Population Growth: 1700–1900* (Washington, D.C.: Government Printing Office, 1909), Table 104, pp. 188–200; *Thirteenth Census of the United States: 1910* (Washington, D.C., Government Printing Office, 1912), Table 28, pp. 65–75; and *Statistical Abstract of the United States* (Washington, D.C.: Government Printing Office, 1953), Table 14, pp. 22–5.

rated city curve (except for small cities) entirely below.[31] This contrast implies that the most meaningful functional definition of a city falls between those of the SMSA and the incorporated place—a conclusion consistent with frequent complaints that some incorporated places are only parts of true functional cities and with the objection that SMSAs are composed of counties, which often contain quite a bit of distinctly nonurban acreage. Accordingly, Zipf's supporters would recommend an intermediate category of definition—a suggestion consistent with existing nomenclature, as the Bureau of the Census established in 1960 the designation "urbanized area" to refer to the built-up area surrounding a central city but not including the urban-rural fringe and rural parts of an SMSA. The rank-size urbanized-area curve, however, though falling between the SMSA and incorporated-place curves, still lies above Zipf's theoretical curve, implying that urbanized areas might be redefined to contain smaller areas and fewer people. Whether Census officials comply with this recommendation depends partly on the extent to which they accept Zipf's thesis.

Zipf and his students at Harvard University collected dozens of illustrations of the application of this and other variations of his "least effort" principle to tremendously varied phenomena, including the frequency of letters of the alphabet in literary works (two statisticians analyzed word counts using Bayes' theorem to establish whether Hamilton or Madison wrote the disputed *Federalist* papers[32]), the use of words in human speech (schizophrenics deviate strikingly from Zipf's $M = RS$ curve), pauses in musical compositions (a composer's style usually has a characteristic pattern in each of his writing periods), and a heterogeneous set of other physical and artistic subjects of great curiosity value. Zipf seems to have been a lineal descendant of the seventeenth-century French philosophers who wanted to find a single formula to describe everything in the universe.

But we must not reject Zipf's idea simply because it seems bizarre. J. C. Russell found that, when modified slightly, the rank-size formula "seems reasonably close" to the urban form in England in 1377.[33] In

---

[31] Ralph Thomlinson, *Population Dynamics* (New York: Random House, 1965), p. 289.

[32] Frederick Mosteller and David L. Wallace, *Inference and Disputed Authorship: The Federalist* (Reading, Mass.: Addison-Wesley, 1964).

[33] Josiah Cox Russell, *Late Ancient and Medieval Population* (Philadelphia: American Philosophical Society, 1958), p. 69.

1952 researchers at Columbia University's Bureau of Applied Social Research, unable to find current figures for certain sizes of cities in a few countries, used Zipf's formula to obtain estimates of the number of cities of given size; census data released later agreed substantially with their estimates. Turning from empirical evidence to theory, this nonlinear inverse relationship between city size and number of cities is in thorough accord with Christaller's ideas of town size and distribution and consistent with the works of Losch and Isard.

Urban growth in most nations constitutes an open system, for there is irregular addition of new cities to the system as old cities grow larger. Because most cities are increasing in size and because new cities at the threshold of urbanization are being added, the result is a dynamic equilibrium in which the relative frequency of communities of each size remains fairly constant while the total urban population and the number of cities are expanding. Individual cities grow larger as the system enlarges, but the over-all shape of the urban distribution remains approximately the same.

○ *Computer Simulation*

City growth is the product of so many forces operating in such varied ways that it sometimes seems to be random; such pseudorandom processes made up of long and only partially known causal chains are labeled "stochastic" (see Chapter 6). In the future, many urban and other phenomena that are now generally regarded as unpredictable will come to be recognized as stochastic processes susceptible to analysis using Markov or similar chains representing compromises between the unrealistic polar assumptions of independence and strict determinism.

The next step—and one that has already been used in a few instances—is computer simulation of dynamic spatial models using Monte Carlo methods of randomizing. In this way, urban sociologists may generate data with which to test their theories. Although use of such semi-fictional data may seem at first to constitute flagrant cheating, the fact is that randomization of data is distinctly different from the deliberate selection of supportive material common to the work of nonscientific "social scientists." Randomization is the antithesis of selection, and Monte Carlo methods have been used in such vital applications as the training of personnel for airport control towers. Simulation is hardly new, as physical replications of reality have been used for many years: for example, wooden mock-ups of new automobiles, wind tunnels used in designing airplanes, and cardboard or papier-mâché models for new downtown malls or civic centers.

There has been relatively little use of urban simulation models dealing probabilistically with movement of people, businesses, industries, and farms in an urban-rural network occupying several thousand square miles. (For example, a computer might be fed data on income, car ownership, place of work, place of residence, and related facts about residents of an area; the computer might then be instructed to simulate the traffic patterns likely to result from specified locations of prospective freeway routes, trying out several routes with little expenditure of public money.) But it probably will be only a short time before such simulations of regional systems yield valuable analytical inferences, a prediction paralleled by the potential application of computer simulation to analysis of the component parts of urban centers—the subject of the next chapter.

chapter 8

THE SHAPE OF URBAN AREAS

THE SECTIONING OF CITIES AND METROPOLITAN AREAS INTO DISTRICTS or quarters is the foremost traditional ingredient of ecological analysis and is possibly the best known of all aspects of urban ecology. This chapter summarizes twelve approaches to ecology on the second or intermediate level—the metropolis. These attempts to discern ecological regularities fall into four categories: spatial (star, concentric zone, sector, and density gradient); natural (polynuclear and surface feature); social (process, sentiment, social area, and cluster analysis); and economic (ecological distance and land economics).

Some of these approaches or systems of hypotheses do not apply to small towns, but all of them can be applied to medium-size or large cities. If several incorporated places cluster together into a metropolitan region, these approaches describe the composite entity rather than any one part; most of them are not truly suited to describing the central city alone or any other single component.

⬡ *Four Spatial Theories*

The star theory of urban ecology is the oldest of all ecological theories. In 1903 R. M. Hurd observed that cities spread out from the center along transportation lines, thus creating an octopus or star shape (see Figure 11).[1] Eventually the interstices fill in, but always later than the points of the star; this observation was especially true before the advent of the automobile. The star outline is particularly common in cities where most commuting is by mass transit. If people

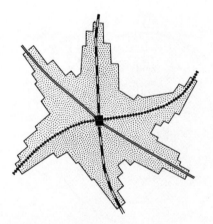

FIGURE 11. The Star Theory

commute by railroad, homes are usually clustered within walking or easy driving distance of the stations, and distance from the city center may be less important in choosing a homesite than distance from the railroad station. Where there is widespread use of the automobile, the spaces between railroad lines are filled in, for cars are not tied to a set route. Most drivers prefer throughways to frequent stop-and-go driving, however, and therefore the star principle still applies, although less decisively. The presence or absence of the star shape is thus

[1] Richard M. Hurd, *Principles of City Land Values* (New York: Record & Guide, 1903).

largely determined by the customary mode of transportation. In underdeveloped countries where most workers walk to their jobs, cities are less likely to develop star shapes than in areas where commuters use bus or streetcar routes.

The most famous ecological theory is the concentric-zone hypothesis of E. W. Burgess and R. E. Park. These University of Chicago professors proposed that a city can be divided into a series of five concentric circles or ovals, usually named, in turn, the central business district, the zone in transition, the zone of workingmen's homes, the middle-class zone, and the commuters' zone (see Figure 12). Sometimes two other zones are added: agricultural districts lying within the circle of commutation, and the hinterland.[2] But Zones

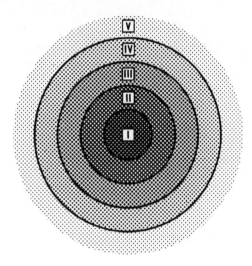

FIGURE 12. The Concentric-Zone Theory

VI and VII do not lie within the metropolis proper and are rarely included in research or discussion using the concentric hypothesis. Zone I is the focus of commercial and civic life; Zone II surrounds Zone I with "areas of residential deterioration caused by the encroaching of business and industry from Zone I" and therefore is an

2 Ernest W. Burgess, "The New Community and Its Future," *Annals of the American Academy of Political and Social Science*, 149 (1930), 161–2.

"area of physical deterioration and social disorganization"; Zone III contains two-family homes for lower-class and immigrant settlement; Zone IV is the home of "small businessmen, professional people, clerks, and salesmen" in apartments interspersed with shopping centers; and Zone V is a ring of dormitory suburbs.

If the Central Business District is predominantly a homeless-men's region; the rooming house district, the habitat of the emancipated family; the area of first immigrant settlement, the natural soil of the patriarchal family transplanted from Europe; the Zone of Better Residences with its apartment houses and residential hotels, the favorable environment for the equalitarian family; then the Commuters' Zone is without question the domain of the matricentric family.[3]

According to Burgess, urban space thus has social implications, location and social background being interrelated. Each zone tends to extend its area by invading the next outer zone; the system of concentric circles "represents an ideal construction of the tendencies of any town or city to expand radially from its central business district." [4] Burgess and Park hypothesized that residents of each zone exhibit characteristic differences from those of other zones; for example, Faris and Dunham's study of the ecological etiology of mental illness disclosed consistent zonal differences in the incidence and types of certain mental disorders in Chicago.[5] The concentric-zone theory has been criticized extensively, usually on the basis that the circular lines are arbitrary, that it neglects natural and man-made topography, or that it does not fit all cities. Nonetheless, the theory's adherents are numerous.

The best-accepted part of the concentric-zone thesis is Zone II, the zone in transition. Sociologists frequently term an area Zone II to depict a blighted or slum area, well supplied with saloons and flophouses and inhabited by homeless men and pariahs. Once a respectable residential district, the area is encroached upon by seedy busi-

---

[3] Burgess, "Urban Areas," in T. V. Smith and L. D. White (eds.), *Chicago: An Experiment in Social Science Research* (Chicago: University of Chicago Press, 1929), pp. 114–23.

[4] Burgess, "The Growth of the City," in Robert E. Park, Burgess, and Roderick D. McKenzie (eds.), *The City* (Chicago: University of Chicago Press, 1925), pp. 47–62.

[5] Robert E. L. Faris and H. Warren Dunham, *Mental Disorders in Urban Areas* (Chicago: University of Chicago Press, 1939).

nesses on the periphery of the central district; with decay come the ghetto, hobohemia, and the red-light district.

Residential areas exhibit an inverse relation between central location and socioeconomic status: the farther out, the higher the status. Some people move to outlying zones because they are moving up; others move out in order to move up. The Massachusetts mill towns are a classic example of this thesis: First the English, then the Irish, then the middle Europeans, then the southern and eastern Europeans settled initially near the center of the city and later moved outward simultaneously with their rise up the social ladder from laborer to skilled worker to foreman to manager.

The sector theory visualizes the city as divisible into pie-shaped wedges or sectors (see Figure 13). Essentially dynamic, it portrays

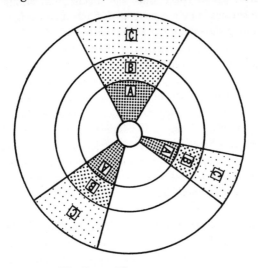

*Place Occupied by
High-Rent Districts*

A   In 1900
B   In 1915
C   In 1936

FIGURE 13. The Sector Theory

change rather than prevailing conditions. Homer Hoyt, who mapped data concerning the high-rent areas of 142 American cities for 1900, 1915, and 1936, deduced the following hypotheses:

1. High-grade residential growth tends to proceed from the given point of origin either along established lines of travel or toward another existing nucleus of building or trade areas.
2. The zone of high rent tends toward high ground which is free

from risk of floods and to spread along lake, bay, river, and ocean ports, where such waterfronts are not used by industry.

3. High-rent residential districts tend to grow toward the section of the city that has free open country beyond the edges and away from "dead end" sections which are prevented from expanding by natural or artificial barriers.

4. The higher-priced residential neighborhood tends to grow toward the homes of the community leaders.

5. Sometimes movement trends of office buildings, banks, and stores pull the higher-priced residential neighborhoods in the same general direction.

6. High-grade residential areas tend to develop along the fastest existing transportation lines.

7. Deluxe apartment areas tend to be established near the business centers in old established residential areas.

8. The growth of high-rent neighborhoods continues in the same direction for a long period of time.

9. High-rent neighborhoods do not skip about at random in the process of movement—they follow a definite path in one or more sectors of the city.

10. It is possible, under some conditions, for high rent areas to "double back," or return toward the center of the city.

11. High-rent areas tend to be adjoined by medium-rent areas, and sharp disjunctions in rental areas are not frequent.[6]

Although these hypotheses are given in terms of high-rent districts, the same trends frequently occur in medium-rent districts, but they occur later and to a lesser extent. The term "rent" is used generically to include house rent, apartment rent, house mortgage or assessment, and apartment mortgage or assessment. Hoyt's theory differs from but is not necessarily in conflict with the star and concentric-zone theories; in some cities, sociologists have used the sector theory to explain residential movement and the Burgess-Park theory to interpret other phenomena of location within the city.

A density-gradient explanation was proposed in 1951 by Colin

[6] Homer Hoyt, *The Structure and Growth of Residential Neighborhoods in American Cities* (Washington, D.C.: Federal Housing Authority, 1939), pp. 112–22.

Clark.[7] Clark and others have generalized that density declines with distance from the city center and that, in time, density falls in the central city and inner suburbs and rises in the outer suburbs as the city spreads out—but this regularity, though of near universal applicability, does vary somewhat between Western and non-Western cultures.[8] The density pattern is expressed by the exponential formula $y = Ae^{-bx}$, in which y is the population density at any given point, A the density in the center, e the Naperian logarithmic base 2.718, b the rate at which the density declines, and x the distance from the city center (see Figure 14). The quantities x and y are variables, e is a

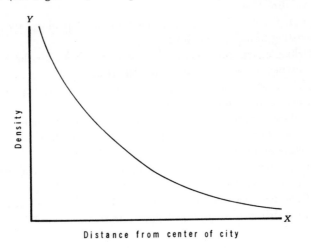

FIGURE 14. The Density-Gradient Theory

constant, and A and b are parameters fixed for each city at any given time. A high value of b indicates a compact city; a low value betokens a sprawling cluster like Los Angeles. In most urban complexes, the value of b is decreasing because of the greater propensity to commute. Assigning a constant value to b throughout a given city is necessary to keep the formula from becoming unwieldy, but in fact the magnitude

[7] Colin Clark, "Urban Population Densities," *Journal of the Royal Statistical Society*, Series A, 114 (1951), 490–6.

[8] Brian J. L. Berry, James W. Simmons, and Robert J. Tennant, "Urban Population Densities: Structure and Change," *Geographical Review*, 53 (July 1963), 389–405.

of *b* varies from sector to sector within the city. Allowing it to vary within the formula, however, would destroy much of the utility of Clark's thesis, as it would no longer provide a single generalization for each city but rather a curvilinear set of density-gradient relations (which might, nonetheless, be a reasonable next step in elaborating this approach).

Plotting density-regression lines for a given city for, say, 1900, 1910, 1920, 1930, 1940, 1950, and 1960 displays graphically the changes in density in the central areas in comparison to outer areas— all, of course, in response to transportation and cultural changes. Trends revealed by this time series can serve as the basis for inferences about 1970 or later years. Although such assumptions about the future entail the possibility of error, they are nevertheless of some value, if only to indicate what the density of various parts of the metropolitan area will be if present tendencies continue unaltered and thus, perhaps, to make a case for altering them if the prospective density gradient is undesirable.

○ *Two Natural-Area Approaches*

Unlike the four spatial theories, which all place strong emphasis on physical location and distance from the city center, the polynuclear theory is founded on the premise that metropolises develop multiple business, industrial, and residential nuclei (see Figure 15). Polynuclear supporters argue that cities tend to develop several separate centers roughly equal in importance, particularly if a metropolis has grown through consolidation of several smaller communities, and that the locations of the nuclei cannot be predicted by spatial generalizations not specific to the given city. C. D. Harris and E. L. Ullman hypothesized that four factors determine the rise of nuclei: certain activities require specialized facilities; like activities tend to group together; certain unlike activities are incompatible; and some activities cannot afford the high rents of the most desirable sites.[9]

The polynuclear thesis is less a theory than a negation of all theo-

[9] Chauncy D. Harris and Edward L. Ullman, "The Nature of Cities," *The Annals of the American Academy of Political and Social Science*, 242 (November 1945), 7–17.

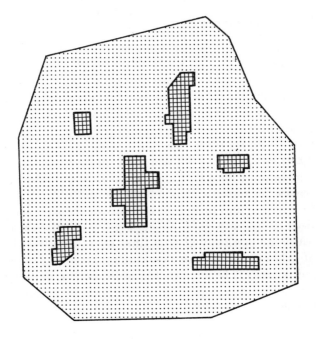

FIGURE 15. A Polynuclear Pattern

ries, and objectors to it claim that ecologists can make reliable generalizations about the spatial-density properties of cities. Lovers of
compromise combine this theory with the concentric-zone or sector
theory by assuming that there are rings and sectors surrounding each
of several nuclei. The polynuclear approach is also in principle com-
binable with Clark's density-gradient formula. In any of these combinations, however, the rings, sectors, and gradient lines overlap, merg-
ing much as do the circular ripples formed by dropping several stones
into a pond; the resulting pattern is apt to be so perplexing as to
discourage generalization.

Reacting strongly against the spatial theories, particularly that putative bellwether the concentric-zone thesis, M. R. Davie and others
claim that topography and pre-existing man-made features like railroads and major buildings render such theories inoperable. "There is
no universal pattern," wrote Davie, "nor even an 'ideal' type." [10] By

[10] Maurice R. Davie, "The Pattern of Urban Growth," in George Peter Murdock
(ed.), *Studies in the Science of Society* (New Haven: Yale University Press,
1937), pp. 131–62.

this Davie meant that concentric-zone and other spatial hypotheses fail; instead, he argued, social scientists should recognize the importance of surface features and use common sense and ingenuity to describe and predict urban ecological trends. Land use is determined by several factors. Topographical features such as rivers, lakes, hills, escarpments, ravines, and swamps interfere with or take precedence over social or geometrical determinants of growth: level land attracts business; high elevations attract residences; low land near transportation routes attracts industry. An erratic arrangement of streets favors central growth; freeways expedite radial expansion. Irregular outlines of cities stem from uneven development of these and other growth factors, supplemented by the idiosyncrasies of private land ownership. The framework of radial growth is laid down by the watercourses, major highways, and railroad tracks.

To be sure, it is hard to object to these statements, but they represent analysis without theory—and such empirical generalizations not bound together theoretically contribute little to knowledge. The surface-feature approach explains urban patterning with a long list of ad hoc descriptive statements that lack the cohesion of other approaches. The purpose of having a theory is to organize a body of data into a compact system of generalizations, thus offering efficient and parsimonious explanations of why events take place as they do. Although the accuracy of the surface-feature approach cannot be denied, as it is principally an organized description of what one finds in each city, it is in essence antitheoretical. And because it provides no systematically arranged hypotheses to be tested, it cannot be proved either right or wrong; it just states what is, whereas a theory promotes a deeper understanding through synthesis. Regardless of these shortcomings, this approach is popular, appealing particularly to those observers of urban life who believe that the spatial theories are too rigid, generalized too far, and ill designed for adaptation to the bewildering variety of city styles.

○ *Four Social Approaches*

Most of the preceding approaches are essentially static portrayals confined to a single time; change is studied by comparing two "photographs" of ecological structure taken at different times. However, the process approach to urban ecology, attributed to R. D. McKenzie,[11] differs by being inherently designed to study change. Although space remains an important feature, this point of view considers it only indirectly, being oriented instead toward the dynamics of movement—the manner in which people and land uses sort themselves out and keep changing their sorting. Some of the seven processes McKenzie named, especially invasion and succession, have passed into the conventional literature of sociology.

1. Concentration is the piling up or massing of people in an area; it is centripetal.
2. Deconcentration is the outward movement from existing clusters; it is centrifugal.
3. Centralization is the gathering of people around a pivotal point. It differs from concentration in that it involves integration around a definite focus; concentration makes no reference to arrangement about a pivot. The most visible illustration is the familiar American central business district.
4. Decentralization is the tendency to move away from the central focus and to shed the urban arrangement of activities and buildings. Deconcentration differs in that it involves an expansion of urbanism; Patrick Geddes' conurbation is deconcentration, not decentralization.
5. Segregation is the clustering together of similar people or institutions—a sifting of population groups and land uses into harmonious types, as through an egg-sorting machine. The operative principle is that like units, whether of people or of specialized functional activities, tend to gather in a given area.
6. Invasion is the penetration of one group or function into an area

---

11 Roderick D. McKenzie, "The Scope of Human Ecology," in Burgess (ed.), *The Urban Community* (Chicago: University of Chicago Press, 1926).

dominated by a different group or function. This encroachment into a segregated area by a group or institution different from the one already there may arouse strong feelings and contribute to interracial tensions.

7. Succession is the complete displacement of the established group or use from an area by an invading group. It is the climax or end product of invasion (until another invasion-succession cycle begins).

These processes are useful for describing the alterations that constantly occur in urban areas, yet essentially they remain merely a set of concepts with accompanying vocabulary rather than a set of hypotheses tested against empirical observations. In other words, although the seven processes generally are conceptually meaningful and consistent with observed urban events, they are descriptive rather than explanatory.

Walter Firey's sentiment theory, like the surface-feature approach, originated in reaction against the idea of spatial determinism in ecological behavior. Firey rejected spatial theories as seeking "some universal regulative principle to explain the spatial orderliness of human activities" and as being "disinclined to consider the *modus operandi* by which people and groups are propelled to their appointed niches in space." Instead, he proposed that ecologists consider values, symbolism, solidarity, and fetishes as explanatory variables.

> If space gets its socially relevant qualities through cultural definition, and if social systems may locate in terms of social values, there is obviously far more to the society-space relation than an intrinsic nexus. . . . A satisfactory ecological theory must conceptualize this non-intrinsic nexus and integrate it with the propositions applying to intrinsic spatial adaptation. . . . Characteristics of space are not those belonging to it as a natural object of the physical world, but rather those which result from its being a symbol for a social system.[12]

Firey points out several areas in Boston that have maintained their special qualities long after McKenzie, Burgess-Park, Hoyt, or Hurd would have expected them to yield to social change: Beacon Hill has remained an upper-class residential district for a century and a half because of sentimental associations; Boston Common has resisted in-

---

[12] Walter Firey, "Introduction," *Land Use in Central Boston* (Cambridge, Mass.: Harvard University Press, 1947).

cursion of business despite restricted land supply because it symbolizes historical sentiments; and the ethnic solidarity in the Italian North End has a retentive power discouraging moving from the district (although some outward migration has recently taken place).

In New York, another observer encountered fetishistic attachment even to filthy tenements scheduled for razing. In a building infested with rats and fleas and piled high with refuse and garbage, a seventy-nine-year-old Italian lady named Rosa lived in a two-room apartment consisting of a tiny living-bedroom and a kitchen with a window opening on a nine-inch air shaft. Rosa, a welfare case, paid $26 a month rent and had been living in the apartment for the fifteen years since her husband had died. In view of the structure's noxious dilapidation, anyone should have been filled with joy at the prospect of being able to move out. When the tenement began to empty, Rosa did become frightened of being alone in it and reluctantly consented to move to an apartment in the same neighborhood. But on moving day she became irascible and refused to budge, finally agreeing to leave only after several hours of strenuous protest. The next day she could hardly be recognized: "She stopped holding her back straight and she stopped cursing at people and she stopped making jokes, and she started complaining about aches and pains she'd never had before." After five months, she hadn't yet unpacked her belongings. At first she returned often to her old building, walked up to her old rooms, and just sat for hours on a box, looking vacantly at the walls. After the last family moved out and the building was boarded up, she took to going every day to stand in front of it or to sit on the steps and wring her hands and mutter. Shortly before demolition a housing official commented: "She's still at it. We're going to tear the place down soon, and I don't know what she'll do then. I think she'll die." [13]

Social-area analysis is a method for preparing a typology of urban districts under the assumption that persons living in one type of social area tend to differ in attitudes and behavior from persons living in other types. Social areas are not spatially determined but are defined solely through socially pertinent characteristics of the inhabitants. The methodological sequence is somewhat the reverse of the spatial theories, which begin with certain assumptions about what kind of

[13] Robert Rice, "Reporter at Large," *The New Yorker*, 30 (April 17, 1954), 103–7.

person lives how far and in which direction from the city center. Rather than starting with a spatial template, social-area analysts first ascertain social attributes and only later put them on a map; space is thus a secondary consideration. The founder, Eshref Shevky, developed eighteen types of social areas based on three indexes computed from seven variables.[14] The index of social rank is calculated from three variables: occupational status, education, and income. The index of urbanization is also prepared from three variables: the child-woman ratio, the proportion of working women, and the percentage of single-family dwellings. The segregation index is based on the proportion of persons in highly isolated population groups. Each census tract is rated as high, medium, or low in social rank; high, average, or low in urbanization; and high or low in segregation—making a cross-tabulation total of eighteen categories.[15] The first two indexes combined are assigned Roman numerals from I to IX; an S is added to indicate high segregation, and absence of S signifies low or no segregation (see Figure 16). All eighteen types may or may not be

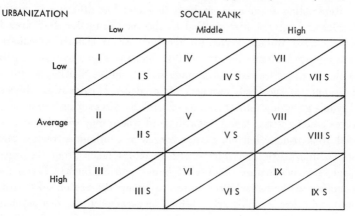

FIGURE 16. A Typology of Social Areas

represented in a given city, and those types that are present may or may not be spatially clustered.

14 Eshref Shevky and Wendell Bell, *Social Area Analysis* (Palo Alto, Calif.: Stanford University Press, 1955).

15 Shevky and Marilyn Williams, *The Social Areas of Los Angeles* (Los Angeles: University of California Press, 1949).

The major objective of this procedure is to classify each small section of the city and then to discover what social attributes are especially prominent in each area. If, for instance, all IIS types tend to have a certain property in common (a high rate of juvenile delinquency, for example), or if, in nearly all of a dozen cities, Type VII areas undergo Negro invasion peacefully and amicably, whereas residents of Type VIII areas generally respond by tossing stones through windows or burning crosses on front lawns, then we shall have learned something useful about the kinds of predispositions common to certain sections of cities—and policy makers can take action with a greater likelihood of success. Proponents of social-area analysis visualize it as having several uses: delineating neighborhoods, expediting contemporaneous and longitudinal comparative studies, and facilitating research on individual attitudes and behavior. This promising typology has been widely applied but frequently criticized (usually for the choice of the seven component variables), so its standing must remain ambiguous.

Resembling social-area analysis in intent but differing in method is cluster analysis, first applied to the San Francisco Bay area by psychologist Robert Tryon for the purpose of classifying subareas and their inhabitants into types. Like Shevky, Tryon avoided starting with any preconceived spatial pattern, but, unlike Shevky, he did not postulate a specified number of predefined categories. Instead, Tryon's grouping into areas was effected by discovering common features among census tracts, regardless of where they were located (social areas usually but not always consist of contiguous tracts). Starting with statistics on thirty-three variables taken from the census (age, sex, occupation, quality of home, and so forth), Tryon used complex mathematical procedures to group the region's 243 tracts into eight demographic areas, which he assumed to be also psychosocial areas: "An area homogeneous in demographic features will also be homogeneous in psychosocial ways." [16]

This assumption is the point of attack for disputants, as jumping the gap between demographic and psychosocial attributes is intellectually hazardous, although perhaps permissible so long as one does not use these areal statistics to make inferences about traits of indi-

[16] Robert C. Tryon, *Identification of Social Areas by Cluster Analysis* (Berkeley: University of California Press, 1955), p. 8.

viduals.[17] Shevky avoided this difficulty by directly seeking social areas; Tryon looked directly for demographic areas and then assumed that they were also psychosocial areas. Obviously, it would be preferable to ascertain attitudes and personality traits directly, but such data are not available for small areas within cities. Collecting this information would require interviewing a large number of people, and the expense would be prohibitive. Methodologically more complicated than Shevky's technique, and related to the elaborate quantitative procedure called factor analysis, this new psychological approach has not yet been tested in enough cities to evaluate its merits conclusively.

◯ Two Economic Theories

Some ecologists believe that impersonal forces like cost, time, distance, site, and competition result in a sorting out and concentration of particular activities in a single area (a wholesale district, heavy manufacturing district, or retail shopping center). Sociologist James A. Quinn has evolved a set of hypotheses based on distance, position, and cost. Quinn suggests that there are three kinds of distance: linear (purely spatial), ecological (referring to the all-inclusive cost of moving men and materials as measured by time, energy, waste, danger, and discomfort), and social (a status variable). He envisions four kinds of positions: geometric (geographic), ecological-spatial (degree of accessibility to transport routes), ecological-functional (dominance-subordination working relation), and social (status).

The meanings of ecological distance and position may be illustrated by considering a family about to decide between two urban apartments, apartment A being nine miles from work and apartment B seventeen miles away; however, apartment B is actually closer ecologically, for its nearness to transportation lines ensures faster, cheaper, and more comfortable commuting than from apartment A. Business and industrial firms face similar decisions, and the shrewd factory

[17] W. S. Robinson, "Ecological Correlations and the Behavior of Individuals," *American Sociological Review*, 15 (June 1950), 351–7.

owner considering building a new plant estimates the total cost of, for example, the salaries and fringe benefits of two men in a truck burning gasoline waiting for lights to change while moving x crates of goods from the plant, plus the truck's depreciation, license fees, and insurance. Quinn uses these notions in three hypotheses:

> Hypothesis of minimum costs: Ecological units tend to distribute themselves through an area so that the total costs of gaining maximum satisfaction in adjusting population to environment (including other men) are reduced to a minimum.
>
> Hypothesis of minimum ecological distance: If other factors are constant in an area, ecological units tend to distribute themselves through it so that the total ecological distance traversed in adjusting to limited environmental factors, including other ecological and social units, is reduced to a minimum.
>
> Hypothesis of median location: In a free competitive system, social and aesthetic factors being equal, a mobile ecological unit tends to occupy a median location with respect to (1) the environmental resources it uses, (2) other units on which it depends, and (3) other units it serves. If several ecological units find their medians located at the same place, that ecological unit tends to occupy the common median which can utilize it most intensively.[18]

Intensity of utilization is measurable indirectly by the amount of money the user is able or willing to pay for a site: Department stores utilize sites more fully than do single-family homes; therefore they will pay more for the land they desire than would a homeowner, however rich.

The first hypothesis is reminiscent of the hedonistic calculus of utilitarians Jeremy Bentham and John Stuart Mill. The third implies that the best ecological pattern is achieved by leaving ecological units alone; that government is best that governs least. In this view, "natural selection" tends to eliminate those activities not sufficiently profitable to permit purchase of land for their pursuit, in favor of the more successful land uses, which proliferate greatly. On this reasoning, zoning regulations should not interfere with these natural competitive-distributive processes but should be confined to a passive role. Quinn implies that if everyone looks after his own interests as well as he possibly can, then the interests of the group will be served best. But

[18] James A. Quinn, *Human Ecology* (Englewood Cliffs, N.J.: Prentice-Hall, 1950), pp. 272–89.

can we support this laissez-faire position that selfish actions by all individual members of society add up to maximum benefit to society as a whole? The balance of intellectual opinion favors a negative answer. In any case, Quinn's theory is not widely accepted.

The last of the twelve approaches is that of land economics. Land economists believe that the determination of urban land use is a market process: The kind and intensity of use made of each parcel of land result from economic competition among the various possible uses. The processes of city growth are seen as economic, and the pattern of urban land use is deemed the result of the land market.[19] Land economists talk of demand, supply, market, income, and property. Under competition, the most valuable land goes to the type of use that can best afford to pay for it: business. Usually the most expensive piece of property in the city (measured per front foot) contains a department store. Because private and industrial users often cannot compete with businesses in bidding for land, and because location downtown is unessential and often undesirable to them, they go elsewhere. A city's structure is thus determined through this dollar evaluation of the importance of various locations. According to this thesis, merchants, industrialists, and homeowners bid competitively for sites on the basis of their felt needs and profit expectations, the highest bidder usually being the one who can extract the greatest return from the site. The entrepreneur who owns a parcel of land attempts to ascertain the use that will yield him the highest revenue, and, as each owner tries to maximize his income, every plot tends to achieve optimum use. Of course, under an economic system in which land is not privately owned, these motives do not apply.

Ecological conclusions of land economists frequently agree with those of the other eleven approaches described here; differences arise in explaining how the various urban activities and land uses sort themselves out as they do, land economists being distinguished by their great stress on competition for accessible sites through direct or indirect competitive bidding. The economic importance of location is mirrored in the manner in which property tax assessments are customarily made in American cities: Valuation is based on front footage, which varies not only with the width of each lot, but primarily according to the nearness of the city center or other nucleus. Depth of

[19] Richard U. Ratcliff, *Urban Land Economics* (New York: McGraw-Hill, 1949), p. vi.

the lot is relatively insignificant, and some assessors simply assign a blanket 10 per cent increase to valuations of unusually deep lots without consideration of how much additional land is involved. Of course, in some residential areas, topographical or other physical features may override distance from the city center as determinants of value.

○ *Soft and Hard Facts and Theories*

The fact that twelve different—although sometimes compatible—approaches to urban ecology have managed to survive the hazards of empirical verification testifies both to the lack of a grand theory and to the diversity of people's reactions to their environments. Some people go one way, some another. Some of the Italians described by Firey in Boston's North End district have risen far enough in social status and income to live in other sections of the city, but their feelings of ethnic identity cause them to stay in the old Italian neighborhood; for similar reasons most of them retain their obviously Italian names. On the other hand, some immigrants or minority-group members abandon their ethnically stigmatizing names and, in some cases, their religious affiliations as they move to "Anglo-Saxon" Protestant neighborhoods in their search for financial and social success. Still others are motivated neither by ethnic solidarity nor by social climbing: "Economic men" respond directly to price changes, selling their homes when profits are offered and refusing to pay for either sentimental associations or conventional names (but often sentiment and "in" labels are worth money in the marketplace and simple-minded purchasers are induced to put dollars into brokers' pockets). In sum, a dozen sets of generalizations are needed because people respond to ecological stimuli in at least a dozen different ways—a fact of life hardly conducive to maximize respect for ecology as a unified scientific system.

This survey of recent and present thinking on ecological structuring within cities thus reflects the strengths and weaknesses of social science, illustrating both the soft and hard facts of social research. This topic is the second of the three levels of ecological analysis, and it is also middling in the rigor of research and depth of sociological sophistication it has so far attracted.

In common with other sociological hypotheses, the generalizations in this chapter have many exceptions. No one can advance a set of generalizations about the cities of a whole continent or major country without encountering a large number of deviations. This chapter summarizes many broad statements, usually not intended by their originators to constitute invariant descriptions. The purpose is to identify as many valid generalizations as facts warrant, without claiming universal applicability. Great individual variations exist from city to city, but common qualities can be found, and the thrust of this chapter has been to identify them, whether prominent or obscure, in the expectation that discovery of similarities will advance our understanding of the cities in which so many of us live.

Spatial sociological research offers a latent benefit: the unanticipated nonspatial accomplishments that have flowed almost incidentally from the quest for a viable theory of urban shape. Park, Burgess, Hawley, and other urban ecologists have come up with important discoveries about social stratification, attitudes toward ethnic groups, crime and delinquency, family life, political affiliation, and many other social problems. A spatial orientation is capable of producing significant contributions to nonspatial fields of considerable concern to all types of sociologists. Still, the major advancement in knowledge to be expected from ecological research remains the understanding of how and why and to what effect men distribute themselves across the face of the earth.

chapter 9

INTERNATIONAL CONTRASTS

THE DOZEN ECOLOGICAL APPROACHES DESCRIBED IN THE PRECEDING chapter were nearly all developed by Americans using data from cities in the United States and a few other industrial nations. But do they apply in other countries and cultures? Or, rather, to what extent do they apply? Which ones are reasonably accurate descriptions of which places? And how much modification of these theories is called for in response to observed cross-cultural variations?

Seven of these approaches—the six spatial and natural ones plus the sentiment theory—are so constructed as to be amenable to quantitative or qualitative testing; that is, the hypothesis can be said either to fit or not to fit the ecological structure of a given city. If a theory describes most cities with reasonable accuracy, it is considered partially verified and entitled to survive, but if it usually fails to describe urban ecological patterns it must be either abandoned, altered, or perhaps accepted as applicable only to a particular type of city. As might be expected, when one attempts to analyze anything as complicated as a city or metropolitan region, none of these dozen ecological schemes is likely under the best of circumstances to provide a perfect description of even one city, for any aggregation of 50,000 or 500,000 people is bound to contain a few exceptions to any rule. The question, then, is not whether the proffered description is accurate in all details but whether it is generally accurate. Block-by-block precision and measurement in yards are practical impossibilities, and realistic ecologists are grateful when they find hypotheses that hold for districts and miles.

The remaining five of the dozen approaches are not truly testable, for their value is ascertained not by the degree of their correspondence to empirical data but rather by the extent of their explanatory utility. They cannot be said either to fit or not to fit—and therefore to be supported or refuted. Instead, their intellectual legitimacy is based on the validity of the descriptive or causal explanations for observed phenomena that they offer.

○ Preindustrial Cities

Preindustrial cities had certain properties in common, despite pervasive variations in the cultural contexts within which the cities grew. One common property was that the upper classes lived near the city centers and the lower classes on the outskirts, the reverse of the typical modern American gradient. An inverse correlation between socioeconomic status and distance from the center of the city was present in most prenineteenth-century cities in all parts of the world, including the United States. And when there were pariahs or slums in the area, they were found on the periphery rather than in the transition zone described by Park and Burgess. The contemporary American gradient-slum arrangement is thus a cultural peculiarity more or less confined to our own time.

Lack of transportation made it necessary to live close to the center if one were to have ready access to the city's offerings; this motivation encouraged a concentration of elite at or near the center in preindustrial cities on all continents. Conversely, the more disadvantaged the person, the farther out from the center he was forced to live: The moderately poor fanned out toward the periphery, and the outcasts lived on the fringe, entire families often occupying flimsy, one-room hovels.

These and other ecological attributes of preindustrial cities were (and in many parts of the world still are) part of the "bazaar economy," in which the "flow of commerce is fragmented into a very great number of unrelated person-to-person transactions"—as opposed to the "firm-centered economy" of the Western world, in which exchanges of goods and money "occur through a set of impersonally defined social institutions." [1] Each of these two marketing systems implies its own ecological ordering of economic activity within a city, the most significant difference being the more sharply defined and temporally constant zone pattern associated with the modern system. By contrast, cities operating under a bazaar economy tended to be characterized by heterogeneous mixing of economic activity and land use; a proliferation of small business establishments were interspersed throughout residential areas, where bargaining and haggling were inescapable parts of the ritual of any purchase and prices fluctuated dramatically in accompaniment to disordered noise, fascinating odors, and colorful tableaux. But this seemingly chaotic merchandising pattern did not have a social-stratification counterpart, for ethnic quarters usually were strictly separated from one another—far more so than in industrial cities—as members of each linguistic, religious, racial, or nationality group resided almost without exception in their own section of the city.

Another common characteristic of preindustrial cities in most parts of the world was the presence of a surrounding wall.

> Typically, all or most of the city is girdled by a wall. Inside, various sections of the city are sealed off from one another by walls, leaving little cells, or subcommunities, as worlds unto themselves. Walled cities have been the generalized pattern throughout the Middle East from North Africa to Central Asia, and in India and China during much of their history. Even certain pre-Columbian cities of Meso-America conformed to this pattern.[2]

The walls and moats encircling the communities of feudal Europe form a familiar picture. Whether these enclosed settlements should be

---

[1] Clifford Geertz, *Peddlers and Princes* (Chicago: University of Chicago Press, 1963), p. 28.

[2] Gideon Sjoberg, *The Preindustrial City* (New York: Free Press, 1960), p. 91.

called towns or castles is often difficult to decide, for medieval towns were usually very small, and castles were so well supplied with the necessities of life as to be fully as self-sufficient as any city. Often a community presented attributes of both; hence such compromises or perplexing terms as "castle-town," "fortress-city," and "castle-burg."

Polynucleation was also a world-wide preindustrial pattern, observable on all continents and in both large and small cities. Some—but certainly not all—of the modern United States ecological patterns are thus seen to be historical irregularities, exceptions, however, that may be rapidly on the way to becoming universal norms for modern industrial cities throughout the world. In many parts of the world, however, cities still adhere to their traditional social contours and have not yet changed—and perhaps may never change—to one of the American ecological patterns. Some nations contain both old-style and new-style cities, and often the old and the new are both present in one city.

As for internal structural comparisons among twentieth-century cities, the available quantity and quality of information permit reliable and detailed generalizations in some regions, but in others there is a crippling scarcity of relevant data. Let us turn next to the continents for which the most and best information can be obtained.

○ *Latin American Cities*

The observed positive correlation between distance from the city center and socioeconomic status in the United States is reversed in the traditional cities of Latin America: There upper-class people live near the city center, and lower-class people live on the periphery.[3] A number of factors underly this ecological inversion between Latin and Anglo American cities.[4]

---

[3] Asael T. Hansen, "The Ecology of a Latin American City," in Edward B. Reuter (ed.), *Race and Culture Contacts* (New York: McGraw-Hill, 1934), pp. 124–42; Norman S. Hayner, "Mexico City: Its Growth and Configuration," *American Journal of Sociology*, 50 (January 1945), 295–304; and Floyd Dotson and Lillian Ota Dotson, "Ecological Trends in the City of Guadalajara, Mexico," *Social Forces*, 32 (May 1954), 367–74.

[4] Theodore Caplow, "The Social Ecology of Guatemala City," *Social Forces*, 28 (December 1949), 113–33.

Traditional Spanish American cities are political centers without the Anglo American emphasis on commerce and therefore without the competition for land that results in steep gradients of prices and emphasizes centripetal trends. Land tenure is also different: Land ownership is nominally vested in the city, and the government has regulatory powers never approached in Anglo America. Land has a value in itself rather than merely as a source of income. There has been much more urban planning in Latin American cities from the outset than in their Anglo American counterparts, which grew in rather haphazard fashion; because of this Latin tradition of city planning, central blight has not compelled the well-to-do people to move to the suburbs. Earthquakes, which seem to offer no benefits, do help to prevent blight by periodically removing weak structures fit for demolition; not only are they selective and frequent, but they also limit vertical building, which automatically limits land values. As the lower classes have considerable difficulty paying taxes, they prefer to move out beyond the city limits into the unimproved areas—a process that keeps the poorest people on the periphery of the community; thus the invasion process associated in Anglo America with the zone in transition does not take place, and the socioeconomic gradient is preserved.

The Anglo American image of downtown as a dirty, noisy, unpleasant place, which one prefers to visit for a "good time" rather than to live in, is the opposite of the Latin stereotype of the city as a place for exciting living in the thick of things, in contrast to the crude, boring, and sometimes dangerous life of the countryside. The Spaniards who colonized Latin America preferred to live close to the center of activities; the natives were thus compelled willy-nilly to live farther out in their mud huts.

Transportation and communications are poorly developed in Latin America, making it impossible to live very far from work and still commute quickly and comfortably; faced with sharing accommodations on a decrepit bus with chickens and pigs, those who can do so willingly pay a premium for the privilege of living near their work or close to the downtown district. Only upper-class people can afford the luxuries of not traveling on slow, overcrowded, dirty buses and of living within walking distance of work so that they can readily make the trip home for the traditional afternoon siesta. And until quite recently very few people could afford private automobiles. Furthermore, the intermingling of small stores in residential areas of all social classes makes extensive daily travel unnecessary and discourages centralization.

Housing as a form of conspicuous display of social status is inhibited by the Latin custom of presenting blank walls to the street; life in a patio-centered residence is directed inward. Also, the patio arrangement promotes low residential density and thereby discourages blight in the residential districts surrounding the central plaza. From the outside it is difficult to distinguish between luxurious homes and very poor ones, and the wealthy Latin American is not motivated to move to the suburbs and to build a home that would show off his expenditure; social mobility is therefore not tied to geographic mobility. The rigid continuity of the social-class system impedes change and promotes both social and ecological stability. Finally, the basic traditionalism permits absorption of many minor alien traits with comparatively little effect on behavior.

Nevertheless, since World War II the traditional Latin American socioeconomic ecological gradient has been moving toward the Anglo American pattern. The patio-centered house is becoming obsolete. The *barrio*—traditionally a very important intra-urban community somewhat larger than an Anglo American neighborhood—is losing its force as a functional unit and a community of identification; today, the larger and more modern the city, the more its *barrios* have declined as autonomous social units. Cities are booming, industrializing, and modernizing. Transportation and communications are improving. Wealthy foreigners build expensive homes on the outskirts. General Motors and Coca-Cola, for example, are Anglo-Americanizing Latin America; in fact, there as elsewhere, the increasing prevalence of the private automobile rivals industrialization as the most influential force in this Anglicization. The result is a mixture of the traditional and the modern.

○ *European Cities*

Clearly, the United States pattern of urban development is not necessarily typical and certainly not universal. Research in Europe on urban ecology supplies additional material suitable for testing hypotheses formulated in the United States. In general, the more rigorous and explicit the theory, the less it applies to European cities.

The concentric-zone theory has been tested in England with varying success. Francis Hauser argues that it is entirely inapplicable to London,[5] but I. M. Castle and E. Gittus maintain that Liverpool, like Chicago, does tend to be arranged in concentric circles.[6] On the other hand, Peter Collison and John Mogey describe an ecological pattern in Oxford resembling that of a traditional Latin-American town, with occupational rank declining with increasing distance from the city center.[7]

On the Continent, Stockholm exemplifies the many European cities shaped by explicit public policies, largely because of government ownership of large tracts of land; concentric rings are discernible, but the socioeconomic gradient is the reverse of that in Chicago, and there is no transition zone with dislocated functions. Vienna has grown in a polynuclear fashion, mingling residential, business, and industrial uses. Budapest and other Hungarian cities show zonal patterns somewhat resembling those of Chicago, but there is no zone in transition, as wealthier classes tend to live close to the downtown district.[8] In many European cities high prestige is traditionally associated with central rather than peripheral residence. One study applying social-area analysis to Rome demonstrated not only the analytical utility of the Shevky approach but also that Rome exhibits both sector and zonal patterns, with the qualification that social rank is highest in the central district, declines slightly in intermediate areas, and decreases sharply in outer areas.[9] Another widespread phenomenon is rapid industrial growth on the fringe since 1900, a pattern found in Berlin, Vienna, London, and Paris.[10]

---

[5] Francis L. Hauser, "Ecological Patterns of European Cities," in T. Lynn Smith and C. A. McMahan (eds.), *The Sociology of Urban Life* (New York: Dryden, 1951), pp. 370–5.

[6] I. M. Castle and E. Gittus, "The Distribution of Social Defects in Liverpool," *Sociological Review*, 5 (July 1957), 43–64.

[7] Peter Collison and John Mogey, "Residence and Social Class in Oxford," *American Journal of Sociology*, 64 (May 1959), 599–605.

[8] Erdmann Doane Beynon, "Budapest: An Ecological Study," *Geographical Review*, 33 (April 1943), 256–75.

[9] Dennis C. McElrath, "The Social Areas of Rome," *American Sociological Review*, 27 (June 1962), 389–90.

[10] Robert E. Dickinson, *The West European City* (London: Routledge, 1951), pp. 228–50.

In France, the sections of cities called "quarters" are far more cohesive than their United States counterparts, being supported by extensive primary relationships, strong sectional identification among residents, and distinctive folkways. The sentiment, polynuclear, and surface-feature approaches all fare well in France. Centrality is less marked than in United States cities; there is less of the disruption of transition, invasion, and succession; density does not diminish regularly with distance from the center; and social class is not consistently associated with residential location.[11] French cities, like those of most other regions whose towns are older than United States communities, present many more variations in ecological form.[12] Because their main periods of growth were usually spread over several centuries, French cities—and European cities generally—present "more alternative types of urban settlement than can be found in the United States; more varieties of internal adaptation, of spatial patterning, of architectural structure, and of change." [13]

Although the spatial theories have had indifferent success in Europe, the polynuclear and sentiment approaches seem especially applicable to many of the older metropolitan areas. Cities that have had long histories are often polynuclear, as seventeenth-century and nineteenth-century nuclei grow together to be joined by twentieth-century centers to form single large communities. Where history is long and well regarded, the ecological scene comes to be dotted with historically understandable contradictions. Rome and the relatively young New York offer contrasting treatment of sports arenas: Although demolition of New York's Madison Square Garden was resisted by athletic diehards who remembered it as the setting for many of their heroes and champions, it was nonetheless razed; but a much older and irreparably dilapidated athletic stadium in Rome has not yet been and may never be demolished, for the Coliseum is a focus of sentiment—and the greatest force maintaining the Coliseum may well be neither beauty, history, nor greed but, rather, sentiment. Similarly, dwellings made famous by literary and historical figures like Haw-

---

11 Gaston Bardet, *Le nouvel urbanisme* (Paris: Fréal, 1948); and Pierre Lavedan, *Géographie des villes* (Paris: Gallimard, 1936).

12 Jacques Tricart, *Cours de géographie humaine*, Vol. II: *L'habitat urbain* (Paris: Centre de Documentation Universitaire, 1951).

13 Caplow, "Urban Structure in France," *American Sociological Review*, 17 (October 1952), 547.

thorne, Dickens, and Balzac are maintained in Massachusetts, London, and Paris (although their influence on their immediate environs is often negligible).

○ *Asian Cities*

Generalizing about the cities of an entire continent is hazardous and calls for many qualifications reflecting the variability of ecological structure from city to city. And if brief summaries of ecological research in all continents verge on the dangerously naïve, then broad statements about Asian cities are particularly susceptible to oversimplification because in that one culturally varied continent reside one-third of the world's urban people. With this caveat, we can proceed to make a few cautious generalizations.

In Asian cities, which are inclined to be amorphous, the polynuclear thesis is apt to be the most appropriate. Many of the cities are overgrown villages with gopher-trail street patterns. Indeed, a large portion of the urban dwellers earn their living in agricultural pursuits.

Both zonation of land use and racial and ethnic segregation are more clearly defined and persistent than in Western cities; metropolises tend to be sharply differentiated into quarters settled by distinct racial or religious groups. Often each quarter has its own head official. City-wide rights are practically nonexistent in traditional cities, where legal claims are sometimes dependent on the power of local clans. Civic pride is likely to be expended on the clan or quarter in preference to the city. Residents of such cities are really urbanized villagers united by kinship or ethnic ties.

Cultural values, sentimental associations, and symbolism are important determinants of community spatial structure in the East. In India the religious and occupational aspects of caste are vital; towns tend to be segmented into distinct caste areas, each with its sacred shrine and headman. Industrialization and Westernization, however, are breaking down these caste-induced ecological patterns.[14]

[14] Radhakmal Mukerjee, "Ways of Dwelling in the Communities of India," *Asia*, 40 (June 1940), 287–90; 40 (July 1940), 375–8; 40 (August 1940), 439–42.

Often several districts are present but imperfectly integrated: a modern commercial, administrative, and upper-class residential district; an "old city" of wayward alleys and densely occupied dwellings; and a mushrooming zone of huts or shacks inside or outside the city limits (but usually on the periphery) that lacks most urban characteristics except high density and nonagricultural employment of residents. In some cases the modern city is completely separate from the old, and the latter has retained its traditional artisan industries, bazaars, social structure, and sharply defined ethnic or religious bases for quarters. The central business districts of such cities as Bangkok, Saigon, Singapore, and Jakarta are "entirely nonindigenous." [15] Some traditionally organized cities have grown to considerable size with only minor admixtures of modern elements.[16]

In many Oriental cities, the rising population has not contributed to suburbanization, for villages have long been located beyond the periphery; enlargement of these cities meant that the perimeters simply moved out to where the villages already were. Such villages are neither suburban nor urban; they are geographically near the city, but they lack urban amenities and ways of life—they are in the city but not of it.

Within Indian cities, members of each religion and stratification level tend to reside together voluntarily in ghettos, although economic segregation sometimes cuts across these caste and religious lines. Slums may be located either on the outskirts or in the heart of the city.[17] Unlike Western cities, where central districts are commonly almost totally devoid of residences, the center is sometimes, as is the case in Rangoon, Burma, "the most densely populated residential area of the city." [18] Shops selling the same type of merchandise are usually clustered together, sometimes occupying entire streets for several blocks. Although central business districts do exist in India, the usual commercial pattern is segregation according to type into a number of

---

[15] D. W. Fryer, "The 'Million City' in Southeast Asia," *Geographical Review*, 43 (October 1953), 474–94.

[16] United Nations, *Report on the World Social Situation* (New York: United Nations, 1958), pp. 131–2.

[17] S. Ghosh, "The Urban Pattern of Calcutta," *Economic Geography*, 16 (January 1950), 257.

[18] Richard W. Redick, "A Demographic and Ecological Study of Rangoon, Burma, 1953," in Ernest W. Burgess and Donald J. Bogue (eds.), *Contributions to Urban Sociology* (Chicago: University of Chicago Press, 1964), p. 38.

minor districts, conforming somewhat to the polynuclear principle. Contributing to the wide diffusion of business is the need for a bazaar in each of the numerous segregated residential quarters. Also, outlying business districts tend to be more independent from the central businesses than in the United States, with its chain stores.[19] The highly mixed residential and commercial land-use patterns have an industrial counterpart: "Industrial activity may—and does—appear almost anywhere in an Indian urban area." [20] This polynucleation is further encouraged by the poverty that compels most residents to walk to stores or their workplaces—a circumstance also inhibiting deconcentration of industry to less congested areas on the fringe and promoting extremely high densities of up to 400,000 people per square mile[21] —higher than in any Western city, although easily surpassed by Hong Kong.

Although their narrow, twisting lanes convey romantic charm to the casual tourist, Indian cities are one of the most unpleasant and noxious environments on the face of the earth; what is appealing to the photography hobbyist becomes appalling when a Westerner contemplates living there. And until imported Anglo American patterns —like functional segregation of areas and arterial streets semisystematically intermingled among local streets—replace indigenous patterns (assuming that they ever do), the legacy of mixed land uses and numerous small foci of activity will continue to prevail in India.

Traditional Japanese cities were not centralized; rather, businesses and residences were scattered at an almost uniform density throughout the towns. This old ecological structure persists today primarily in small municipalities; some large industrial cities are coming to be patterned similarly to those in the United States.[22] Tokyo, says R. P. Dore, "divides satisfactorily into the concentric zones" of Park and Burgess.[23] Manufacturing and trade, however, still tend to be dis-

[19] Noel P. Gist, "The Ecology of Bangalore, India: An East-West Comparison," *Social Forces*, 25 (May 1957), 356–65.

[20] Gerald Breese, "Urban Development Problems in India," *Annals of the Association of American Geographers*, 53 (September 1963), 258.

[21] John E. Brush, "The Morphology of Indian Cities," in Roy Turner (ed.), *India's Urban Future* (Berkeley: University of California Press, 1962), p. 64.

[22] Amos H. Hawley, "Land Value Patterns in Okayama, Japan, 1940 and 1952," *American Journal of Sociology*, 60 (March 1955), 487–92.

[23] Ronald P. Dore, *City Life in Japan* (Berkeley: University of California Press, 1958), p. 11.

persed throughout all sections of metropolitan agglomerations, largely because of the continuation of household-based production and commercial units, which results in a high degree of functional homogeneity within many metropolitan areas, in contrast to the greater differentiation customary within United States and other Western metropolises.[24]

○ *African Cities*

African cities vary greatly. One major distinction is between the urban communities of the Mediterranean littoral and those of the rest of the continent. Cities in North Africa, a part of the Near East, fit the traditional Asian patterns remarkably closely. But sub-Saharan Africa is quite different in urban style from Asia or any other continent.

The urban communities differing the most from those in the West are probably those of Africa. In the first place, cities are relatively scarce in Africa; and second, those indigenous cities that do exist are considerably different in character from the ones dominated by Europeans. In non-European cities, there tends to be a homogeneity of buildings, most of which are residential, with a few larger structures designed as palaces, churches, or markets—representing the three factors most frequently responsible for the creation of African towns. Ecological differentiation is almost nonexistent, for many cities tend to be collections of compounds, each housing an extended family. Streets often are simply those spaces not occupied by compounds, although in African cities of 50,000 or more population, arterial avenues are customary. Otherwise, the street arrangement is best described as a maze. Many—and often most—of the residents are farmers by occupation; the people are less urban than the physical setting.

Partly because African cultures are so little urbanized and partly because there has been scant research on the morphology of African cities, not much can be said about their ecological structure. Perhaps the main point is that some African cities have long histories, antedating by many years the arrival of white invaders; the Yoruba and

[24] Thomas O. Wilkinson, *The Urbanization of Japanese Labor, 1868–1955* (Amherst: University of Massachusetts Press, 1965), pp. 185–7.

other West African tribes have lengthy urban traditions. Centuries of caravan trade have introduced ethnic heterogeneity, and there is considerable division of labor among various specialties, but spatial ordering seems to be difficult to discern in indigenous cities in the face of the relatively uniform array of small houses. The one ecological regularity that can be discerned with confidence is the segregation of Europeans, Africans, and Asians into distinct residential quarters brooking no racial intermingling.[25] The degree to which invasion will be tolerated in the foreseeable future is still highly uncertain.

Forces affecting the locations of cities springing from indigenous African cultures, as opposed to cities drawing on the industrial revolution and other Euro-American traditions, nonetheless frequently resemble the forces influencing siting of Western cities. Timbuctu, for example, prospered as a commercial center on the banks of the Niger River because the spot was accessible to both land and water traffic; Horace Miner identified three important siting and growth factors:

1. Its position at the point where the Niger penetrates the desert most deeply, favoring the junction of river and desert-borne traffic.
2. Its location just beyond the area of wide inundations making possible a port settlement open to land traffic the year round.
3. The early political and commercial dominance of the area to the west and southwest.[26]

Two case studies of social topography in African cities suggest some of the change that is now taking place. The small West African city of Lagos, Nigeria, grew rapidly during the century of European domination beginning in 1852; today, despite its location in an underdeveloped country, it has a pattern of land use "not unlike that in a medium-size city in the more advanced countries of the world." [27] In East Africa, the developing city of Khartoum, Sudan, bears a vague resemblance to the concentric zones of the Park-Burgess conception, implying that perhaps "when the same forces and factors that are operative in Western cities are at work in Eastern cities, the same

[25] See for example Ronald W. Walmsley, *Nairobi: The Geography of a New City* (Nairobi, Kenya: Eagle, 1957), pp. 27–35.

[26] Horace M. Miner, *The Primitive City of Timbuctoo* (Garden City, N.Y.: Doubleday, 1965), p. 307.

[27] Akin L. Mabogunje, "The Evaluation and Analysis of the Retail Structure of Lagos, Nigeria," *Economic Geography*, 40 (October 1964), 304–23.

results occur." Khartoum, however, manifests several deviations from the Chicago-inspired pattern, some resulting from the tropical climate and others signifying cultural differences. In tropical Africa, the water front is refreshing and attracts the upper classes, whereas in colder latitudes, the water front frequently is shunned by the rich in favor of hilltop sites. Another interesting difference is the relation between color of building and social class—"the higher the status, the brighter and lighter the tint of the residence"—a relationship "so prevalent that it can be considered a social index." [28]

○ *Underdeveloped Areas*

In African as in many Asian and other underdeveloped nations, certain kinds of activities have no fixed locations and are therefore not truly part of the land-use pattern. Many functions that would occupy specific parcels of land in Western cities are performed on streets or sidewalks or other public places—wherever space is available for temporary pre-emption. Sidewalk vendors display their wares wherever there are passersby, barbers cut hair on chairs along sidewalks, and pushcarts offer vegetables or other goods at curbs. Such markets are familiar to travelers in non-Western areas and also to those Americans old enough to remember their counterparts in United States cities, especially in lower-class and immigrant districts.

Another practice contributing to the greater functional mix in cities in underdeveloped regions is the custom of storekeepers living in, behind, or over their shops—an inherently mixed land use that can also be observed in the older sections of many industrial cities of Europe and the United States. In some cities the sorting of land uses seems more vertical than horizontal; that is, there is little or no territorial separation of activities, but within almost every block the ground floor is used for commerce or small industry, and the second and higher stories are devoted to residences (although in some instances the second story is reserved for office and warehousing use).

Perhaps the most frequently differentiated kinds of land use in

[28] G. Hamdan, "The Growth and Functional Structure of Khartoum," *Geographical Review*, 50 (January 1960), 21–40.

cities in newly developing lands are the very lowest and highest residential categories—which, ironically, tend to be located near each other on the periphery. Squatter areas often develop on the fringe of the city; they are inhabited by impoverished migrants from rural areas who seek unskilled employment. At the other extreme of the socioeconomic scale, high-income people are shifting away from their traditional loci adjacent to city centers and are now building imposing homes on the most attractive sites at the outer edges of the city, from which their automobiles permit more comfortable commuting than was possible before the twentieth century.

For millions of people no permanent residence exists. In many urban areas, large segments of the people live in temporary huts, as in the hills around Rio de Janeiro, or sleep in the streets huddled next to buildings when adverse weather threatens, as in Bombay, India, or Lagos, Nigeria. Sleeping in the street is a familiar predicament in the surging cities of underdeveloped nations: In Calcutta, some 600,000 people sleep in the streets, a way of life permitting "no privacy, no relief from heat, no escape from cold or rain, and no decent means for disposing of human waste. It is the way of the stray animal." [29] Nor is there dignity in death, for Hong Kong street cleaners on their morning rounds have grown accustomed to finding forsaken carcasses awaiting disposal.

Because rapidly growing cities frequently contain insufficient permanent housing to accommodate the numerous newcomers, temporary shacks—often lacking water, electricity, gas, and drainage—are permitted (or carefully ignored) in what has come to be called the "septic fringe." The shanty-towns of Caracas, Venezuela, increased from 16 per cent of the city population in 1943 to 23 per cent in 1961, when they housed 285,000 people. Also in 1961, Jakarta, Indonesia, hosted 750,000 squatters, amounting to one-fourth of the total metropolitan population. There are nearly 500,000 squatters in Lima, Peru, and in Ankara, Turkey, almost half the population are squatters. Of the 900,000 residents of greater Baghdad, an estimated 400,000 live in peripheral zones in reed huts devoid of latrines and other amenities. A few squatter colonies even subsist in junks or houseboats, which may or may not be improvements over improvised shacks on

[29] Charles Abrams, *Man's Struggle for Shelter in an Urbanizing World* (Cambridge, Mass.: M.I.T. Press, 1964), pp. 3–4.

refuse dumps. This tale of marginally habitable shelters, thrown together from waste materials and situated on land that does not belong to the habitants, is being repeated in one underdeveloped country after another in the face of human multiplication in both rural and urban regions. Few people enjoy these squalid slums, but nonetheless, in the emerging cities of newly industrializing lands, many millions of people live in shanties. Sometimes shanty-towns persist for generations, and their universality is so great that nearly every nation has its own special name for them, which is known to most citizens—including those fortunate individuals who never have to see this evidence of human wretchedness in their own community.

Housing misery, ironically, is often felt most grievously in those underdeveloped nations that are doing the most to industrialize and modernize. "In Southeast Asia it is the squatter settlements which are the symptom of modern city growth. . . . In most cities, squatter settlements proliferate and slums persist." [30] In peasant-agricultural societies, most housing is inadequate by modern standards, but the simplest of habitations may be sufficient to satisfy the demands of the nonabundant way of life. Mud huts that lack running water and electricity are not regarded as slums or problems in such cultures. But rising expectations among peasants reaching out for the material benefits of modern technology may evoke sensations of deprivation. It might even be claimed that one of the criteria identifying the first arrival of modern civilization is dissatisfaction with housing conditions. But changed perceptions and aspirations are only part of the story, for many newly urbanized people were in fact better housed in the rural villages they left to seek their fortunes in the metropolis. And the governments of the newly developing nations—especially the usually inexperienced administrators of the new countries of Africa—generally lack both the knowledge and the capital to cope with the complications inherent in sudden urbanization. Enthusiastically adopted panaceas turn into disheartening fiascoes, encouraging the less expensive policy of apathy. And the faster the pace of modernization, the more drastic the shock of urban revolution. When the urban population grows faster than the number of dwellings, cities come to be faced with a housing famine under which the prime requisite is

[30] T. G. McGee, *The Southeast Asian City* (New York: Praeger, 1967), pp. 156, 170.

more homes of any sort; given conditions of intense overcrowding, quality becomes secondary, and even demolition of slums must be discouraged in the face of the imperative need to put a roof over everyone's head.

○ *Cross-Cultural Comparisons*

The most salient conclusion to be drawn from these cross-cultural comparisons, in which each city may, with qualifications, be viewed as constituting a separate experimental group, is that ecological patterning of cities varies considerably from culture to culture. This conclusion should not come as a surprise, for, as cultures vary, so consequently might one expect urban structures to vary. A corollary finding is that modern industrial cities tend to resemble one another the world over; that they also are marked by ecological variations is evidenced by the viability of twelve different theories explaining urban structure.

Despite the similarities among the more up-to-date industrial cities, the anthropologists' familiar cross-cultural message applies here also: Not all cities are alike. Ecological examination of non-Western cities —and, for that matter, even of European cities—induces awareness of the exceptional uniformity of United States cities from Maine to California. Like so many other products of mass production, American cities lack the diversity encountered within many far smaller nations. Although such a degree of uniformity may be efficient, it can also be boring. To consider one index of variation: Neither the narrowest nor the widest streets are found in American cities; Paris, for instance, contains both broader and narrower streets than any in New York City or Chicago (with the possible exception of multilane throughways). Types of streets, too, are more varied in many other countries, where residents may traverse divided streets, covered streets, arcaded streets, streets for pedestrians only, canal streets, streets so winding as to remind one of a corkscrew, and so forth. But, appealing as this sheer diversity may seem to the would-be anthropologist, impracticality in the face of the automobile and other twentieth-century developments seems to be on the way to eradicating many of these traffic ways in favor of near-carbon copies of the avenues of Detroit and Oklahoma City.

Mutual resemblance of cities in all cultures may increase in the future, as cities everywhere approximate more and more the characteristics of United States cities. A major element in this tendency is the automobile: When—not if—the day comes that the ordinary citizen everywhere can afford a car and therefore when nearly everyone has a car, then most cities will have freeways and parking lots, drive-in restaurants and banks, and other automotive appurtenances. With the adoption of the car will come a remaking of cities to fit the car. Such automobile-induced morphological change is illustrated by Kirman, an Iranian city of 60,000 residents: "A hallmark of the Islamic city—the labyrinth of twisted alleys—is being replaced by regular street patterns which can be used by automobiles and trucks." [31] Already many American cities are being redesigned to conform to the preferences of motorists—which gives rise to cries of dismay from lovers of traditional cities. But so long as 150-pound men insist on transporting themselves to work in 4,000-pound projectiles, so long will city patterns be affected, whether pedestrians and mass transit riders like it or not.

Another focus of present complaint and future speculation is personality, for urban ecology contains implications for each individual's adjustment to his environment. Although favorable effects are discernible, negative influences are more often affirmed; allegations are frequent that cities—and especially certain parts of them—exert disruptive influences on the character traits of their residents. If these objections are valid, then alterations in the physical layouts of cities may alter the personalities of their inhabitants. And the greatest potential influence in this connection, according to certain social scientists, is the immediate neighborhood.

[31] Paul Ward English, *City and Village in Iran* (Madison: University of Wisconsin Press, 1966), p. 46.

chapter 10

NEIGHBORHOODS AND OTHER SUBAREAS

AFTER DISCUSSING NETWORKS OF INTERRELATIONS AMONG CITIES AND then the patterning within cities, a logical next step is to turn to urban subareas. Accordingly, this chapter inspects homogeneous clusters within cities: their physical constitution, human composition, and major causes and consequences of the changes therein. If, as has often been alleged, a city is a mosaic of differing social worlds, ecologically detached, partially insulated socially, and culturally differentiated from one another, then these bounded subcommunities must play crucial roles in social interactions among urban residents.

These local districts are, at their most cohesive, neighborhoods in which people are intimately and empathically associated with one another. But there are increasingly numerous allegations that neighbors are being replaced by mere nigh-dwellers—a term designating adjacent residence coupled with anonymity and indifference. Is urban life inescapably impersonal and lonely, or does the neighborhood or another local group offer a substitute for the weakening bonds of kin-ship? Sociologists study this question, and city planners face its consequences.

○ *Neighborhood Groups*

Sociologically, the most significant city segment having territorial aspect is the neighborhood. In certain situations, other areal units are more meaningful—wards, precincts, quarters, blocks, parishes, tracts, or districts—but the subcommunity most frequently identified as a social unit remains the neighborhood. The *Dictionary of Sociology* defines a neighborhood as "a small community, characterized by lim-ited area and highly developed personal, face-to-face relations"; a neighborhood group is "an association, frequently informal, of per-sons living near one another." [1] Three components dominate these definitions: The generic term "community" denotes an aggregate of people having enough in common to be called a group, although both size and degree of cohesiveness vary greatly; second, a small area is requisite, for without a territory there would be no neighborhood; and third, social relations are ordinarily, although not invariably, personal rather than impersonal, friendly—or antagonistic—rather than distant.

Because of these properties, neighborhoods are persistent forces affecting the personality and behavior of residents. The converse is also true: The character of a neighborhood is determined by its in-habitants. A closely knit neighborhood plays an important part in socializing its members in accordance with the prevalent norms through face-to-face interaction and a daily stream of reinforcing stimuli.

Partly because the neighborhood so frequently exerts a potent pres-sure on individual behavior, social scientists have given it considerable attention. Some sociologists, however, deny the neighborhood as a legitimate social entity. In fact, the neighborhood's significance does seem to be declining, although to report its death at the present time

[1] Henry Pratt Fairchild (ed.), *Dictionary of Sociology* (Ames, Ia.: Adams, 1944), pp. 203, 134.

would be decidedly premature, especially regarding cities in the Old World.

The recently posed question of whether neighborhoods actually exist, particularly within great cities, seems a singularly academic one, indeed downright absurd in the suggestion that neighborhoods are wilful mental creations of romantic sociologists. Paris, for all its formal Cartesian unity, is a city of neighborhoods, often with a well-defined architectural character as well as an identifiable social face. The Parisian neighborhood is not just a postal district or a political unit, but an historic growth; and the sense of belonging to a particular *arrondissement* or *quartier* is just as strong in the shopkeeper, the bistro customer, or the petty craftsman as the sense of being a Parisian.[2]

Alive, dead, or dying, the neighborhood is conceptualized and delimited differently by sociologists of various bents. Shevky's social-area analysis and Tryon's cluster analysis define neighborhoods in terms of the characteristics of the inhabitants—a well-accepted procedure. Most sociologists, however, focus on the kinds and extent of social interrelations: A neighborhood is generated by personal, almost daily interactions among people living near one another.

Not all subareas form neighborhoods, however, and not all urban residents live in neighborhoods. Some sections of cities—and large portions of many cities—contain no neighborhoods, for their inhabitants have little or no feeling of communality or identity with others living in the vicinity.

To know whether or not a given area can properly be called a neighborhood, several criteria may be applied: Is there face-to-face interaction? Is there a feeling of cohesion or unity among the residents? When asked where they are from, do residents often name their immediate district rather than a larger area?

Interviews of householders in small sections of Boston and Chicago showed that residents perceived themselves as living in a neighborhood having a commonly accepted name but only approximately agreed-upon boundaries;[3] however, conflicting results have been obtained in other American and European cities. Residents are often ascribed status according to the social levels generally attributed to

[2] Lewis Mumford, "The Neighborhood and the Neighborhood Unit," *Town Planning Review*, 24 (January 1954), 256–70.

[3] H. Lawrence Ross, "The Local Community: A Survey Approach," *American Sociological Review*, 27 (February 1962), 75–84.

their neighborhoods. For illustration, try ordering goods to be delivered from a store on two different occasions, using in one instance a "good" address and in the other a "working class" address; the response of the sales clerk is sometimes dramatic, quickly becoming respectful obeisance or condescending familiarity, depending on the status of the neighborhood.

○ *Neighbors Versus Urbanites*

Much of the point of neighborhoods lies in their face-to-face relations. In contrast to the city at large, with its prevailing impersonal relations, a neighborhood is a place where nearly everyone knows everyone else. Some urban dwellers are neighbors in this sociological sense, and some are not.

A neighbor, in the strict usage of the word, is not just someone who lives nearby. Nor is he a friend or relative, for the roles played by the latter dominate the role of neighbor; indeed, in villages in which all inhabitants are related by blood or marriage, the concept "neighbor" is not meaningful. A neighbor is a semistranger with whom one maintains a pleasant but formal (although not always recognized as such) relationship. Neighbors help one another with advice about garden care or the loan of a household tool or small item of food. Anyone who goes much beyond these or similar limited contacts ceases to be just a neighbor and becomes a friend. One gains a friend through choice based on common interests and enjoyments; one gains a neighbor by moving next door and being polite. And because a necessary (but not sufficient) condition for a neighborly relationship is physical nearness, neighbors are lost when one moves away.

In some cultures the degree of formality becomes far greater than is customary in the United States. In some European villages, mutual obligations are expressed in a contract, and Japanese villagers live under an elaborate system of collective responsibility. Even in giant cities like Tokyo, behavior of neighbors is made highly predictable by inbred rules specifying in detail what actions are acceptable and what are not.[4]

[4] Ronald P. Dore, *City Life in Japan* (Berkeley: University of California Press, 1958), p. 255.

Even the largest cities in the world include numerous small parcels having a degree of social intimacy superficially associated only with rural villages. The largest metropolis in the world, New York, generally regarded as the antithesis of a small town because of its depersonalization and absence of neighborhood gossip, contains hundreds of more or less coherent subcommunities equivalent in many respects to small towns. In some neighborhoods, an insider walking into a grocery store is known to the proprietor by name, occupation, family status, and hobbies. And if he runs out of cigarettes in the evening and elects to send his son to the corner drugstore, the druggist knows by sight whose child he is and puts the price on the tab.

On the other hand, some urbanites have no intimacy with the people in the next apartment. When a delivery boy asks the occupants of apartment 4C if they would accept a package for the Levines, who live next door, they may have to check the card on the door to be certain that apartment 4B is actually occupied by a couple called Levine. Even after living many years in this apartment, they do not invite the other people on the floor to evening parties or morning Kaffeeklatsches. Just the circumstance that someone lives on the other side of a plaster wall is not sufficient reason for making friends; after all, they tell themselves, one encounters thousands of people in a day, and the less attention given to these many others, the less fatigue results and the more of oneself is left at the end of the day.

Yet many New Yorkers and Chicagoans know everyone else on the same floor and quite a few others in their own building. These true neighbors patronize local merchants (especially in an ethnic neighborhood where a foreign language prevails), attend the neighborhood movie house, and exchange friendly remarks with the cop on the beat. In this way, they convert the metropolis from a gigantic impersonal force to a more manageable place that they can call their own, where they are as respected and well known as many a villager. Sometimes, like villagers, several generations maintain stability of residence and friendship, trusting each other for a few dollars until the end of the week and chastising one another's children. A few of these urban villagers spend their entire lives in their own neighborhood, never venturing out into the inhospitable world of the great metropolis.[5]

Neighborhood cohesion and identification appear stronger in the

[5] Herbert J. Gans, *The Urban Villagers* (New York: Free Press, 1962).

traditional cities of Asia and Europe than in American cities and their modernized Old World counterparts. Where ethnic segregation is marked and persevering, strong neighborhood identities prevail. Where migration is frequent, neighborhoods tend to be weak; for this reason, real-estate salesmen sometimes try to impress on prospective customers the permanence of residents as a demonstration of the stability of the neighborhood. It has also been suggested that the intensity of neighborhood feeling may vary according to the type of city (see Chapter 4).

Clearly, sections of the city and their inhabitants differ considerably in the form and frequency of their personal communications. Some interaction is transitory and superficial, according to the urban stereotype. But casual and fleeting contacts are characteristic of only some parts of the city, for many blocks are marked by mutual exchange of favors, visiting, and other social intimacies.

In an attempt to determine whether residents were neighborhood or city oriented, Donald Foley interviewed residents of a middle-class district in Rochester, New York, that contained a well-balanced selection of local facilities. He relied on three criteria: use of local versus nonlocal shopping and entertainment facilities, amount and intensity of informal visiting, and sense of residing in a definable (by name and boundaries) local community to which one owes allegiance. Foley concluded that inhabitants of the area were partly neighborhood oriented and partly city oriented. About three-fourths of them acted in a neighborly fashion by having at least a "chatting relationship" with other people in their block, but only two-fifths extended this relation to all residents in their block. One-fourth rarely chatted with neighbors, two-fifths did not exchange favors, and three-fifths never visited informally in the homes of others in the area. Evidently, neighboring ranged from complete avoidance of friendliness to frequent intimate social contacts. Informal neighboring tended to be restricted to adjacent homes and the summer months, when conversation centered about lawn care. Added to this observation that relationships were generally shallow was the conclusion that neighboring seemed to be less important than in previous decades: "People just don't neighbor as they used to." [6] Other studies of residential subareas have also

[6] Donald L. Foley, *Neighbors or Urbanites?* (Rochester, N.Y.: University of Rochester Department of Sociology, 1952).

concluded that intimate association within city blocks has decreased considerably—so much that some sociologists challenge the utility today of the traditional concept of the neighborhood.

Instead of stemming from propinquity, informal social contacts are increasingly founded on mutual interest. People appear to be becoming more discriminating in their primary-group associations, selecting their friends because of shared interests and congenial personalities rather than nearness and convenience, and joining voluntary organizations because of the functions they perform rather than as semiobligatory neighborhood activities. Consequently, residents of urban areas frequently go considerable distances to visit friends— greater distances, in fact, than they go for most shopping. A study of 300 Los Angeles residents disclosed that housewives traveled an average of 4.8 miles to engage in personal contacts, much farther than the 2.1 miles they averaged on shopping trips.[7] Among the factors encouraging friendships outside the neighborhood, the most significant shown by the Los Angeles study was ownership of a car, which markedly increased the radius of social contacts.

○ *Informal Neighboring*

Whatever the decline in neighborly visiting, people continue to engage in informal social contacts and sometimes to form cliques. In studying a middle-class commuting suburb near Chicago, W. H. Whyte noted that many wives and a few husbands participated in informal bull sessions, largely about immediate problems: child care, home management, and occupational promotion. Whyte summarized his findings for single-family homes: People tend to be friendliest with neighbors whose driveways adjoin theirs; deviates or feuding neighbors tend to define the boundaries of social groups; persons residing in the most central locations make the largest number of social contacts; width of street and amount of traffic determine whether or not residents make friends across the street; and people make friends with neighbors adjoining their rear lot lines only when some physical

---

[7] Svend Riemer and John McNamara, "Contact Patterns in the City," *Social Forces*, 36 (December 1957), 137–41.

feature creates traffic.[8] In apartment developments, social contacts and even lasting friendships are affected by such mundane matters as distance, convenience, and where the car is: In apartment units formed around parking bays, social life is oriented inward; wings whose entrances face each other facilitate social contacts; buildings sited ambiguously—neither toward one side or the other—tend to isolate their residents or divide their allegiance; and small courts are usually more cohesive than large ones.[9]

The web of friendship appears to Whyte to be as neatly ordered as a spider's web—although, of course, there are many exceptions to such tendencies, however present they may be in the aggregate.[10]

1. Filiarchy: The children, not the parents, set the social framework: childrens' friendships are translated into mothers' friendships, which in turn may affect the fathers' social engagements.
2. Play areas: The wives' Kaffeeklatsch destinations tend to follow the flow of wheeled juvenile traffic; children try to play where they feel like playing, and mothers chat where they can keep an eye on their offspring.
3. Placement of driveways and porches: Driveways—especially adjoining ones—form a natural setting for baby-watching and accompanying gossip with other mothers; hence friendships more often flower on that side of the house than on a side having only lawn and shrubs. Similarly, apartment dwellers sharing adjacent porches or stoops looking out on play areas tend to be drawn together.
4. Lawns: Since the front lawn rather than the rear receives the most attention from homeowners, the consequent borrowing of tools and offering of advice tends to encourage friendships along and across the street, rather than across back yards.
5. Centrality: The closer to the center of a block one lives, the larger the number of neighborhood social contacts he is likely to have, for the focus of activity is generally in mid-block, whereas the families residing on corner lots are less frequently included in social gatherings.

[8] William H. Whyte, Jr., *The Organization Man* (New York: Simon & Schuster, 1956), p. 345.
[9] *Ibid.*, p. 344.
[10] *Ibid.*, pp. 342–8.

6. Size of groups: A clique normally contains no more members than can be accommodated together comfortably in a living room—so the size of the clique may be influenced by the usual size of the rooms in the neighborhood.

7. Chronology of arrival: Families who move in at about the same time form friendships, based originally on common problems; once established, such informal visiting patterns tend to perpetuate themselves long after the original problems cease to exist.

8. Barriers: Physical or invented barriers set limits to social contacts in several ways. Streets may become boundaries for adults when their width or the frequency of passing automobiles motivates mothers to forbid their children to cross. A house containing a family that doesn't mix may serve as a social watershed, discouraging mothers from following tricycles across this alien territory; so persistent are these habits that even when that family moves out, their successors are likely to inherit the function of serving as a social boundary.

Such relationships are not unique to the United States; similar social patterns have been disclosed by research in Coventry, England, and other European cities.[11]

Although middle-class neighboring seems largely a matter of wives assembling on one another's lawns and around their kitchen tables, working-class people exhibit a different style of sociability. Neighboring seems to be a more important part of working-class life, possibly because their opportunities outside the neighborhood are generally more limited than are those of the better-educated middle-class people, whose neighboring is more selective and whose social life is less tied to the immediate vicinity. Observers in both England and the United States have pointed out the greater significance of the local community to lower-class people in nearly all aspects of their lives. In London many poor people work, amuse themselves, quarrel, shop, marry, and spend their entire lives in one small district of the city, to which they are bound financially and emotionally; some families have continued to reside in the same district for several generations.[12] A study

---

[11] See for example Leo Kuper (ed.), *Living in Towns* (London: Crescent, 1953).

[12] See for example Elizabeth Bott, *Family and Social Network* (London: Tavistock, 1957); and Roger Wilson, *Difficult Housing Estates* (London: Tavistock, 1963).

of four settlements in New York showed that low-income families make a larger proportion of their purchases in neighborhood stores or from door-to-door peddlers than do medium-income families.[13]

Working-class neighboring seems more often to take place outside or away from the home, particularly in the pub in Britain, the bistro in France, the café in Latin countries, or the saloon in the United States, where the sexes are often segregated by preference of the customers. The urban working-class recreational center tends to be the local bar—traditionally, but not exclusively, a male institution. Taverns generally draw a collection of "regulars" from their immediate areas, and patronization of some bars is virtually confined to members of a certain nationality or race. Blue-collar men meet their friends or neighbors each evening to drink in a relaxed, comfortable, congenial atmosphere, carrying on running jokes implying a primary group relationship. In contrast to this informal continuity, upper- and middle-class bar patrons tend to be irregular, transient, and anonymous. That the number of hours a week spent in drinking emporia is inversely correlated with social class is indicative of the extent to which the tavern is an important social center for lower-class workers.[14]

With the bar as a lower-class men's club and the midday hen session as a middle-class female counterpart, formal neighborhood clubs have formidable opposition. In fact, organized neighborhood associations generally tend to be weak, having little influence on the opinions or behavior of the residents and tending to collapse under any threat of adversity. In many cases, however, the reverse is true: Single-purpose formal neighborhood organizations arise in response to such specific threats as the usually chimerical danger of declining property values following invasion by Negroes. One exception to these generalizations is the P.T.A., which occasionally plays an important part in bringing together residents of the neighborhood surrounding a public school, especially if the school supplies facilities for adult and teen-age activities in the evenings; most P.T.A.s, however, fail to solidify the neighborhood. People who seek more formal or purpose-

---

[13] David Caplovitz, *The Poor Pay More* (New York: Free Press, 1963), pp. 49–57.

[14] David Gottlieb, "The Neighborhood Tavern and Cocktail Lounge," *American Journal of Sociology*, 62 (May 1957), 559–62; see also Sherri Cavan, *Liquor License* (Chicago: Aldine, 1966).

ful organizations can find them in the multiplicity of special-interest groups available in all but the smallest cities.

Several sociological studies have shown that suburbanites are less inclined than central-city residents to join formal associations but are appreciably more inclined toward local neighboring. Returning to that familiar ecological variable, distance, research discloses that "neighboring gradually increases with distance from the city center." [15] This correlation is caused in part by the circumstance that a frequent reason for moving to the suburbs is the desire to maximize opportunity for informal neighboring.

○ *Invasion and Succession*

Sometimes people act in violently antineighborly ways, particularly when confronted with invasion of minority groups they do not like or fear may cause property values to deteriorate. Whatever its deficiencies as ecological theorizing, the social-process approach is invaluable in studying such movements of minorities and other groups. Initially, a small number of individuals or families move into an area, to which the original occupants may react in various ways and with varying degrees of intensity. Resentment is common but rarely achieves high intensity if the newcomers are Italians, Poles, Greeks, or other whites —especially if they are of about the same economic level as the older residents. But Negroes usually—and Jews and Orientals occasionally —arouse powerful opposition, particularly if they arrive in large numbers.

If the newcomers become sufficiently numerous, the old residents may begin moving out—a phenomenon known as "tipping"; the tipping point occurs when minority-group invaders reach a proportion beyond which majority-group residents leave. Tipping points vary according to the characteristics of the city, the neighborhood, and the minority group. Social class is especially influential, sometimes overriding the older residents' propensity to abandon the area to the newcomers; if the invaders are of sufficiently high status, their nationality

[15] Sylvia F. Fava, "Contrasts in Neighboring: New York City and a Suburban County," in William Dobriner (ed.), *The Suburban Community* (New York: Putnam, 1958), p. 126.

or religion may be overlooked, although this response rarely extends to Negroes. William Myers, who in 1957 was the first Negro to move into Levittown, Pennsylvania, aroused strong pro- and anti-Myers factions. Favoring his moving in were the college-educated and career-oriented cosmopolites, who refused to define the situation exclusively in the light of its impact on their own suburban community. Opponents were largely from the less-educated working class, especially those in uncertain transition to the middle class.

A high degree of ethnocentrism is a common phenomenon in the sub-college stratum, and as might be anticipated a goodly number of Levit-towners had chosen to live in this community precisely because it offered an escape from "mixed" neighborhoods and those facing imminent desegregation. Moreover, these initial biases among industrial workers were frequently reinforced by status anxieties arising from their equivocal position in the class structure. A skilled or semi-skilled laborer employed by the United States Steel Company, Kaiser Metal Products, or other local enterprises might well sense the disparity between his relative economic affluence and his modest occupational prestige. One method of resolving this ambiguity consists of borrowing prestige from his community, which if it is to serve this purpose satisfactorily must then represent a pure distillate of middle-class life styles. The working class addiction to the coy middle-class symbolism so prevalent in Levit-town, its "Sweetbriar Lanes" and "cook-outs," its "patios" and enthusiastic agronomy, is to an appreciable extent a simultaneous exercise in self-persuasion and ritualistic affirmation whose purpose it is to demonstrate that life patterns in the community, and not the job, constitute the only valid basis for class assignment. The appearance of a visible threat to the social status of the community in the persons of a Negro family could be expected to produce considerable apprehension among the inhabitants of a poorly defined no man's land on the margins between two classes.[16]

Blocking invasion is attempted in several ways: Neighborhood "protective associations" or "betterment committees" try to exclude unwanted ethnic groups; property owners and real-estate companies agree not to sell or rent to such undesirables; attractive profits are offered to the first invader if he will resell his house; local merchants are prevailed upon to refuse to transact business with him; 3:00 A.M. telephone calls attempt to disturb his sleep and equanimity; symbolic

[16] Marvin Bressler, "The Myers' Case: An Instance of Successful Racial Invasion," *Social Problems*, 8 (Fall 1960), 133.

crosses or "K"s are burned in public places or on his lawn; physical violence is sometimes applied to make life miserable for the newcomers by defacing their homes or threatening personal injury. Less destructively, recent attempts have sought instead to persuade old residents to remain, on the assumption that stemming their exodus will stabilize the neighborhood.

If these efforts fail, or if they are not tried, invasion may proceed to its climax: complete displacement of the original population. Sometimes the neighborhood changes drastically and is hardly recognizable, as when Jewish delicatessens are replaced by Mexican-American stores whose proprietors have different notions of conducting business. Other cases of succession may involve almost no alteration except for the change of names on mailboxes. Ethnic invasion may thus maintain the existing neighborhood structure or replace it with another of different type.

○ *Minority-Group Enclaves*

Once established, most minority-group neighborhoods either form permanent enclaves of stable character or exhibit the same gradual alteration more or less common to any white-majority area. Some minority enclaves have grown so large as to constitute virtual cities in their own right: for example, Harlem and Chinatown in New York and Chicago's "Black Metropolis." [17] These districts are much too large to be called neighborhoods, but their residents are generally united by common bonds, strongly encouraged by the refusal of the white majority to accept them outside these ghettos. Such large areas are subdivided, then, into smaller social worlds, distinguished from one another by social class and other criteria in much the same manner as majority-group neighborhoods.

Smaller enclaves are formed of Armenians, Japanese, or other immigrants who came from the same region or even the same small town in the old country. One block may house a Sicilian settlement, with grocery stores and restaurants catering to their preferences and managed by Sicilians. The next block may contain Neapolitans or Atheni-

[17] St. Clair Drake and Horace R. Cayton, *Black Metropolis* (New York: Harcourt, 1945).

ans, and their own kinds of music can be heard from the sidewalk. A few immigrant neighborhoods support movie theaters showing foreign language films without subtitles.

Europeans immigrating to United States cities from rural villages often changed as little as possible from their old nonurban social norms and institutions to the prevailing urban milieu, and villages were created within the city. For that matter, many rural-to-urban migrants remaining totally within the United States also cling to their familiar folkways and mores. Surrounded by an urban culture, peasant immigrants strive to maintain a semirural subculture in the three or four blocks designated as "Little Italy" or the like.

Aside from their function of providing a modified replica of the native culture, these enclaves offer other residents of the city an opportunity to experience an exciting range of food, music, and cultures —whether it be baklava, goat cheese, bouzouki music, and belly dancers in a Near East café or the Indonesian or Japanese equivalents. This fascinating cultural variety is one of the major reasons why large cities are so extolled by their partisans and why threats of disruption to these cultural enclaves arouse vigorous opposition from aficionados of exotic smells and suspended cheeses and salamis.

Immigrant enclaves are not the only interesting neighborhoods. Native-born citizens with a yen for something different may set up small colonies of artists, beatniks, hippies, or whatever next year's label may be. Rejecting middle-class standards of family life, sexual morality, church going, and financial success, these people may gather together in one or another Bohemian settlement, of which the best known was Greenwich Village in New York City. There as elsewhere, however, the reputation for unorthodox cultural flavor has tended to draw pseudo-Bohemians seeking the appearance of casting off social restrictions without actually doing so.

○ *Areas of Social Disorganization*

Superficially similar to but in fact far removed from intellectual and artistic Bohemias are subareas characterized by high rates of personality disorganization and social problems. Often located in the zone in transition adjoining the central business district are areas of homeless men, gambling houses, red-light districts, and other breeding grounds for crime and vice. In these retrogressing neighborhoods—assuming that they ever were neighborhoods, for they certainly do not merit the designation on the basis of present characteristics—are the highest frequencies of poverty, dilapidated housing, juvenile delinquency, family disintegration, and physical and mental disease. Impersonality and anonymity are of such high degree that an integrated social neighborhood cannot truly be said to exist. At best rooming-house districts and at worst slums, these subareas have been studied extensively by sociologists for many years.[18]

A specialized field of study entitled "social disorganization" concentrates on alcoholism, prostitution, mental disorders, suicide, drug addiction, divorce, delinquency, and crime. Areas characterized by these problems are not ordinarily composed of any one racial or nationality or religious group but are populated generally by the lower classes without much regard for ethnicity. Isometric or dot maps of the incidence of arrests, illegitimacy, and other forms of social disorganization support the generalization that, with the exception of occasional pockets elsewhere, the rate of deviance increases the closer one approaches the city center.

Disorganization may be either personal or social, the former occurring to an individual (mental illness, assault or the like) and the latter occurring to groups (like failure to work together harmoniously or effectively as indicated by high rates of adult crime, juvenile delinquency, and so forth). This distinction, however, is somewhat forced, as the two types of disorders overlap. Disoriented persons may flock together into the more impermanent and anonymous subareas of the metropolis, and the areas themselves may spawn subcultures placing positive value on an individual's delinquency and deviance.

Subcultures or variants of the dominant culture have their own normative standards of behavior to which members must conform or suffer rejection; adolescent delinquents are probably the most patent case in point.[19] Consequently, most deviant subcultures form fairly

---

[18] See Harvey Zorbaugh, *The Gold Coast and the Slum* (Chicago: University of Chicago Press, 1929) ; Louis Wirth, *The Ghetto* (Chicago: University of Chicago Press, 1928) ; and other products of the Department of Sociology of the University of Chicago from about 1925 to 1945.

[19] Clifford R. Shaw and Henry D. McKay, *Juvenile Delinquency and Urban Areas* (Chicago: University of Chicago Press, 1942).

cohesive neighborhoods. In contrast, disorganized areas not dominated by deviant subcultures do not function as neighborhoods; although they may fit the defintion of a neighborhood by occupying a clearly demarcated territory, they lack cohesiveness and primary social interaction.

○ Involvement and Continuity

Every culture or subculture has both conformist patterns and sanctioned deviations therefrom. One of the most striking facts about any society or subgroup is that essential functions are performed, year in and year out, with some degree of consistency. Similar behavior in response to the same obligations may be seen time and time again by virtually all members of a society, and the conclusion must be that there is a consistently ordered—indeed, almost automatic—patterning of human actions. Although perfect conformity is never attained, the various segments of the culture or subculture do tend to reinforce one another, thus adding to the stability of the whole. Where nonconformity persists, it is often attributable to an unusually rapid rate of change in the technology or social organization that creates strains in related aspects of the culture; this situation is especially prevalent in industrializing areas and rapidly growing cities.

One of the most potent forces in preserving traditional values is the family. Whether an urban resident migrated from a rural village or grew up in urban surroundings, adherence to basic norms was instilled in him from early childhood by parents and peers. If a newcomer's initial encounter with the city is made alone, he feels isolated and perhaps dispirited; if he arrives in a family group, his awe of the multifarious and sometimes incomprehensible new environment is eased by familial security and the comforting knowledge that other family members share his uncertainty and ignorance. But as time passes, the migrant-turned-resident is exposed to many forces outside the family that contribute to an erosion of family control over his thinking and feeling.

Men are more directly and immediately influenced by the new urban environment than their wives are. Most men must work, and to do so they usually must learn the language and folkways of their associates. Women often stay at home, where they continue to play familiar roles and can avoid social relationships that might disrupt habitual patterns of behavior. Ethnic neighborhoods often provide protection against unwelcome change, as in an Italian immigrant district of first-generation settlement, where few of the women learn to speak English and from whence they seldom venture. The family member most likely to be affected by urban or neighborhood relocation is the child, whose classmates may represent many cultural heritages and who comes to share, more deeply than his parents ever learn to do, in the dominant cultural values and norms.

Contact with peer groups affects all family members, of whatever age or status; informal neighborhood cliques are one of the most influential forces that either solidify or alter the attributes of the individual. From block parties to boys' gangs, neighborhoods contribute to the formation of personality and the engagement of each individual in the life of his community. But neighborhood and other cohesive influences are sometimes insufficient to prevent disengagement, as in New York's infamous 1965 case of the murder of Catherine Genovese while onlookers avoided becoming "involved."

○ *Idealization of the Neighborhood*

Despite such negative examples of local social organization and socialization, the neighborhood is often extolled as the ideal toward which urban civilization should aim. Many social workers and city planners have posed themselves the task of creating city neighborhoods that would maintain the social advantages of earlier eras while respecting the contemporary desire to be left alone. Most of these ameliorators seem agreed that neighborliness should be encouraged, generally on the implicit assumption that traditional rural primary relations are best for rearing children and keeping adults on the "straight and narrow" path to virtue. Of course, these old-fashioned farm communities were not deliberately designed, but many modern planners still hope to foster neighborhood friendliness by proper sectioning and physical design of the city.

This sentimental preference for close fellowship over purposeful organizations was expressed definitively by Ferdinand Tönnies, originator of the untranslatable concepts of *Gemeinschaft* and *Gesellschaft*.[20] By *Gemeinschaft*, Tönnies meant a social order characterized by sympathetic communal feelings as expressed in family and neighborhood groups; the contrasting *Gesellschaft* describes social relationships characterized by more formal and consciously ordered actions, as in cities and nations. Tönnies felt that city life or *Gesellschaft* was not a good life; people tend to get psychologically lost in the city. The family and the village community provide the essence of the good life, and therefore governments should try to destroy *Gesellschaft*, which brings decay to the family and doom to the traditional culture, and replace it with *Gemeinschaft*, which offers a superior prospect of vital religious spirit and community fellowship.

Many large apartment developments in the United States and Europe, as if attempting to invoke Tönnies' principle, provide for local services and participation of residents in one form or another of quasineighborhood activity: swimming pools, day nurseries, health centers, playgrounds, branch libraries, coin-operated laundries, and recreation rooms with ping-pong or billiard tables. The facilities themselves do not necessarily betoken neighboring, for they often resemble those available at a modern motel, than which nothing is more transient. Increasingly popular are apartment buildings for "singles"—swinging men and women under thirty-five who enjoy the excitement of having some organized activity to titillate their senses every hour of each weekend and every week night. Such establishments are not neighborhoods but rather social clubs—often modified, ironically, from the spirit and activities of "senior citizen" communities.

Of all residential forms, single-family houses are probably the most amenable to neighborhood organization, largely because they usually offer greater permanence and the largest number of children, who are often regarded as the backbone of neighborhood socializing. City planners try to design physical settings conducive to a feeling of living in a spirited neighborhood having stable property values, honest merchants, good schools, hospitable playgrounds, and a sensation of togetherness, preferably immortalized by a name that outsiders will

[20] Ferdinand Tönnies, *Gemeinschaft und Gesellschaft* (1887), trans. by Charles P. Loomis, *Fundamental Concepts of Sociology* (New York: American Book, 1940).

recognize, such as Brentwood or Bonnie Doon or, if one must, the pejorative Shantytown—or, worst of all, such precious but popular labels as Shady Crest.

The persistent quest for community in our urbanized and therefore seemingly depersonalized civilization is a continuing theme of diverse writers owing allegiance to various movements. Poets, planners, and prophets from T. S. Eliot to Lewis Mumford and Timothy Leary have encouraged people to approach closer to one another in humane sensitivity. For this as for other objectives, it is helpful to have concrete, practical means to forward their attainment—and that is the subject of the following chapters.

part three

HOW URBAN AREAS MIGHT BE ARRANGED

chapter 11

CITY-PLANNING PRINCIPLES

LIFE IS CHANGE, AND WHATEVER DOESN'T CHANGE IS DEAD. THEREFORE cities should be expected to change, citizens might do well to seek change, and planners should try to ensure that change is beneficial rather than disruptive.

The planning of cities is regarded variously as an ivory-tower vision, a practical and necessary program for development, or an undesirable interference with the citizen's freedom to do as he wishes with his own property. Some citizens see planning as a dictatorial force compelling people to do as the government directs. Planners see themselves as servants of the people who are trying to make the city a better place in which to live but who are circumscribed by legal and political restrictions. The truth lies somewhere between these extremes.

○ *Purposes of Planning*

A former President of the Borough of Manhattan and Chairman of the Board of the New York Regional Plan Association said:

> City planning simply means getting ready for the future in city growth. It is the guidance into proper channels of a community's impulses towards a larger and broader life. On the face it has to do with things physical—the laying out of streets and parks and rapid-transit lines. But its real significance is far deeper; a proper city has a powerful influence for good upon the mental and moral development of the people. It is the firm base for the building of a healthy and happy community.[1]

The two key words are "future" and "influence": Planning is by definition a preparation for the future; as Simonides of Ceos said in the fifth century B.C., "The city teaches the man"—that is, good cities make good men. Fully as much, good cities are made by good men (the man teaches the city), or as Winston Churchill said, "We shape our buildings; thereafter they shape us."

City planning is the ordering of physical elements to serve the residents as efficiently, economically, healthfully, and agreeably as possible. At first glance, physical elements seem dominant: Streets, buildings, utility lines, and other structures are the things that planners manipulate. But these things are really just means to the end of serving the inhabitants, to make their lives more pleasant, comfortable, and meaningful.

Beauty is crucial, as much for cities as for the automobiles that people so avidly covet or the women that men so enthusiastically admire. Yet urban grace, like a woman, is "a sometime thing." [2] Reacting against the squalor of the ill-conceived factories and tenements of the industrial age in England, a former Vice-Chancellor of Oxford University remarked: "It is strange that a people . . . which created the most beautiful villages in the world should have built Leeds and Manchester and Sheffield." In the United States as in England, it has

---

[1] George McAneny, quoted in Harold MacLean Lewis, *Planning the Modern City,* I (New York: Wiley, 1949), 7.

[2] George Gershwin, *Porgy and Bess,* 1935.

traditionally been the privilege of factory directors and landowners to despoil nature. During a 1961 congressional debate on an amendment to restrict billboards along Federal highways, Senator Clifford B. Case read from Mark Twain's *A Tramp Abroad*, describing the verdict awarded by a judge to an American patent-medicine peddler who had painted a slogan on a rock in Switzerland:

> You are from a land where any insolent that wants to is privileged to profane and insult Nature, if by doing so he can put a sordid penny in his pocket. But here the case is different. Because you are a foreigner and ignorant, I will make the sentence light—you will immediately remove every trace of your offensive work, you will pay a fine of ten thousand francs, you will suffer two years imprisonment at hard labor, you will then be horse-whipped, tarred, and feathered, deprived of your ears, ridden on a rail to the edge of town, and be banished forever. The severer penalties are omitted in your case—not as a grace to you, but to that great republic which had the misfortune to give you birth.

○ *History and Development*

Organized control over individual use of property has a long history. Many ancient Chinese and Japanese towns show traces of city planning, usually in the form of chessboard designs of straight streets, right-angle intersections, and symmetrically placed gateways where streets meet the outer city walls. These practices probably go back two or three thousand years and appear to have been derived in conformity with religious, military, and agrarian customs.[3]

Egyptian pyramids were planned, but they were not cities; however, temporary cities were constructed at their sites to house workmen. One such temporary community, Kahun, was built about 2000–2500 B.C. to house slaves and artisans. Its twenty acres contained about 300 four- or five-room dwellings, twenty-five larger homes for foremen and officials, a central meeting place, and street drainage.[4]

[3] Francis J. Haverfield, *Ancient Town-Planning* (London: Oxford, 1913), pp. 147–8.

[4] Martin S. Briggs, "Town-Planning from the Ancient World to the Renaissance," in Charles Singer and others (eds.), *A History of Technology*, III (London: Oxford, 1958), 269–70.

Although we do not know definitely that they were planned, Babylonian and Assyrian cities show evidence of planning; that is, some of these cities are so regular in pattern (the majority of cities "just grew" into various irregular shapes) that some systematic direction must be assumed. The Greek historian Herodotus described Babylon as having many right-angle intersections and straight streets, whereas unplanned ancient cities tended toward meandering paths that changed direction and intersected randomly.

In classical Greek cities, main thoroughfares were generally planned as processional avenues and as vistas for stately buildings, but residential areas remained undisciplined. It was not until the Hellenistic age that the Greeks devoted attention to planning residential areas. Many Greek cities show evidence of planning: Rhodes had streets radiating from the center; Cumae was planned in 1050 B.C.; Miletus, in Asia Minor, was rebuilt in 479 B.C. (after destruction by the Persians) with a rectangular street pattern. The fourth-century colony of Priene in Asia Minor is probably the best example of ancient Greek planning. Hippodamus of Miletus, the first man to be called a city planner, designed Piraeus in the fifth century B.C. Aristotle described Hippodamus as a picturesque, idealistic dreamer—not unlike current complaints of our more adventurous planners:

> Hippodamus, son of Euryphon, a native of Miletos, invented the art of planning cities and laid out the street plan of the Piraeus. . . . He planned a city with a population of 10,000, divided into three parts, one of skilled workers, one of farmers, and one to defend the state. The land was divided into three parts: sacred, public, and private, supporting in turn the worship of the gods, the defense of the state, and the farm owners. . . . Hippodamus introduced the principle of straight wide streets and provided for grouping of dwelling houses, also paying special heed to the integration of the different parts of the town into a harmonious whole, centered about the market place.[5]

Roman towns were often rigidly platted into rectangular sections. Their military outpost towns were so uniform that it was said that, if a soldier were dropped into the middle of any town, he could not tell which one he was in. Most town planning was done by military engineers, but the Roman who is best remembered as a planner is the first-century B.C. architect Vitruvius, whose writings influenced urban

[5] Aristotle, *Politics*, ii, 8, 1267[b].

planners for many centuries. Vitruvius' preferred (but never built) octagonal city with eight radial roads intersecting at the city center has inspired many formal plans.

After the ancient Greek and Roman efforts, city planning—like so many intellectual endeavors—entered a sterile phase for the next millennium and was not revived until Renaissance utopians proffered their fanciful and artificial schemes. Although actual medieval cities grew haphazardly, the utopians produced in theory perfect and static cities. Rather than fitting plans to existing conditions, they preferred to declare those conditions (such as topography) irrelevant and proceeded to ignore them. Unrealistic though this approach might be, it did generate some intellectually fascinating designs. Among these men were several painters, sculptors, and architects of enduring fame, including Alberti, Palladio, and Vasari. Vincenzo Scamozzi's ideal city was shaped as a twelve-pointed star; the points were both aesthetic and practical, serving as bastions along the city walls for enfilading by defenders. In 1593 Scamozzi built Palma Nuova, a small city in the shape of a nine-pointed star. Jacques Lemercier designed the town of Richelieu in 1631 for the famous Cardinal. The epitome of this insistence on symmetrical perfection was expressed at Versailles, whose gardens, palaces, and town were planned as a unit by the architects Le Vau, Charles Le Brun, Jules Mansart, and Le Nôtre.

Another monumental undertaking also occurred in France when, in 1853, Napoleon III directed Georges Eugène Haussmann to replace large slum sections of Paris with broad avenues offering attractive vistas and, not incidentally, conducive to moving troops quickly from one side of the city to another. In seventeen years Haussmann supplemented and in some areas replaced the maze of winding medieval lanes with long, sweeping boulevards radiating from plazas, transforming the city into the thing of beauty it is today. But masterful though his boulevard system was, it was not sufficiently comprehensive to be called true city planning. Traffic circulation was improved, some festering slums were cleared, and the city was beautified; but many areas of Paris were not touched at all.

The most noteworthy early British contribution to planning was Christopher Wren's unadopted but ingenious plan for rebuilding London after the disastrous fire of 1666. Later British plans were motivated partly in reaction to the appalling living conditions in the industrial cities and partly because some industrialists saw advantages to setting up factory towns, of which several were planned and built in the nineteenth century.

Cities in several other European countries kept pace. The growth of Stockholm has been consciously guided since the formation of a city-planning office in the 1630s. Stockholm did not just grow. Founded as a fortress in the thirteenth century, it developed into a port and then became the national capital in the seventeenth century. Built mainly of wood and thus susceptible to severe fires, early Stockholm turned disaster into opportunity by rebuilding according to orderly plans. Further encouragement to planning was provided by public ownership of most of the land (private persons owned houses but leased the land on which they stood), an advantage that declined sharply with increasing private land ownership after 1850. But even today the power of the planning office is greater than in the United States, and Stockholm owes much of its oft-admired beauty to an over-all guidance on aesthetic and social matters.[6]

The Netherlands too has contributed to the advancement of city planning. "Amsterdam is one of the few cities of our times which shows a continuous tradition in town planning, unbroken since 1900."[7] In Rotterdam, J. J. P. Oud built carefully planned apartment buildings for low-income groups beginning in 1919, and in the 1930s W. van Tijen erected tall slablike apartment houses similar to the slab blocks first conceived by Walter Gropius and Marcel Breuer in the mid-1920s.

Although city planning, like other planning, might be expected to reach a high point of development under socialism, the Soviet Union has not been a pioneer. Early Soviet city planning was "extraordinarily haphazard, socio-ideologically confused, and technically experimental. The 'sanitary norm' was the only principle that guided the development of urban centers and residential blocks."[8] However, in 1944 the government set limits to the growth of large cities, espoused the superblock as a basic unit, and encouraged detailed and complete plans for every city. Since the Plenum of June 1931, more than 500

---

[6] Goran Sidenbladh, "Stockholm: A Planned City," in Scientific American, *Cities* (New York: Knopf, 1965), pp. 75–87.

[7] Sigfried Giedion, *Space, Time, and Architecture* (Cambridge, Mass.: Harvard University Press, 1941), p. 517.

[8] Maurice F. Parkins, *City Planning in Soviet Russia* (Chicago: University of Chicago Press, 1953), p. 50.

new towns are reported to have been constructed in the U.S.S.R., many of them in Asiatic Russia as a consequence of the national policy of decentralizing industry and population.

○ New Towns

Both facets of planning—building new towns and rebuilding old ones—have been practiced for thousands of years, but concerted programs for new town construction are relatively recent. One of the most important historical policies guiding the building of cities was the Laws of the Indies, ordinances proclaimed by Philip II of Spain in 1573 to govern new cities in the New World. This document, which was followed almost without exception throughout Spanish possessions, contained about forty specifications and admonitions dealing with the selection of site, location of plazas and streets, and character of public buildings and private dwellings. These formal regulations closely follow the principles advanced by Vitruvius but with admixtures from Alberti, monastery planning, and castramentation resulting in rectangular shapes with straight streets and right-angle intersections.[9]

In addition to missions and presidios from Florida to California, the Spanish colonists established pueblos, or self-contained urban-rural units like the Greek *polis* consisting of towns surrounded by closely integrated farms and ranches; a few of these pueblos grew into major cities, notably Los Angeles. Not only were the Laws of the Indies required to be followed; they were also useful handbooks for builders of new cities, who usually had no relevant education and may well have been grateful for the instruction. That they were followed in later enlargements as well as initial construction is the principal explanation of why Latin American ecological patterns differ from those of Anglo America.

Planning has continued in both Americas. Belo Horizonte, a provincial capital in Brazil, was planned in 1898 by Aarao Reis in a geometric pattern of radial streets and ring boulevards superimposed

[9] John W. Reps, *The Making of Urban America* (Princeton: Princeton University Press, 1965), pp. 26–55.

on a gridiron plan. In 1956 a new site was selected for the national capital, Brasilia, located in the interior some 600 miles from Rio de Janeiro. Architects Lucio Costa and Oscar Niemeyer designed the completely new city in the shape of an airplane, a symbol suited both to the air age and to the regrettable circumstance that at first the only access was by plane, an expensive way to transport building materials (to certain religious persons, this pattern of a major axis crossed by a minor axis represents the sign of the Cross, but irreverent enemies of the government prefer to describe it as the cross they have to bear). Separate centers for government, commerce, and recreation are located along one axis, and housing is situated along the other. Proceeding with great haste, the Brazilian government has treated the world to a spectacle of frenetic building of this attractive city of concrete and glass, which opponents have proclaimed to be as economically ruinous as Versailles. "The positive conviction, uncompromising courage, and daring forms represented in this new city are inspiring. Perhaps a faint question can be heard through the powerful thrusts of this dynamic place: is it really for people?" [10]

Venezuela is also building an air-age metropolis, not as a capital city but as part of its effort to advance the national economy. Like other new cities, Ciudad Guayana seems an answer to a planner's dream—maximum freedom of design without the need to compromise with existing structures, entrenched property interests, and recalcitrant residents. Such a new undertaking is beset by many handicaps, however, particularly the lack of the basic ingredients for building a city: a trained labor force, established community loyalties, consumer supplies, and public facilities. As a result, skilled workers must be imported, homes and apartments constructed for workers and their wives, schools built and staffed for their children, and such amenities as water, electricity, and local transportation provided—all before plans are effectuated. Makeshift shacks and impatience with long-range plans exacerbate problems associated with temporary shelters and facilities, which often become incorporated into the new city despite being grossly inconsistent with long-term plans. The temporary shanties often remain because, with the rapid population increase and consequent housing shortage in Latin America, destruction of any housing—no matter how miserable—is difficult to justify. With all

[10] Arthur B. Gallion and Simon Eisner, *The Urban Pattern* (Princeton: Van Nostrand, 1963), p. 352.

these compromises, it is no wonder that planners of new cities so frequently complain that their dreams and intentions are drastically violated.[11]

With the founding of the United States came the desire for a new capital city, culminating in the decision to build Washington, D.C. Rejecting Thomas Jefferson's plan, national leaders employed Pierre L'Enfant, whose 1791 design added to Jefferson's gridiron plat a set of sweeping diagonal avenues, with monuments or important buildings at major intersections. Although the diagonal boulevards facilitated movement in and out of the city and relieved the monotony of the gridiron system, they permitted the growth of triangular lots and the baroque *patte d'oie* ("goose-foot") intersections that still confuse motorists. But L'Enfant's plan had dignity and grandeur, which can still be detected despite the designer's contention that his plan was "most unmercifully spoiled and altered." After several disputes, L'Enfant was dismissed in 1792 and only partly paid for his extensive efforts. Washington is still admired—although Dickens called it a city of "magnificent intentions" and broad avenues leading nowhere—and L'Enfant became the spiritual father of plans for other American cities and inspired indirectly the "city beautiful" movement that dominated American planning from 1893 until World War I.

Less grand but more practical were the industrial towns that mushroomed across the country in the nineteenth century, following the railroad lines and the spread of industry. Depressing factories were surrounded by grimy tenements and company stores, to which overworked laborers remained in perpetual debt; as Tennessee Ernie Ford sang: "I load sixteen tons, and what do I get—another day older and deeper in debt. . . . I owe my soul to the company store." [12] But such exploitation, portrayed bitterly by Upton Sinclair and piquantly by John Steinbeck, was not the only employer-worker relationship: Benevolent paternalism also motivated the founding of industrial and railroad towns intended to improve social welfare. Not always unpleasant and sometimes blandly attractive, factory towns were generally reproductions of older communities, for industrial leaders, who might legitimately pride themselves on their imagination in business

[11] Lloyd Rodwin, "Ciudad Guayana: A New City," in *Scientific American*, *op. cit.*, pp. 88–104.

[12] "Sixteen Tons," Copyright, 1947 by American Music, Inc., Elvis Presley Music, Inc., and Noma Music, Inc. Used by permission.

technology, remained fundamentally conservative and remarkably un-inventive in planning settlements for their workers. Consequently, no new ideas or practices were added to city planning knowledge by the sponsors of company towns.

New ideas were being produced, however. From the 1893 Chicago fair, nicknamed "White City" in contrast to the soot and gloom char-acteristic of many cities of the time, the Classic Revival was launched, altering architectural taste and inspiring city planning. The fair's de-signer, Daniel Burnham, cried, "Make no little plans; they have no magic to stir men's blood"—and thereafter plans did become more comprehensive and stirring. Burnham prepared a plan for San Fran-cisco in 1905 containing gridiron streets intersected by diagonals and marked by a considerable increase in land devoted to parks and play-grounds. When in the following year much of the city was destroyed by fire, his plan provided an opportunity for city remodeling unparal-leled since the London fire of 1666. But Burnham's plan was no more followed than was Wren's for London. When a city burns down, the residents generally hold rebuilding so imperative that they refuse to take time to decide how it might be done better (Stockholm provides one of the few exceptions to this understandable but short-sighted tendency). By ironic contrast, Burnham's 1909 plan for Chicago, which was not followed by any such disastrous but facilitating event, was partially effected, leading to many improvements in Chicago and stimulating similar accomplishments in other cities.

Across the world, the Australian national capital was built follow-ing an international contest; the winning design was submitted by Walter Burley Griffin, an American. Begun in 1918, the city of Can-berra has low density and strict separation into residential, govern-ment, and commercial districts. Evaluations vary from "perhaps the most carefully planned city in the world" [13] to "the most inconvenient little town in the world" [14]—the latter remark being inspired by the transportation difficulties flowing from the fact that stringent separa-tion makes trips to work and grocery stores longer than they might otherwise be. A further complaint was that Canberra's early leaders

[13] Egon Ernest Bergel, *Urban Sociology* (New York: McGraw-Hill, 1955), p. 516.

[14] Benjamin Higgins, "Canberra: A Garden Without a City," *Journal of the Royal Architectural Institute of Canada*, 28 (September 1951), 245–56.

closely translated civil service rank into residential location, parceling the land segments into sharply defined status clusters. This high degree of residential exclusiveness has not been maintained, however, and areal differentiation among social classes does not now seem any more marked than that in other Australian cities.[15]

When India and Pakistan were partitioned, a new site was selected for the capital of the Punjab, and Prime Minister Nehru appointed the famous French architect Le Corbusier to plan the new city, Chandigarh, which was intended ultimately to grow to 500,000 population. The 1951 plan, gradually being converted into concrete, calls for a huge gridiron divided into superblocks constituting self-contained neighborhoods of 15,000 people apiece, each with shopping and other facilities. Although giant superblocks divided into many small blocks with access through narrow cul-de-sacs are familiar in many American cities, Le Corbusier's superblocks differ in being planned as units. Whereas in the United States the residences, shopping center, and school are usually sited and built by three different groups, the superblocks of Chandigarh were designed from the beginning as single entities, thereby facilitating more thoughtful location of schools and markets. At the heart of this square city is a major commercial center, and along one boundary is the large capital complex. Although Le Corbusier's plan is unquestionably bold, creative, and imposing, the scale is so monumental, the landscape so stark, and the form so abstract that visitors are more awed than charmed, and some residents complain that they do not feel at home among the majestic edifices. But perhaps this grand concept may one day be compromised enough to offer some of the intimacy of the indigenous urban styles.

In 1966 bulldozers began the transformation of twenty-five square miles of Maryland countryside into a city expected to grow to 100,000 people. Midway between Baltimore and Washington, the new city of Columbia, backed by a $25 million loan from a life-insurance company, represents the largest attempt in the United States to plan an entirely new community complete with houses, apartments, business, and industry. Developer James W. Rouse claims to be motivated by the familiar idealization of small-town neighborhood values and complains that cities are out of scale for people, being "too big for people

[15] F. Lancaster Jones, "A Social Profile of Canberra, 1961," *Australian and New Zealand Journal of Sociology*, 1 (October 1965), 107–20.

to comprehend, to feel a part of, to feel responsible for, to feel important in." Fundamental to this conception are Columbia's neighborhood units of 300 to 600 families; each unit will be built around an elementary school, nursery, and small shopping center and surrounded by grassy and wooded "buffer" space. Five or six neighborhoods will constitute a village, and each village will contain a high school whose auditorium and library form the nucleus of a village center, supplemented by various shopping facilities. In this way, say the developers, recurring needs can be met locally, and the tendency of transportation to tyrannize suburban lives will be avoided.

When suburbs and new towns are mentioned together, the name "Levittown" almost inevitably springs to mind. Shortly after World War II the first Levittown was begun on Long Island, offering each buyer a house with two bedrooms and a den for appreciably less money than he would have had to pay anywhere else in the New York metropolitan area. These low prices were made possible by mass-producing the homes. In fact, the head of the company, William J. Levitt, prefers to call himself a "manufacturer" of houses. Imitating industrial production lines was a new concept in housing, and it was educational to watch the houses and yards come into being: A truck would drive slowly down the street, and as it passed each house a workman pushed off a sapling; half a block behind the truck a tractor with a spiral digger bored a hole in each front lawn; following the tractor, a workman placed each tree in its hole, and a companion shoveled the dirt back. In this way five men managed to plant more trees more economically than had been thought possible. The result was not inspired, but the construction method was effective and efficient—and because of the low prices made possible by mass-production techniques, the Levitt brothers sold their houses in large numbers. Their success was so great that similar Levittowns were built in Pennsylvania beginning in 1951 and New Jersey beginning in 1958.

A UNESCO bibliography reports some 200 new towns built between 1940 and 1960. Purposes of building are varied: creation of capital cities (Chandigarh, Brasilia, Canberra); strategic or military reasons (Oak Ridge, Tennessee; Los Alamos, New Mexico); exploitation of natural resources or development of private enterprise (Kitimat, Canada; Alcoa, Tennessee; Wolfsburg, Germany); collective planning (Magnitogorsk, Russia); relieving congestion in existing urban centers (Harlow, England; Vallingby, Sweden; Park Forest, Illinois); and escape from population pressure (Wadi-Faliq, Israel).[16]

○ *Garden Cities*

Of all self-contained communities deliberately created, one type has had an especially powerful influence on twentieth-century urban planning: the garden city, introduced by Ebenezer Howard in 1898. The principles put forth by Howard were not totally new. Four centuries earlier Leonardo da Vinci had suggested a plan to Ludovico Sforza, the Duke of Milan, for dispersal of Milan into ten satellite cities of 30,000 inhabitants apiece, thereby separating "the great congregation of people who herd together like goats one on top of another, filling every place with foul odor and sowing seeds of pestilence and death." But Leonardo did not influence Howard.

Direct antecedents may be found in Thomas More's *Utopia* of 1516, John Bellers' *Colledge of Industry* of 1696, and the proposals of various nineteenth-century English factory owners. Indeed, nineteenth-century England was rich in utopian ideas, as benevolent industrialists, inspired by such rallying cries as Benjamin W. Richardson's "Instead of a gutter, the poorest child would have a garden," sought to produce factory towns reminiscent of rural cottages and village greens. Protesting the filth and ugliness of the early industrial cities, Robert Owen successfully attempted social regeneration in New Lanark, Scotland (where he became proprietor of a cotton mill in 1799), and later—without success—in New Harmony, Indiana. In 1849 James Silk Buckingham published a proposal for a model town (never built) to be called Victoria and to contain 10,000 inhabitants, whose occupations would be divided between farming and manufacturing, and to be surrounded by 10,000 acres of agricultural land. Ironically, a major purpose of the community, which was to be completely planned before settlement—and all of whose land, factories, residences, businesses, and farms would be owned and managed by a

[16] Jean Viet, *New Towns*, UNESCO Reports and Papers in the Social Sciences, No. 12 (Paris: UNESCO, 1960), pp. 16–52.

single parent company that would provide free medical service, nurses, and education—was "to avoid the evils of communism."

Factory owner Titus Salt was more conservative than Owen and Buckingham—and more practical. Opening a new textile plant in 1853, he spent the next eighteen years completing a contiguous town called Saltaire; this community of 4,400 people on the River Aire represented a notable improvement in living conditions of workers. Chocolate manufacturer George Cadbury, seeking room to expand his business, founded Bourneville in 1879; built on a greater scale than Saltaire, Bourneville was never intended to be a one-company town, and in fact about half the working population was employed elsewhere than at the Cadbury factory. Another model factory town, Port Sunlight, was begun in 1888 by William H. Lever, a soap manufacturer. Although these paternalistic planned towns demonstrated the disparity between the prevalent sordid living conditions and the improvements possible under enlightened management, it was Edward Bellamy's utopian community portrayed in *Looking Backward* in 1888 that inspired Howard to put forward his proposal for garden cities.

The garden city, said Howard, "is not a loose indefinite sprawl of individual houses with immense open spaces over the whole landscape; it is rather a compact, rigorously confined urban grouping. It is not a suburb but the antithesis of a suburb; not a more rural retreat, but a more integrated foundation for an effective urban life." [17] The central five or six acres contain civic buildings, a lecture hall, theater, library, and so on. Stores and shops are nearby. Around them is a ring of houses, each with its own yard, and scattered schools, churches, and small parks. An outer ring contains the factories and warehouses, fronting on the highway or railroad line. Six boulevards radiate from the center. Beyond the 1,000 acres of the city itself is a greenbelt area covering 5,000 acres and, beyond it, an agricultural belt not a part of the community. This layout is illustrated schematically in Figure 17.

The greenbelt is essential in Howard's scheme, for this integral part of the city supplies elbow room for the confined urbanites. This preserve of natural fields and woods must never be encroached upon for housing, business, industry, or even farming (although pasturing is

[17] Ebenezer Howard, *Tomorrow* (1898; 2nd ed., *Garden Cities of Tomorrow*, 1902; Cambridge, Mass.: M.I.T. Press, 1965).

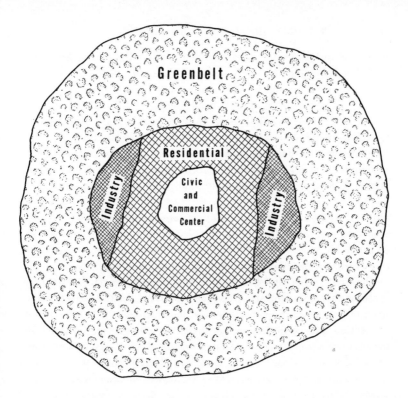

FIGURE 17. The Garden-City Concept

permissible); it is intended for recreation—cricket, football, love making, or bird watching. Encircling the city, the greenbelt halts urban sprawl and is thus a form of girth control, making is impossible for the city to grow larger than was originally planned.

Howard's garden city is a self-sufficient town planned for healthy living and a balance of workers and employment, large enough to have a full measure of amenities but not so large as to choke itself with transportation woes. With a population of 30,000, there would be several basic industries, with the attendant advantages of diversification: If one plant were crippled by a recession in its industry, the others might keep going, and unemployment would not hobble the town. In other words, the economic base should never consist of only a single factory.

Because land is owned not by individuals but by a limited dividend company, there is no land speculation and no temptation to increase density in order to raise rental income. Land and buildings are never sold, but leases may be for a lifetime. Unearned increments of land value are used to reduce utility rates or to improve the parks and schools. Road repairing and other city maintenance work is done by the private corporation that owns the land, supported by income received through rental of property to families and industries.

A garden city has balanced employment and is definitely not a commuting suburb. In Howard's conception, it should not exceed 30,000 residents, for the greenbelt cannot be encroached upon, and the houses and apartments simply will not hold much more than that number. The permanent surrounding reserve of parks and pastureland thus eliminates the possibility of deterioration through success. This combination of the virtues of urban life plus easy access to the countryside inspired other men to write books and build cities.[18]

The first garden city, Letchworth, was begun in 1903, followed by Welwyn in 1920. Howard personally founded, helped govern, and lived in both cities, and such was his unquenchable confidence in his conception that he undertook construction of the second city before the first was sure of success. Growth was disappointingly slow in both cities, largely because of manufacturing firms' reluctance to move from London; consequently, many residents commuted—a practice strongly disapproved by Howard. Several decades were required to reach the appointed 30,000 population, but both towns survived, and the shareholders received dividends. Today these prototype garden cities are stable, successful communities. Letchworth, which Howard planned in conjunction with Raymond Unwin, is about thirty-five miles north of London and contains light and diversified industry. Welwyn also has industry, but because it is only twenty miles from London, many residents commute, a fact inconsistent with Howard's original plan.

In the 1940s the garden-city movement was transformed into the new-towns movement, aided by the Barlow Report of 1940, the Distribution of Industries Act of 1945, the New Towns Act of 1946, and the Town Development Act of 1952. These acts called for the construction of fifteen new garden cities of 25,000 to 60,000 people (eight near London as part of the decentralization plan for greater London) and

18 For instance, Herbert George Wells, *Anticipations of the Reaction of Mechanical and Scientific Progress upon Human Life and Thought* (New York: Harper, 1901).

for controlled expansion of many existing towns. Unlike Letchworth and Welwyn, which were owned and operated by private companies, the post-World War II cities were government enterprises.

An American sociologist who visited England in 1952 was "favorably impressed" by what he saw.

> With all the mistakes, all the fumbling and stumbling, all the misinformed and uninformed idealism, the new towns program could hardly be judged a failure, even though the objectives will never be realized in full and the efforts will be unnecessarily costly. In a sense the mistakes may, in the long run, be triumphs for they will demonstrate to the world valuable lessons in the art and science of planning.[19]

Local interests were sometimes antagonistic to these reforms and in some instances were able to block or modify government proposals.[20] Each new town had its fiascos in getting under way, but after the first, Stevenage, the number of administrative blunders and disheartening obstacles decreased.

> New towns have been built and old ones renewed since the earliest times. But a national policy of building within a few years complete communities to serve new needs and to help recast our urban environment is something unique in urban history. Only in 1946 in Britain did this first become official government policy.[21]

This step forward was not taken hastily. During the half-century between publication of Howard's book in 1898 and the adoption of the national policy in 1946, only two garden cities were built—and it is possible that without World War II and the rise to power of the Labour Party, recent progress would have been equally slow. Once the New Towns Act was passed, however, action was rapid: From 1946 through 1949, fourteen new towns were begun, and a fifteenth was added in 1955. A total of twenty-two new towns were started by 1965, sited in various locations throughout England, Scotland, Wales, and Northern Ireland. Their total population has grown to about half a million and will reach nearly a million when the cities are fully constructed.

---

19 Noel P. Gist, book review in *American Sociological Review*, 21 (October 1956), 647.
20 Harold Orlans, *Utopia Ltd.* (New Haven: Yale University Press, 1953).
21 Lloyd Rodwin, *The British New Towns Policy* (Cambridge, Mass.: Harvard University Press, 1956), p. 3.

○ *Garden Suburbs*

The garden-city idea caught on in the United States, where the best-known adaptation is Radburn, New Jersey, planned by Henry Wright and Clarence Stein in 1928 as an "answer to the problems of the motor age." The basic unit in Radburn, a community of 2,500 people located sixteen miles from New York City, is the superblock; front doors face inward toward a park and recreation area, and rear doors open on cul-de-sac service lanes for deliveries and family cars, thus ensuring almost complete separation of pedestrians and automobiles. Figure 18 provides a generalized diagram of what has come to be called "the Radburn idea." Radburn is not, however, a true garden city; it is a commuting town, is not incorporated, lacks a greenbelt, and has no industry. Yet Radburn shares much of Howard's spirit. Its developers used good judgment in adapting several of Howard's ideas, but they turned out to be poor economic prophets in beginning the new community just before the Depression. As a result, Radburn was never completed, and financial vicissitudes forced the corporation into bankruptcy. But the homes and parkland survive, and residents generally report favorably on Radburn's pleasures.

One of the designers of Radburn, Clarence Stein, also planned Baldwin Hills Village in Los Angeles. This 1941 expression of the Radburn idea consists of a set of one- and two-story dwellings, most with walled gardens, in a large superblock. Pedestrian and automobile traffic are separated, as all homes face open space along the communal backbone. The acreage of Baldwin Hills Village is 85 per cent greenery.

Also embodying some of Howard's garden-city principles were the three "greenbelt" towns of the 1930s: Greenbelt, Maryland; Greenhills, Ohio; and Greendale, Wisconsin. A fourth community, Greenbrook, New Jersey, was begun in 1935 but ended in 1936 following legal squabbles. These New Deal creations combined the garden city, the Radburn idea, and the neighborhood-unit principle. Located near Washington, Cincinnati, and Milwaukee, respectively, all three towns were designed to have each neighborhood focused around a school, shopping center, and communal facilities, and each town had its pe-

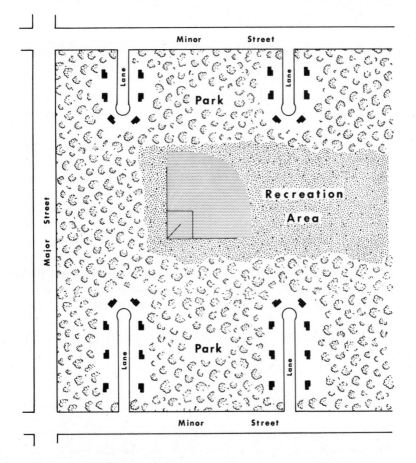

FIGURE 18. The Radburn Idea

ripheral greenbelt. But limited funds and continual attacks by real-estate interests so hampered their construction that they became merely small dormitory villages, lacking their own sources of employment. In the 1950s the government sold the greenbelt space to private developers, and today the three towns hardly differ from numerous other garden suburbs and apartment developments.

In Sweden, France, Finland, and Germany, the garden city also became a garden suburb for commuters, a sentimental adulteration that Howard would not have accepted. Although some, like Vallingby near Stockholm, do contain a little industry, most of these communities are not self-contained, they have no greenbelt, and residents do not live exclusively in single-family homes. In sum, they are merely low-density dormitories for the central city's workers. Such perambulator havens do have the virtue of more grass and trees than ordinary apartment developments, but otherwise their resemblance to garden cities is faint.

The garden-city concept has also been perverted by retirement communities like Leisure World, Sun City, and other housing tracts in California and the Southwest that cater to the needs of aged persons by offering a great variety of services. Although such "adult communities" sometimes attempt to achieve the garden-city spirit of independence from outside communities, they nonetheless represent a distortion of Howard's idea, for they have few active workers, they are economically unproductive, and there is little or no greenbelt. Perhaps the only respect in which they bear a close resemblance to the English garden cities is the strong control exercised over the land and its occupancy—and, some say, the occupants—by the directors of the establishment.

○ Optimum City Size

That planners in different countries disagree on the most desirable form of organizing urban networks is not surprising in view of other cultural differences among nations. Even the seemingly simpler matter of deciding the most effective or congenial size for urban agglomerations has aroused discord from the earliest times to the present.

Hippodamus recommended 10,000 citizens plus their wives, children, and slaves. Plato preferred 5,040 citizens, or a probable total of about 50,000 people, although the number could vary somewhat according to size of territory. Aristotle said that "ten people would not make a city, but with a hundred thousand it is a city no longer." In 1516 Thomas More suggested 6,000 large families. Ebenezer Howard recommended a population of 30,000. The U.S. National Security Resources Board agreed with the English Ministry of Town and Country Planning in selecting 50,000 as the optimum. English town planner Thomas Sharp spoke up for cities of 100,000. French architect and planner Gaston Bardet advocated 200,000 as the maximum, lest city residents lose touch with rural environments. The Indian sociologist G. S. Ghurye agrees with Russian city planners in favoring 300,000. The renowned French designer Le Corbusier considered 3 million ideal. Contributing to these variations in proposed optimum size are their essential subjectivity and the inconsistencies in the criteria chosen. Several American sociologists have attacked the problem not by setting up a single optimum but by estimating a separate optimum for each of a dozen criteria.[22]

An optimally sized city should be small enough to permit ready access to the countryside and a reasonably quick journey to work; it should also be large enough to support a bus or streetcar system for those who do not use private cars. Most cities of 25,000 or more in the United States have some form of mass transit. Difficulty of access to the various parts of a city increases proportionately with the radius of the city; time, cost, and convenience all seem better served in the medium or small city. Also, the distance traveled from home to work tends to increase in direct proportion to the diameter of the city. Traffic congestion too increases with city size.

Transportation between cities is also important: Lack of intercity personal and freight service isolates communities and retards the spread of new ideas, customs, and products—which means, to look on the obverse side, that disruptive social change is less likely. All cities of 100,000 or more population and about half of all towns of 7,500 or more are located on or near an Interstate or Defense Highway. Small towns generally lack airports, and many medium-size cities are served only by local routes; a resident must take a short flight to a major airport to travel a longer distance.

Health is a crucial criterion. Health expenditures per resident appear to increase as the size of the city increases; in other words, health care costs more in large cities. Whether the greater cost is due to better facilities and more skilled physicians or to some explanation

[22] See for example Otis Dudley Duncan, "Optimum Size of Cities," in Paul K. Hatt and Albert J. Reiss, Jr. (eds.), *Cities and Society* (New York: Free Press, 1957), pp. 759–73; Fenton Keyes, *The Correlation of Social Phenomena with Community Size* (Ph.D. dissertation, Yale University, New Haven, 1942) ; and William Fielding Ogburn and Duncan, "City Size as a Sociological Variable," in Ernest W. Burgess and Donald J. Bogue (eds.), *Contributions to Urban Sociology* (Chicago: University of Chicago Press, 1964), pp. 129–47.

less flattering to metropolises is difficult to say. We do know, however, that not only the number but, more important, the per capita ratio of physicians, nurses, hospital beds, and diagnostic and therapeutic equipment varies directly with city size; also, certain medical specialists and facilities are found only in metropolitan centers. But in small towns there are fewer opportunities to contact carriers of disease. To avoid getting sick, perhaps one should live in a small town; but if one becomes sick, treatment is most effective in large cities. Probably the best arrangement is to live in the smallest city that has a good hospital. Pollution of water and air is generally higher in large cities, but many small communities also have pollution hazards; in fact, smoggy air and waste-laden water are coming to be hallmarks of modern civilization regardless of city size.

Public safety is a fourth factor. Reported crime rates (many crimes go unreported) generally increase with city size—though not for all types of crimes. Deaths resulting from automobile accidents are greater in large cities—but miles driven are also greater. Other variables also yield ambiguous results: For instance, the number of fires per capita varies inversely with city size, but the per capita fire loss in dollars is not consistently associated with city size.

Municipal efficiency is also difficult to evaluate. Police and fire protection cost more per capita as city size increases, and large cities spend more money per capita for schools, public welfare, sanitation, roads, and nearly all other public services. But the quality of these services probably increases with the amount disbursed, because more and better equipment is bought and trained professionals can be hired: For example, large cities usually pay larger salaries to policemen and other public servants and can therefore employ more competent personnel.

Educational opportunity is greater in large cities. By offering higher salaries, they are more likely to attract good teachers, and they spend more money for books and equipment. Expenditure per pupil is much higher in large cities, and it is probable that the quality of education is superior. Small communities often have smaller classes, however. Finally, residents of large cities are more likely to have access to the library and other facilities of a college or university.

Cultural offerings are nearly always superior in large cities. Museums, symphony orchestras, zoos, opera houses, radio and television stations, multiple-ownership newspapers, auditoriums, gourmet restaurants, religious diversity, and informal educational advantages are not often found in respectable quality in cities under 100,000 population.

Social welfare services also are more plentiful in large cities. Specialized services for dependent children, delinquents, the aged, psychoneurotics, and the indigent are not usual in small towns—but possibly they are less necessary. When a small-town mother goes to the hospital for an appendectomy, neighbors may take turns baby sitting and supplying casserole dinners to the family. In large cities, with their greater tendency toward aloofness and impersonality (although close-knit neighborhoods are more common in metropolitan centers than is generally supposed), the husband and children are more likely to have to fend for themselves. (Insurance companies are well aware of this difference; they sell policies to urbanites to provide the security that is supplied informally in small towns through folkways of mutual assistance.)

Merchants in large cities are more specialized, and purchasers have the opportunity to make price comparisons. For some commodities, this distinction is irrelevant: Corn flakes and soap are sold in quantity in all sizes of communities. But in any town, only a small percentage of homes have pianos; therefore only a large city can support a store selling only pianos, and only a metropolis can offer Steinway versus Baldwin versus other franchises. The metropolite thus has a wider choice—and perhaps a more convenient one—than the small-towner does. Merchants' preferences vary: Some like to specialize and compete in the metropolitan setting, and others prefer the relatively limited but captive market in a small town.

Individual income is greatest in very large cities and smallest in very small villages. Not only are the highest-paid occupations best represented in metropolises, but even when the type of job is held constant, income is positively correlated with city size. The National Bureau of Economic Research reported in 1967 that average hourly wages of industrial workers in 1959 varied as follows: rural, $2.00; population 2,500 to 9,999, $2.12; 10,000 to 99,999, $2.23; 100,000 to 499,999, $2.41; 500,000 to 999,999, $2.56; $1,000,000 and over $2.84. This city-size wage differential is present in all regions and for all races; however, differences are particularly large in the South and among Negroes and workers of limited education.

On the other hand, the cost of living tends to increase directly with city size; this differential, however, is considerably smaller than the income differential. Metropolitan housing is more expensive, but it is often more modern and in better repair. Small towns have a higher proportion of homes lacking running water, indoor toilets, and refrigerators. Surprisingly—to anyone who has never seen a rural or small-town slum—there is more overcrowding (as measured by the number of people per room) in small cities than in large ones.

Density of settlement is higher in large cities than in small towns. In fact, there is a fairly direct correlation between the total population of a city and the number of persons per square mile, from "millionaire" cities down to the smallest incorporated places. But whether high or low density is preferable is a value-laden question differently answered by different individuals.

Ideas and inventions diffuse outward from large cities. Not only the absolute number but also the per capita proportion of patents granted in the United States varies directly with the size of the community. Whether technological and humanistic advances are good or bad, anyone who wants to live among cultural innovators and intellectual leaders would be wise to move to the metropolis.

Variation and its pejorative, deviation, are both greatest in large cities. The bigger the city, the more likely it is to contain divergences from the average that disturb conventional people and excite the enterprising. Whether fondly or disparagingly regarded, unusual occupations and personalities are generally found only in great cities: Competent oboe players and pickpockets are rarely encountered in villages.

The ability to live one's life as one wishes is claimed by most people as central to their satisfaction with life, but where this desideratum is best met is a moot question. Small towns offer a degree of freedom from encountering undesirables one does not wish to meet or even to see, and they are free of crowds and rush-hour traffic which dominate the daily schedules of many urban residents. But it is only in large cities or in completely isolated nonurban areas that one can achieve freedom from friendly but inquisitive neighbors. Small towns may seem confining and large cities depersonalizing; which set of virtues and liabilities one prefers—and to what extent and in what manner they affect him—is an individual matter. Increasingly, however, people do seem to choose the metropolis, although the choice may not necessarily indicate preference.

No one knows where people are happier. Villagers say that small towns are friendly, comfortable, relaxed, and stable and that large cities breed anxiety and fear. Metropolites reply that hamlets are stagnant and that "big brother" is always watching, whereas large cities are dynamic, varied, exciting, and unrestrictive. There is no optimum size for happiness; rather, each individual's preferences and propensities are supposedly matched to the properties of his chosen community.

In sum, each person's choice is largely subjective: Which qualities are most important to him? Good reasons may direct him toward either the metropolis or the small town; similarly, both community and national well-being may be advanced by each individual's proper choice of either a large or small city. For an average person and the nation as a whole, the balance favors cities of about 50,000 population—which is what Plato recommended 2,300 years ago and what the British new towns are averaging today. Intelligent social policy, however, should recognize that many variables and purposes must be considered before national leaders can decide what size to encourage.

chapter 12

PLANNING PRACTICES AND PROBLEMS

NEW TOWNS ARE DESIGNED FROM TIME TO TIME, BUT THE OVERWHELM-
ing majority of all planning activity consists of reworking existing
cities. To this end, city governments set up bureaus to oversee the
daily working out and modifying of their master plans. The first official city planning agency in the United States was established in Hart-
ford, Connecticut, in 1907.

This pioneering occurred during planning's "city beautiful" phase,
when the intent was aesthetic, planners were landscape architects, and
plans dealt mainly with civic centers and parks. The second phase, the
"city practical," began during World War I and lasted about a decade. In this stage, when the first professional planners went to work,
the main emphasis was on zoning and public works, and planning
commissions were created in hundreds of cities. Stage three, the "city
welfare" of the 1930s, responded to the national Depression by shifting attention to social problems, especially bad housing.[1]

---

[1] Harvey S. Perloff, *Education for Planning* (Baltimore: Johns Hopkins University Press, 1957), pp. 54–61.

The first academic planning departments were established at Harvard University in 1929, Massachusetts Institute of Technology in 1935, Cornell University in 1935, and Columbia University in 1937. In stage four—after World War II—the scope of planning broadened: New graduate schools opened, nearly all cities came to have planning boards, and planners turned their attention to subdivisions, zoning laws, public housing, urban renewal, transportation, capital programing, and public relations. Planning had come of age. A professional planner today is expected to have a bachelor's degree in architecture, engineering, political science, sociology, economics, or a related discipline, followed by a master's degree in city planning.

○ *The Master Plan*

The basic framework for directing the planning of a city is the master plan, which ordinarily is prepared by a staff of planners—and which may or may not be adopted by city officials. The master plan sets forth a program recommended to achieve goals projected over ten years or so. In some cases, the city council refuses to support the plan; more often, it endorses the recommendations, sometimes even vigorously setting out to implement the proposals.

The size of a master plan varies with the size of the community, some plans being only a few dozen pages and others filling several thick volumes. The range of topics usually includes land use and value, population, public transportation, traffic and parking, recreation and parks, schools, housing, subdivision regulations, neighborhoods, public and private utilities, capital investment and financing, and zoning ordinances. Like ecologists, planners do much of their work on maps, and a large—and perhaps the most important—part of any master plan is its maps supplying basic information about the community and recommending programs for stabilization or change.

In the United States more than 90 per cent of all cities with more than 10,000 population carry on some sort of planning, the prevailing form being the independent or semiautonomous commission.[2] This

[2] Donald H. Webster, *Urban Planning and Municipal Public Policy* (New York: Harper, 1958), p. 102.

commission or board usually consists of perhaps six private citizens —lawyers, prominent businessmen, or other community leaders— who are appointed by the mayor to terms of about three years and who act as an advisory body to the mayor, city council, or other branches of the city government. The commission hires whatever professional staff it can afford; the number varies from none to more than 100 in New York and Los Angeles. The larger cities house their planning staffs in extensive offices and provide annual budgets amounting in a few cases to more than half a million dollars. The American Institute of Planners recommends a minimum annual per capita budget of 15 cents for the largest cities and $1 for very small ones.

Planning activity is not confined to professionals; in fact, some city planners strive to interest the citizenry in planning decisions. One prominent practitioner, Hugh Pomeroy, has listed several contributions that ordinary citizens can make to planning the cities in which they live.

1. Assist in interpreting the thinking of the people of the community to the planning board.
2. Perform various kinds of direct service for the planning board, such as in the making of surveys, tabulating material, etc.
3. Collaborate with the planning board in the development of various phases of the community plan and of neighborhood plans, and in the formulation of the various measures for carrying plans into effect.
4. Assist in informing the people of the community as to the purposes and methods of planning in general, and as to the plans of the planning board in particular.
5. Provide organized support for carrying out the recommendations of the planning board.
6. Be alert to protect the integrity of the community and neighborhood plans, and of zoning and other measures for their furtherance.
7. Insist on the provision of adequate means for the planning board to do its diligent and systematic work, and effective performance on the part of the planning board.[3]

[3] Hugh R. Pomeroy, "The Planning Process and Public Participation," in Gerald Breese and Dorothy E. Whiteman (eds.), *An Approach to Urban Planning* (Princeton: Princeton University Press, 1953), p. 34.

When citizens feel threatened by an enterprise—usually commercial or industrial—that they view as likely to lower property values or otherwise to detract from the neighborhood, they may rise up in force to protest. But unless an issue affects them personally, most citizens remain apathetic about planning and zoning matters.

○ Zoning and Land Use

The major tool of city planners is zoning—the establishment of districts to regulate the use, bulk, and height of buildings, the density of population, and the use of land. Zoning orginated in the late nineteenth century as a method of controlling nuisances in the interest of public health and welfare. To twentieth-century planners, zoning is not merely a means of controlling noxious or disagreeable activities, but it also promotes the future comfort and happiness of urban residents by guiding city growth along orderly lines. The first comprehensive zoning law in the United States to stand up under court test was New York City's Zoning Resolution of 1916, which set up elementary land use and bulk regulations. In the next dozen years, other states enacted enabling laws permitting hundreds of municipalities to set up zoning ordinances, and today even small towns without planning boards or master plans often have zoning maps and statutes.

Strictly speaking, a zoning ordinance (or subdivision regulation) is neither a plan nor part of a plan; rather, it is a legal instrument for effecting a plan. One application of zoning that has not received court sanction is racial and religious segregation, but a more drastic step—retroactive zoning—may soon be acceptable. Already time zoning—the forced removal of nonconforming uses within a specified although lengthy period of years (with provision for amortization of investment)—is in effect in a few cities, and it is but a short step to wider and faster application of this reasoning.[4]

Major categories of land use and zoning are: residential (comprising several subcategories of houses and apartments); commercial (local shopping, central business area, heavy commercial such as

[4] Robert A. Walker, *The Planning Function in Urban Government* (Chicago: University of Chicago Press, 1950), pp. 54–104.

laundries and garages); industrial (garden factories, light industry, heavy industry such as steel mills and oil refineries); and public (schools, churches, hospitals, streets, and so on). Planners attempt to distribute the activities within the city so that no one category of use occupies an undue proportion of the area. They also try to avoid abrupt disjunctions (for example, high-rent housing next to factories), spot zoning (assigning to a small plot a land use sharply separate from that of the surrounding area), overevaluation (restricting areas to higher-level activities than is realistic), and other dysfunctional arrangements common to unplanned or badly planned communities. When a mistake is made, correction may be attempted by changing the zoning map or, if the error is small, by granting a variance or exception—a practice that unfortunately is sometimes extended not only to redress legitimate grievances but also to favor politically powerful landowners. Fortunately, however, most planning actions are rational and impartial.

A special case is a zoning ordinance for new subdivisions, for which a separate set of rules is often drawn. Zoning of areas already in existence must usually be limited either to the status quo or to minor modifications, but when totally new tracts are subdivided it is possible for planners to exercise a freer hand, unhampered by existing structures and facilities. Many subdivision regulations specify, for instance, that builders must install proper utilities and reserve adequate acreage for schools, parks, and other public conveniences so that new tracts will not consist entirely of houses that produce income for the developer and taxes for the city but that inevitably require costly services from the community government.

○ *Open Space and Parks*

One zoning objective in the face of urban population growth is the withholding of land for open space. With increased incursion of people and buildings into areas of previously low human and structural density, concern has arisen that so much land will soon be covered over with buildings and pavement that little open space will be left to the residents. Conservationist efforts to preserve the beauties of nature in national parks might well be paralleled by civic insistence on retaining the few open spaces that remain in and near cities.

Open spaces are not necessarily unused space; in fact, in urban areas they are usually hives of activity. Golf courses are manicured, parks are landscaped, and playgrounds are supplied with baseballs. Benefits are many: In small neighborhood parks children can play close to home, and mothers can trundle baby carriages; golf courses and tennis courts provide exercise and relaxation for adults; and all types of open areas keep down density levels, thereby offering a more varied and attractive cityscape.

Few American cities have a tradition of reserving at least one area in each neighborhood for strolling and playing, with or without sand pits, wading pools, and stretches of greensward for hitting balls and playing catch. A likely explanation is that such open areas not only fail to supply salable lots to developers and taxable property to the city, but they also require planting, seeding, and recurrent maintenance. Such superficial expenses, however, may be advantageous in the long run, for they tend to make houses more marketable and communities more livable. Whatever the cost, open space is a coveted luxury and is probably a sufficiently desirable necessity to warrant continual attention to its preservation or, if need be, its creation.

Aside from lowering residential density and providing recreation areas, greenery offers respite from cement facades, sun-baked sidewalks, and exhaust fumes. Bushes and trees are not merely aesthetic props, for they supply cooling shade to homes and passersby, absorb noise, alter humidity, and create refreshing natural odors. Paris, Copenhagen, Rome, and certain other cities are supplied with numerous small parks and plazas that give a city grace and charm and encourage residents to walk or sit outdoors; few American cities, however, possess such partial retreats from commerce and clangor.

A final virtue claimed for parks since the pioneering public-health movement of the 1840s is their function as "lungs" or "ventilators" that absorb or dispel impurities exhaled into the atmosphere by the urban environment. Probably the major impetus behind New York's Central Park—the oldest city park in the United States designed to be a natural landscape—came from the conviction that trees were nature's own laboratory for preserving health; aesthetic or recreation arguments might never have sufficed to put into effect the 1856 plan of Frederick Law Olmsted and Calvert Vaux.

○ *Neighborhood-Unit Planning*

Almost as enthusiastic for reform as the nineteenth-century fighters against disease-producing vapors are the twentieth-century advocates of neighborhood-unit planning. This principle, hazily foreshadowed in earlier centuries, was definitively enunciated in 1929 by Clarence Perry, who believed that a residential area should contain within reasonable walking distance every convenience required by the average family, including an elementary school, parks and playgrounds, and a retail shopping district. The distance from home to school or play or shopping should not exceed one-quarter mile if possible, or one-half mile at the maximum. Ideally, the population of a neighborhood unit should not exceed 5,000, but considerable latitude must be given to adapt to local conditions and the preferences of the residents. Perry's writings indicate that he was deeply influenced by Ebenezer Howard's garden city idea, trying, however, to adapt the neighborhood notion to existing cities and districts as well as to newly created ones. Perry's definitive statement was included in the New York Regional Plan of 1927–1931:

> Size. A residential unit development should provide housing for that population for which one elementary school is ordinarily required, its actual area depending upon its population density.
> Boundaries. The unit should be bounded on all sides by arterial streets, sufficiently wide to facilitate its by-passing, instead of penetration, by through traffic.
> Open Spaces. A system of small parks and recreation spaces, planned to meet the needs of the particular neighborhood, should be provided.
> Institutional Sites. Sites for the school and other institutions having service spheres coinciding with the limits of the unit should be suitably grouped about a central point, or common.
> Local Shops. One or more shopping districts, adequate for the population to be served, should be laid out in the circumference of the unit,

preferably at traffic junctions and adjacent to similar districts of adjoining neighborhoods.

Internal Street System. The unit should be provided with a special street system, each highway being proportioned to its probable traffic load, and the street net as a whole being designed to facilitate circulation within the unit and to discourage its use by through traffic.[5]

Hundreds of urban planners have tried to apply Perry's neighborhood-unit concept to their own communities, in the hope that they might thereby disrupt existing patterns of social relationships as little as possible and construct an abiding setting for the social maturation of the coming generation. Recognizing that bulldozers may pulverize the social system along with the physical setting, modern planners strive to revitalize neighborhood life along with the physical facilities.

Many developers have come to favor a watered-down adaptation of neighborhood planning applied to the increasingly popular superblock, which offers a distinct separation of local from through automobile traffic in an endeavor to diminish noise and danger to playing children. In Figure 19 the superblock is defined by a six-foot wall obstructing access from the surrounding major streets in any way except through the two entrances at top and bottom. Pedestrian as well as vehicular traffic is further discouraged by the layout of internal streets, which favors cul-de-sac and circular patterns. The layout illustrated here is common in working-class neighborhoods; middle-class superblocks often exhibit the superficially imaginative variation implied by curving streets; upper-class people rarely live in superblocks.

The neighborhood-unit concept evokes sharp affirmative and negative reactions. Although there is strong support for deliberately arranged neighborhoods, a few planners and many social scientists believe the neighborhood-unit idea is a symptom of unwise social engineering, invoking the questionable principle that the conscious maneuvering of neighborhoods by government authorities or private

---

[5] Clarence Perry, "The Neighborhood Unit," in Committee on Regional Plan of New York and Its Environs, *Regional Survey of New York and Its Environs*, VII: *Neighborhood and Community Planning* (New York: Regional Plan Association, 1929), 34–5. See also Perry, *Housing for the Machine Age* (New York: Russell Sage, 1939), pp. 50 ff.

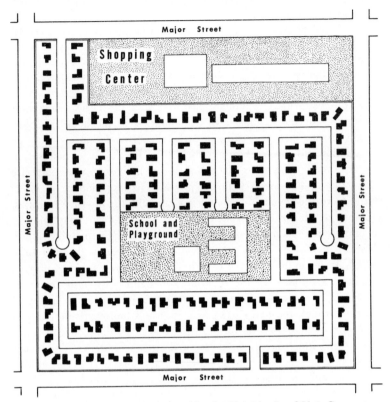

FIGURE 19. A Superblock Influenced by the Neighborhood-Unit Concept

developers is contrary to the spirit of personal freedom. Prominent among opposition leaders has been Reginald Isaacs, who regards neighborhood planning as a fruitless effort to create static residential areas in the midst of dynamic cities; worse yet, Isaacs argues, is their frequently unanticipated or deliberately ignored consequence of promoting racial or ethnic segregation.[6] But the antineighborhood-planning faction has not won over many planners, principally because no alternative has been established as superior to this mode of giving careful consideration to the immediate vicinity of people's homes.

[6] Reginald Isaacs, "The Neighborhood Theory," *Journal of the American Institute of Planners,* 14 (Spring 1948), 15–23.

○ *Housing and Building*

One of the foremost aspects of the master plan is housing. In fact, housing legislation often precedes comprehensive planning, especially in cities having a history of poor housing conditions.

The "railroad" apartments common in New York City around 1850 were representative of large cities in all industrialized nations. The typical lot was 25 feet wide and 100 feet deep, and the plan covered the full width, leaving no front yard and usually a 10-by-25-foot rear yard. There were no interior bathrooms or toilets, and privies were located in the back yards. Each of the five to seven stories contained four apartments, each with a bedroom barely large enough for a double bed, a living room only slightly larger, and a small kitchen. With four units and a stairway squeezed into a 25-by-90-foot floor plan, rooms cannot be made spacious. Since there were no side yards, only one room in each apartment had a window; this room became the living room, facing either the tiny back yard or a noisy street; in some cases, there was no back yard. With no cross ventilation, the foul air became suffocatingly hot in summer. Small children were bathed in the kitchen sink, and adults used a portable tub stored under the sink; but, as water had to be carried upstairs in buckets, perhaps baths were not a great pleasure.

After decades of complaints of health hazards arising from such living conditions, New York City passed the nation's first tenement law in 1867. The following improvements were specified: Ceilings in cellar dwellings were required to be at least one foot above the ground; a toilet had to be provided for every twenty persons; every building had to have running water either inside or in the yard; and all buildings were required to have rear yards at least ten feet deep. Twelve years later a more progressive law prohibited rooms without windows but resulted in what became known as the "dumbbell" plan, offering little improvement except for narrow air shafts down each side of the building. The shafts magnified noise, admitted little light or air (and what there was became fetid on the lower floors), and were excellent repositories for garbage (the alternative being to carry it down several flights of stairs to an already overflowing trash can) ;

tenants soon learned to keep the windows closed. Heating remained inadequate, except in summer, when temperatures were fearsome. The only real gain in the dumbbell plan was provision for the one or two toilets on each floor, to be shared among the residents of the four apartments, who might number more than twenty persons. Bathtubs were not provided. And yet people became attached to these places—in keeping with the sentiment theory described in Chapter 8.

These layouts were finally outlawed by the "New Law" of 1901, which prohibited building on more than 70 per cent of a lot, thus virtually eliminating the 25-foot-wide lot because 70 per cent of it was not a large enough space on which to build an apartment house. Side yards became common, many apartments acquired more than one bedroom, and toilets were installed in each dwelling unit. Since 1901 apartment construction has continued to improve, but, as none of these laws required that earlier structures be torn down, many "Old Law" tenements as well as some prelaw buildings remained to house several more generations.

In 1950 only two-thirds of the nation's dwelling units contained private toilets and baths with hot running water; the other third were largely rural rather than urban, and unquestionably the worst housing in the country was—and remains today—rural. Few cities would now tolerate families living in rusting buses, as can be seen in some rural areas; in a city, the bus would be condemned and dragged away, and in many cases social workers would ply the family with canned food, a subsidized apartment, and offers of jobs.

Cities were similarly laggard in sanitation. In 1900 Philadelphia and St. Louis had twice as much street mileage as sewer mileage, and Baltimore and New Orleans still relied on open gutters for drainage. Those cities that did improve sewage disposal were often more or less forced into it by catastrophe: Memphis built a sewer system only after being partially depopulated by a yellow-fever epidemic in 1879.[7]

It is no wonder then that areas of substandard housing require more than their proportionate share of urban expenditures and account for high proportions of the total crime, delinquency, illegitimacy, vice, desertion, and disease. It is unwise, however, to conclude that removal of slums and blighted areas would eliminate these social ills, for, although substandard housing is statistically associated with these and other indexes of social disorganization, it has never been

[7] Walker, *op. cit.*, p. 7.

demonstrated that poor housing per se is a cause of social pathology. The widespread slum clearance, urban renewal, and redevelopment schemes that followed World War II often paid little regard to planning, neglecting the basic fact that housing improvement is nugatory unless it is compatible with a city-wide program of comprehensive planning.

Housing deficiency is often the result of inefficiency in the building trades, for housing is one of the few major industries in the United States that still rejects mass production. Prefabricated houses are resisted and sometimes declared illegal by building codes, and obsolete methods are maintained. Management, labor, and the public cling to traditional belief in the superiority of custom-built homes, though they drive mass-produced automobiles and wear prefabricated clothing—a far more personal item than one's house. Unions and workmen resist innovations that might make work go faster without sacrificing quality, and builders are too often untrained and unprincipled.

The desire to keep costs down for price-conscious buyers often results in high annual maintenance expense and premature deterioration. To save $500 on the initial cost of a house, builders skimp on the furnace, roof, wiring, hot-water heater, bathroom fixtures, waterproofing, insulation, and plumbing—at an eventual expense of $200 a year in upkeep to the owner. Savings of $10 a month on mortgage payments are more than counterbalanced by the need to install a new $800 heating system within nine years or to pay an extra $7 a month to heat the poorly insulated house. Why spend $100 after moving in to install an item that the builder could have provided during construction for $20?

Building codes are also guilty of impeding progress. Local building regulations are often obsolescent.[8] Frequently designed by our grandfathers, they have not been changed since to permit builders and architects to use the new plastic and other materials and construction techniques invented in recent decades. Building rules hamstring honest developers in the dual interest of preserving ancient folklore and of controlling dishonest builders.

"The chisel was the tool most often used to construct the postwar development house, and the chisel's popularity with builders has not decreased with the passing years. It is one of the touching love affairs

---

[8] Charles K. Agle, "Housing and Urban Redevelopment," in Breese and Whiteman, *op. cit.*, pp. 54–76.

of all time." [9] A congressional committee investigating housing built under the G. I. Bill found linoleum substituted for tile in bathrooms, screens and weatherstripping missing, bathtubs not connected to sewer pipes, iron or lead pipes instead of copper, pine taking the place of oak, concrete slabs two inches thick instead of twelve, one coat of paint rather than three, and refrigerators so situated that their doors could not open all the way. A few inches trimmed off the depth of each closet may not be noticed until after the tenant moves in and finds he has to hang his suits diagonally, but the builder constructing a few hundred houses or apartments stands to reap a tidy profit from such shortcuts.

Even when solidly constructed, many homes and apartments leave much to be desired. Vitruvius said that "well-building hath three conditions: Commodity, Firmness, and Delight"—meaning that architecture is governed by three standards: practical, scientific, and aesthetic. A building should thus be useful, sturdy, and attractive. Whether density is high or low, or expenses great or small, buildings and their settings should be carefully planned to encourage beauty and harmony in the composition of urban land and space. "When we build we do but detach a convenient quantity of space, seclude it, and protect it." [10]

○ *Slum Clearance and Rehabilitation*

Whether initially well built or slapped together, all houses deteriorate in time, especially if their upkeep is neglected. When most of the dwellings in a neighborhood become deteriorated, particularly if there is an accompanying rise in rates of juvenile delinquency and adult crime, the area comes to be known as a slum—the second "shame of the cities," fully as heinous and persistent as the corrupt politics denounced by Lincoln Steffens. Districts approaching such social and physical decay are called blighted areas. Although both degrees of

[9] John C. Keats, *The Crack in the Picture Window* (Boston: Houghton Mifflin, 1957), p. 24.

[10] Geoffrey Scott, *The Architecture of Humanism* (New York: Scribner's, 1914), p. 227.

decay are deplored, the distinction between them involves corrigibility as well as the stage in the cycle of decline: Blighted areas can be reclaimed and perhaps restored to respectable status, but slums generally must be destroyed because attempts at renovation are ineffectual.

Clearance of slums is superficially simple: Existing tenements are razed and replaced by modern dwellings of greater habitability—although not necessarily of lower density. The popular belief that slum clearance consists of replacing overcrowded tenements with structures accommodating fewer persons per acre is misleading. Replacements for razed slums often are many stories taller, and apartments are not always larger; improvement lies not in more space but in more facilities (hot running water, private toilets and baths, and similar amenities) and in supposed quality of construction (no holes in walls, leaking roofs, or sagging floors). Ordinarily, government subsidies are needed, for the inhabitants of slums are not generally in the area by choice but live there because they cannot afford better housing; if they could pay the full rental cost of the new projects, they usually would not have been living in the slum in the first place. Consequently, rentals are usually low; sometimes a uniform monthly rent is charged throughout a development regardless of the size of the apartment, and the number of rooms occupied by a family is determined by the number of persons in the household without relation to their incomes.

Some persons contend that slums result from various forces outside the control of the residents and that removal of the physical elements of slums will solve the slum problem. Others argue that slums are created by slum-prone people having ingrained "slum" mentalities and habits and that placing these people in clean new buildings is ineffective; in this view, such people will soon convert the new apartments into another slum. Which position is correct no one truly knows, although there is some evidence that the hope offered by dwellings that *can* be kept clean and in repair, coupled when necessary with not-too-obvious instruction in the care and maintenance of a home, results in more-or-less permanent elimination of the slum. It cannot be denied that there are people in all social classes who are chronically sloppy, dirty, and irresponsible (although it is sometimes claimed that such people can be educated into more acceptable habits), but that they are proportionately more numerous in the lower classes is highly debatable. In any case, it is probable that the nature of the area makes as great—and possibly greater—contributions to ecological decadence as does the character of the individual.

Arguing with the antireformers, who blame the existence of slums on the repellent habits of the slum dwellers themselves, are the reformers who place the onus on the landlord. For centuries mercenary property owners have been derided for contriving to stow the greatest possible number of tenants into filthy, seldom-repaired tenements. As long as landlords are motivated primarily by profits and not constrained by community housing regulations, it is almost certain that some will try to draw the maximum income from the smallest investment in their property, disregarding the comfort and health of the renters; after all, "People who don't like it can always move out."

When deterioration is under way but not so advanced as to warrant designation of the district as a slum, the so-defined blighted area is improved not by demolition and reconstruction but by rehabilitation —restoring existing structures and yards to some approximation of their former condition in the hope that social improvement will follow. Sometimes such expectations are merited and sometimes not; sometimes repairs are financially feasible and sometimes impractical; sometimes property owners are cooperative and even enthusiastic, but often—particularly in the case of absentee landlords—they are reluctant or antagonistic; consequently, rehabilitation is sometimes successful, but often it fails. In any event, the cost is less than that of slum clearance, there is less relocation of families and disruption of friendly cliques, and the final product is occasionally as edifying if not as impressive.

Rehabilitation often is viewed by city officials as a stop-gap measure in the unceasing battle against urban decay: It may not cure the ills of their city, but it holds the enemy at bay until the next administration is elected. The upper and upper-middle classes may regard both rehabilitation of blighted districts and extirpation of slums as gracious benevolence helping the unfortunate and incompetent toward a better way of life. The lower-middle and lower classes may consider such programs normal community responses to inevitable urban troubles. Adherents of the political right, whatever their social standing, may condemn such government-encouraged or subsidized efforts as inappropriate, self-defeating, or degrading. Liberals and radicals, on the other hand, tend to applaud meliorative actions to help the oppressed. These are broadly generalized stances, however, and deviation from the group image is often encountered. But regardless of differing attitudes, and however extensive or scanty may be the actions in a community, throughout the nation many thousands of dwellings are renovated or replaced and the families moved—with frequently ambiguous but hopeful consequences.

○ *Municipal Services*

When men cluster together in large numbers, services become necessary that are not needed (because they are individually supplied) in sparsely settled rural areas. Urban areas cannot survive, let alone gratify their inhabitants, without providing water, food, housing, heat, sewage disposal, trash collection, and transportation. Whether supplied by private organizations, public utilities, or, as in the United States, an erratic mixture, these necessities must be made available without fail.

In rapidly growing cities these sometimes complex and always high-capital-cost facilities have difficulty keeping up with swelling populations—especially in regions where financial and other resources are stretched to the limit to cope with the demand for a higher living level. Municipal utilities require metal pipes for water and sewage, rolling stock for transportation and trash collection, concrete and wood for construction, and an economic system capable of supporting such industries. These problems particularly beset underdeveloped nations; the relatively minor difficulties in industrial countries arise largely from the need to allocate financial responsibility.

Because utilities are necessities, many people insist that they should not be operated for private profit—or, worse yet, be means of profiteering at the expense of public health. The tendency in modern industrial cities to shift from private to publicly owned and operated utilities was motivated in part by the large initial cost of the installations and the continuing maintenance of pipes under every street and massive plants for generating or transforming electricity, processing gas, treating sewage, and purifying and pumping water. Some cities depend on hundreds of miles of aqueducts bringing in water from reservoirs and artificial lakes far beyond the city limits, thereby adding to the complexity of the web of government. Maintaining permanent police and fire departments further increases the burdens of local governments.

In the United States all of these utilities and services, including the police, are inconsistently governed, being controlled in some cities by state authorities, in others by local commissions, and elsewhere by leases or franchises granted to monopolistic private or quasi-public corporations. Financial support also differs from city to city and from utility to utility, the services sometimes being paid for out of the general tax fund, sometimes by special direct taxes, and sometimes by consumers in amounts determined by meter readings or substitutes for them. Because of increasing city populations as well as increasing per capita usage of city services and occasional additions to the number of services supplied, taxpayers in most nations must support ever larger city budgets. And when civic obligations are extended to opera houses and athletic stadiums, amortization of indebtedness becomes a major part of the urban enterprise.

Investments in public utilities are generally large and must be distributed over a period of years; otherwise, taxpayers may suffer from wildly fluctuating annual obligations to the community government. With a ubiquitous "why plan?" attitude among the citizens and a chronic shortage of municipal funds, professional planners must cope with compromises of doubtful viability and with property owners who complain that tax rates are unduly high yet who would probably complain even more loudly if the services they have come to take for granted were to fail or diminish in quality.

In this and related connections, "watchdog" citizen groups keep tabs on professional planners in city hall. Despite the gadfly quality of such grass-roots spirit, planners often try to encourage their formation and spread in the conviction that people should have some power over the ordering of their environment.

○ *Transportation*

To the traditional three necessities of food, clothing, and shelter and the fourth necessity of sanitation, there has been added a fifth need: mobility. The speed and flexibility of automotive transportation constitute one of the most amazing developments of the age, paralleled only by the irritating congestion and delays it induces. One can fly across the United States in five hours, yet it sometimes takes two hours to get from the edge of the city to downtown, the vehicular density being so great that a triple-carbureted 400-cubic-inch automobile is often slower than a bicycle. The American (and world-wide) love affair with cars being as passionate as it is persistent, such interference with high-gear movement is not well tolerated. Superhighways are built, and traffic engineers attempt to enable more cars to speed downtown to insufficient parking places, which are increasing to the point of taking up more space than the buildings they purportedly serve. But as much as we may deride it, the automobile is a crucial factor in urban life: It not only moves people and goods through cities but also strongly influences the spatial arrangement of human activities inside urban areas.

Urban transportation problems are not new. In the first century A.D., Rome was obliged for a time to relieve congestion by restricting vehicular traffic to the night hours. But oppressive congestion was not common until the nineteenth and twentieth centuries, when the industrial and transportation revolutions brought swelling numbers of people into the metropolitan centers. Traffic problems are not isolated, and many zoning ordinances attempt to channel traffic in certain directions by controlling the patterning and density of land use. Despite limited success with such manipulation of traffic flow, urban traffic congestion remains an unsolved problem, especially with regard to commuting. Collection and delivery of commuters must be made over widely dispersed locations, and three-fourths of total daily traffic volume occurs between 7:00 and 9:00 A.M. and between 4:30 and 6:30 P.M. Such sharp peaks lead to high operating costs, because enough equipment must be bought and employees hired to handle peak loads, only to stand idle or circulate half-empty during noncommuting hours.

One answer to overcrowded buses and streetcars is the private automobile, to which commuters turn with great frequency. Between 1955 and 1965 the number of motor vehicles in the United States increased by 24 million to a total of 85 million; during the same ten-year period, transit patronage declined by 3 billion rides, or 25 per cent, and thousands of miles of expressways were constructed at a cost of several billion dollars. The over-all expense of operating a car averages 12 to 15 cents a mile if fixed expenses (insurance, license, and depreciation) are included, but the variable or marginal cost averages only about four cents; thus, if one owns a car anyway, the daily out-of-pocket cost of commuting by car is fairly low and in some communities may be lower than the bus fare. In such cases, commuting by automobile is economically rational. And the cost of parking, which might be prohibitive if paid directly by the consumer, is frequently subsidized by community taxes, thereby making driving seem cheaper than it is, for the indirect cost paid in taxes is rarely considered. Nevertheless, automobile expense is estimated to consume 6 per cent of personal income in New York, 10 per cent in Chicago, and 15 per cent in Los Angeles; all other transportation consumes an additional 3, 3, and 2 per cent, respectively. People enjoy driving their cars, and if anyone thinks it foolish for a 110-pound secretary to take 3,800 pounds of metal and miscellany on her way to work, he can just take the bus—along with some fifty other people occupying little more street space than the secretary's car and requiring no parking space.

One response to congestion and commuting problems is the movement of manufacturers from central areas to the periphery of the city, whereupon they may advertise to prospective employees the advantage of an easy drive from one's home to the company's spacious parking lot. In fact, one of the most significant differences between commuting to the central business district and peripheral commuting is the extent of use of the automobile. In Chicago, for example, more than 80 per cent of the commuters to peripheral areas use private cars, in contrast to only 30 per cent of commuters to downtown areas.[11] This is true partly because of the convenience and comfort of commuting by car and partly because mass-transit facilities are ill adapted for routing commuters to peripheral locations; most rush-hour buses and trains move toward the city center in the morning and toward the outskirts in the afternoon. People desiring public transit perpendicular to these in-and-out routes must put up with infrequent service and circuitous routes. But most fringe commuters have the advantage of traveling shorter distances to work than those bound for center city. Also, the strong correlation between occupational status and length of journey so often observed for city-center workers contrasts with a weak status-versus-distance gradient among fringe com-

11 Edward J. Taaffe, Barry J. Garner, and Maurice H. Yeates, *The Peripheral Journey to Work* (Evanston, Ill.: Northwestern University Press, 1963), p. 105.

muters. Whether to augment the relatively few peripheral mass-transit routes or to expedite automobile travel is a dilemma to which planners will have to devote added attention. With accelerated centrifugal movement of large factories and businesses, the now relatively frictionless commuting through the rural-urban fringe may one day become sufficiently heavy to discourage both industrial and residential relocation to the outer suburbs (in commuting, nothing ruins success like success). In the meantime, the dispersed industrial pattern in suburban and satellite communities provides relatively unharried trips to work.

The need for faster movement of geometrically increasing numbers of commuters is one of the greatest challenges facing cities today. "Of all the forces reshaping the American metropolis, the most powerful and insistent are those rooted in changing modes of transportation." [12] Mass movement of people has resulted in an outward spread of suburbs, a schism between workplace and home, and such intensification of land use in the metropolitan center that downtown districts are in danger of choking to death. The center of the city traditionally has been the most valued site because it is the most accessible; front-footage property values and the location of retail stores are determined by this accessibility. But now the central business districts are coming to be painfully inaccessible, and some ecologists predict that they may vanish unless drastic action is taken.

The automobile, like other far-reaching technical innovations, requires new urban forms. Establishing one-way streets is a temporary palliative. A more permanent solution might be to ban all motor vehicles (except perhaps taxis) from the downtown area; pedestrian malls like those designed by Victor Gruen Associates for Fort Worth, Texas, and Fresno, California, convert downtown districts into variegated pedestrian islands surrounded by enormous parking lots. Another suggestion is to remove from the center some of the functions traditionally associated with it: Many centrally located hotels are failing or being demolished while motels prosper on the outskirts, and peripherally situated shopping centers are flourishing partly because central stores lack ample nearby parking. Although the central business district as an urban form cannot yet—and perhaps never will—be said to be disintegrating, it is clear that automobile

[12] Francis Bello, "The City and the Car," in The Editors of Fortune, *The Exploding Metropolis* (Garden City, N.Y.: Doubleday, 1958), p. 32.

transportation is altering the city as we know it. One way or another, cities must come to terms with the private car. But until they do, wise urbanites will be forced to heed Thoreau's advice: "The swiftest traveler is he that goes afoot."

One solution to urban traffic and parking problems would be to cease separating land uses into zones that rigidly exclude differing uses, in favor of a mixture of uses in which housing is integrated with stores and workplaces. In many modern tracts, someone in need of a loaf of bread or pack of cigarettes must get into his car and drive to a mile-distant shopping center; earlier generations walked to the corner store. Mixing of uses might also make the neighborhood a more cohesive unit, by making it more than just a place where one's house is located. Advocates of this strengthening of the traditional urban neighborhood maintain that a larger number of facilities for work, shopping, and entertainment within walking distance of the home could go far to alleviate urban transportation—and many other—problems.

Two of the most eloquent opponents of overuse of the private automobile in cities are Victor Gruen and Lewis Mumford. Gruen contends that we must treat the automobile as "a servant to mankind and not a deity" and stop designing cities around freeways and parking lots.[13] Mumford pleads for a return to nature:

> In the utopia that highway engineers have been busily bulldozing into existence, no precinct of the city and no part of the surrounding countryside are to remain inaccessible to automobile traffic on a large scale. This means that people who live in cities are not to be permitted the refreshing contrast of escaping to an island, to a mountaintop, or even to a swath of open country whose isolation from urban traffic makes it possible to still engage in farming or fruit-raising. By means of many-laned highways, every acre everywhere is to be made accessible for the real-estate speculator and the subdivider, and in another generation a drab, standardized, low-grade settlement, lacking both the advantages of the country and those of the city, will stretch along the Eastern seaboard from Maine to Florida.

> Because this principle has been treated as sacred, our growing cities have already lost most of the recreational advantages that the surrounding countryside once afforded them, and one suburb after another has filled in the natural green belt that—when the railroad stations were

[13] Victor Gruen, "Save Urbia for New Urbanites," *Journal of the American Institute of Architects*, 33 (February 1960), 35–8.

a few miles apart and commuters lived within walking distance of them —gave it a pleasantly rural flavor. This has happened all over the country. . . .

Unfortunately, there is a huge vested interest in raising hell with nature, and there is very little money in letting well enough alone.[14]

Recognizing the urgency of transportation problems, President Johnson established in 1967 the Cabinet-level Department of Transportation. Government has subsidized transportation for some years in the form of remission of taxes to railroads, assistance to mass transit, and tax support for interstate highway construction and maintenance. Some four-fifths of all households in the United States have cars, and in many cities there is at least one car in 90 per cent of all consumer units; 30 per cent own two or more.[15] Every metropolitan area in the country is threatened by congestion, and some cities seem to be choking to death with commuters—a situation probably destined to become more aggravated in the future. That cities in many nations are becoming increasingly oppressive to work in and sometimes unpleasant to live in may be attributed in large part to the difficulty of moving around within them. In the United States the private automobile is at once the cause and the solution, for two-thirds of all workers commute by car, the other third being (in rank order) people who walk, take a bus, work at home, ride a subway or railroad, or use a less conventional means (bicycle, boat, and so forth).[16] Consequently, traffic volume on city streets has more than doubled since 1940.[17]

○ *Planning for Places or People*

These and related recommendations and plaints return us to the initial rationale for cities: the pleasure of people. City planning, like cities, is for people, not for land. Although some plans seem to have

14 Lewis Mumford, "The Sky Line," *The New Yorker*, 35 (November 14, 1959), 186–7.

15 Wilfred Owen, *The Metropolitan Transportation Problem* (Washington, D.C.: Brookings Institution, 1966), pp. 27–8.

16 *Automobile Facts and Figures* (Detroit: Automobile Manufacturers Association, 1964), p. 40.

17 Owen, *op. cit.*, p. 29.

been prepared to look good on paper or to airline passengers, most are designed to promote enjoyable living of their inhabitants. Cities have long been lauded for their stimulation of the human spirit, and one of the charges of city planners is the continuing promotion of vivid stimuli.

In downtown areas, the moving eye of the pedestrian must meet changing panoramas and lively, heterogeneous crowds on sidewalks and squares; beautiful but formalistic perspectives become oppressive or boring because they are impersonal and empty of whims and eccentricities. Professional planners are sometimes accused of lack of respect for the vitality and enterprise found in the more fascinating— because varied and unorganized—urban neighborhoods. "Instead of identifying and appreciating the innate values that have spontaneously grown up in a neighborhood, and attempting to reinforce and build on these values, the planner's approach is apt to be one of distaste for all the messiness that life has generated without his assistance." [18]

Cities should have character; they should not be bland, routinely ordered batches of buildings. Cities are where most human energy is expended and where national styles of life are set. The past is highly important: Urban beauty and character result from the accumulated activities and artifacts of generations of residents of varying types, and this cumulative individuality and ethnic variety convert cities into living dramas. Seemingly chaotic or random historical development lends character to an area, and any planner who disregards such historical accidents, however absurd they seem on purely rational grounds, is foolish indeed. "We need to cherish with great care all the personality our cities have left." [19]

In a new city, it is almost impossible to build character into the plat; planners just have to hope for the best. Carefully segregated use areas are inclined to be dull because of their sterile regularity and homogeneity; the strict separation of land uses (and therefore of

[18] Bernard Taper, "A Lover of Cities—II," *The New Yorker*, 42 (February 11, 1967), 45.

[19] John Ely Burchard, "The Limitations of Utilitarianism as a Basis for Determining Urban Joy," in Elizabeth Green, Jeanne R. Lowe, and Kenneth Walker (eds.), *Man and the Modern City* (Pittsburgh: University of Pittsburgh Press, 1963), pp. 18–24.

types of people in the area) so beloved of modern planners is monotonous and boring. Cities benefit from having history written into their buildings and neighborhoods; otherwise they are antiseptic and lifeless. Compare walking through a typical suburban tract with traversing the central city: One tract house after another quickly bores the viewer; on the other hand, walking through the downtown or an ethnic district of a metropolis offers captivating variety. It is this seductive quality of excitement and drama that makes big cities such irresistible lures.

In heady contrast to the carefully planned new towns of England, Brazil, and India, few places are more heartwarming than Paris. "The charm of its monumental spaces, the saucy animation of its avenues, the delight in its varied perspectives, seem less to have been planned than to have blossomed. Perhaps, more than an efficient arrangement of its streets or the abstract shape of its buildings, it takes 'the music of men's lives' to give a city character." [20] The moral of Paris for city planners is succinctly summed up in the dictum of Miës van der Rohe: "More is less."

Jane Jacobs extols the value of diversity in her panegyric to great cities, especially New York: Mixed uses contribute to the safety and socialization of children, and cross-cultural contacts on sidewalks and in parks generate more of the hum than the humdrum of human existence.[21] Integration of uses might eliminate the sameness of many housing tracts and shopping centers, each looking very much like the next and without a hint of individuality or surprise or an indication of "a city with a tradition and flavor all its own"; such sterile projects deaden rather than revitalize.

> They work at cross-purposes to the city. They banish the street. They banish its function. They banish its variety. . . . Almost without exception the projects have one standard solution for every need: commerce, medicine, culture, government—whatever the activity, they take a part of the city's life, abstract it from the hustle and bustle of downtown, and set it, like a self-sufficient island, in majestic isolation.[22]

[20] Arthur B. Gallion and Simon Eisner, *The Urban Pattern* (Princeton: Van Nostrand, 1963), p. 356.

[21] Jane Jacobs, *The Death and Life of Great American Cities* (New York: Random House, 1961).

[22] Jacobs, "Downtown Is for People," in The Editors of Fortune, *op. cit.*, p. 141.

Bulldozed projects tend to be joyless, quarantining one aspect of human life from another in an effort to put all single-family homes here, all local businesses there, and all industry somewhere else. But in this separation of conflicting interests and demands, something of value may be lost, for indiscriminate mixing of people and activities enlivens the human spirit. In short, chaos can be fun.

chapter 13

METROPOLITAN PLANNING

IF CITIES ARE CHAOTIC, WHAT THEN ARE METROPOLITAN REGIONS, whose municipalities sometimes are merely stretches along a cluttered highway, identifiable only by signs declaring "You Are Now Entering ————" followed a few miles later by "You Are Now Leaving ————." Often metropolitan residents are embarrassed by the visitor's query, "What town are we in now?"—for they do not know. Nor need they know, as each suburb blends into its contiguous replica. Yet metropolitan areas do contain certain internal demarcations sharper than those of rural or small-town areas because of the diversity springing from large numbers of people of varied national origins and cultural persuasions. Although transportation changes facilitated metropolitanization, its advent antedates the automobile. H. G. Wells wrote in 1903:

> You will find that many people who once slept and worked and reared their children and worshipped and bought all in one area, are now, as it were, delocalized; they have overflowed their containing

locality, and they live in one area, they work in another, and they go to shop in a third. And the only way in which you can localize them again is to expand your areas to their new scale.[1]

○ *The Need for Regional Planning*

Local political boundaries are being made obsolete by social, economic, and technological developments, but they have always been of limited value. Disease germs do not respect political boundaries, yet each district may take health actions independently of neighboring areas. But chasing the bugs out of town in a manner analogous to the treatment of varmints in the cowboy West is not a rational way to safeguard public health. If one town dumps sewage into a stream or harbor, it jeopardizes the health of a wide area. A single city with an unsatisfactory health organization can spread disease throughout the region.

Crime prevention is sometimes hampered by the separate jurisdictions of police forces. An offender in one municipality may escape to another and there be immune to arrest, although the trend toward police reciprocity is putting an end to this means of defeating the law. Still, criminals may benefit from the jurisdictional disputes that arise between the sheriff and the municipal police, between city police and park-district police, and among other law enforcement agencies.

Colleges, libraries, museums, auditoriums, and hospitals serve an entire metropolitan area, not just the people living in one city. If the whole region supports a large museum or zoo, it is likely to be better than one that remains dependent on the resources of only one city; and because residents of contiguous cities often come to see the paintings and animals without having contributed to their purchase through taxes, the financial burden is more fairly distributed by adopting a tax base applying to the entire region.

Some city zoning ordinances are set up without consideration or even knowledge of zones immediately across the municipal boundary line. To improve health, law enforcement, zoning regulations, and

[1] H. G. Wells, "A Paper on Administrative Areas Read Before the Fabian Society," *Mankind in the Making* (London: Chapman & Hall, 1903), p. 406.

other municipal efforts, a regional approach is far more likely to be effective than letting each municipality do as it pleases, in ignorance of—or opposition to—what its fellows are doing.

> The importance of dealing with zoning on the regional basis does not lie in the territorial expansion as such, but rather in the fact that a city seldom, if ever, is a complete social, commercial, or physical unit. Usually a city is found to comprise but a portion of such a complete entity. It is at best a bit of geography, usually well populated, artificially distinguished from its neighboring areas by arbitrary and usually unnatural boundary lines. The introduction, therefore, of the regional idea permitted taking the fullest advantage of the physical or social and commercial unity of a given area.
>
> Regional areas consequently seldom bear direct relationship to arbitrary political boundaries. . . . And yet, if zoning is to be used as a preventive as well as a cure, the regional approach is almost essential.[2]

The urban planning that has taken place to the present time has been nearly entirely by and for individual municipalities rather than metropolitan regions, leaving unintegrated and contradictory local plans designed to meet purely local needs. When each incorporated community seeks a solution to its own problems in its own way, the interests of other parts of the metropolitan area are not always well served. A regional planning agency is both necessitated and impaired by "the near-feudal isolationism and internecine rivalry that exists among the various governmental units that make up the metropolis."[3]

Comprehensive regional planning means ecological planning, which is defined by Benton MacKaye as "the cultivation of habitability" of areas of human settlement, by Artur Glikson as "the regulation of the relationship between human and environmental factors,"[4] and by Lewis Mumford as "the modification and relocation of various elements in the total environment for the purpose of increasing their service to the community" and "the conscious direction and collective integration of all those activities which rest upon the use of the earth

---

[2] Gordon Whitnall, "History of Zoning," *Annals of the American Academy of Political and Social Science*, 155 (May 1931), 3–4.

[3] John C. Bollens and Henry J. Schmandt, *The Metropolis* (New York: Harper, 1965), p. 306.

[4] Artur Glikson, *Regional Planning and Development* (Leiden: Sijthoff, 1955), p. 9.

as site, as resource, as structure, as theater." [5] These men do not confine their definitions to metropolitan regions, and, in fact, the foremost attempt at regional planning in the United States occurred in a nonmetropolitan area, the Tennessee Valley. Given the dearth of metropolitan planning, this model may serve to illustrate what can be done on a regional basis through a large-scale, multipurpose yet unified attack on communal problems.

After earlier attempts had been vetoed by Presidents Coolidge and Hoover in 1928 and 1930, the Tennessee Valley Authority was launched in 1933 to promote navigation on the Tennessee River, aid flood control on the lower Mississippi River, develop agriculture, encourage industrial development, increase recreational facilities, generate inexpensive electricity, and otherwise foster economic advancement in this destitute area. Several dams were constructed, and state agricultural experiment stations developed local demonstration programs of modern farming techniques. Electric rates fell drastically, and service became almost universal. River traffic doubled in five years, and flood crests were diminished, saving millions of dollars and many lives. Malaria rates plummeted. Per capita income among area residents increased appreciably more than did national income during the same period, and residents came to pay almost twice as large a percentage of the country's income tax as they had paid before T.V.A.

Evaluations of this multisided project range from Admiral Ben Moreell's claim that T.V.A. is socialism and therefore "economically and morally wrong" to Senator Lister Hill's proclamation that "it has promoted the prosperity of the people, added to their security, multiplied their resources for enjoyment, and brought new beauty to the valley and strength to the nation." Attitudes vary according to the stress placed on means versus ends: People who evaluate the program primarily in terms of its results tend to laud T.V.A., whereas those who regard means as more important than ends may question the legitimacy of government action replacing or competing with private efforts. Imitations of T.V.A. are numerous, notably in Pakistan and India. Although differing in details, programs of this scope have been undertaken for metropolitan areas in England and other nations. In the United States, however, the structuring of local governments severely restricts efforts to plan a metropolitan region as a unit.

[5] Lewis Mumford, *The Culture of Cities* (New York: Harcourt, 1938), p. 374.

○ *Governing Metropolitan Regions*

A politically defined city seldom, if ever, is a complete social, commercial, or physical entity. Rather, it is separated from adjacent municipalities by arbitrary boundary lines that have been determined by one or another historical accident. Duplication and overlapping of government agencies, perpetuated by the growth of great urban clusters, is leading to inadequate and financially inefficient government.

Antiquated government institutions can no longer cope with the complexities of modern metropolises. Most city charters were set up in the days when a city was a cohesive, compact cluster of people surrounded by farmland, but today's incipient megalopolises strain the archaic charters almost to the breaking point. Functional economic and social consolidation has already occurred, but political consolidation, if it is to take place at all, is some years in the future. Metropolitan government is highly fragmented: The 212 SMSAs in the United States in 1962 averaged eighty-seven government units each. Although some young southern SMSAs got along with fewer than twenty government units and Baltimore had only twenty-three, others were burdened with far more superstructure than any ship of state can comfortably manage: St. Louis, 439 units; New York, 555; Pittsburgh, 806; Philadelphia, 963; and Chicago, 1,060.[6]

The most important of these government units are incorporated satellites and suburbs, of which the largest metropolitan areas have a hundred or more. When such areas are characterized by petty municipal grudges and animosities, the term "balkanization" is used—a usage derived from southeastern Europe's division into small states that appear to outsiders inconsequentially different but that assert their individuality by intermittent hostility toward one another. Historical circumstances aside, it is possible that the very fact of metropolitan subdivision into autonomous units, each governed by its own small bureaucracy, may breed rancor taking the form, for example, of denying to residents of neighboring suburbs such emergency assis-

---

[6] U.S. Bureau of the Census, "Governmental Organization," *U.S. Census of Governments: 1962* (Washington, D.C.: Government Printing Office, 1963), p. 11.

tance as ambulance or fire equipment. Such enmity often originates either in threatened annexation or in discrepancies in local property taxes. Whatever its origins, the consequences are frequently disruptive and usually expensive. Whether or not amicable relations between neighborhoods would be promoted by lessening of balkanization, two likely results would be greater economy in municipal services and more effective long-term planning. Fortunately, most local communities get along very well with neighboring towns; those that do not create trouble disproportionate to their importance. Balkanization is not completely lacking in virtues, however, for, insofar as the small separate communities differ in their laws, metropolitan residents are offered the opportunity to choose the set of regulations and tax rates they prefer; the variation, however, is not generally very great.

Citizens must pay for all this government, and the overlapping authority is rarely justified by the facts of urban life and often contributes to metropolitan problems. Freeways, public transit systems, water and sewage systems, air-pollution controls, fire protection, and inspection of food and restaurants have no intrinsic connection with incorporation lines. This fragmentation is one reason why existing government units have trouble handling the tasks set them by their growing populations. The diminishing relevance of municipal boundaries and the jumbled and disordered agglomeration of local governments have converted metropolitan areas into governmental nightmares. Wealthy suburbs sometimes capitalize on their separate incorporation to adopt zoning ordinances preserving their aloofness and exclusiveness, expecting other municipalities to zone for less expensive houses, shops, and gas stations. An industry may incorporate itself as a nonresidential city so that it can pass to nearby residential suburbs the costs of educating the offspring of its employees as well as the welfare problems of laid-off workers, or it may fend off incorporation entirely, with much the same financially expedient result.

One response to the inequities generated by such selfish but understandable dodges has been the appeal for a more streamlined form of metropolitan government—one that will fit the modern realities of urban interdependence and avoid territorial overlapping and duplication of functions. Victor Jones proposes two sets of solutions to these problems, the first requiring few or no structural changes in existing local governments and the second necessitating major structural revisions. Devices in the first category are

1. The grant of jurisdiction to, and the provision of services by, the central city outside its boundaries.
2. Establishment of ad hoc authorities to handle special problems on a metropolitan basis.
3. Intergovernmental arrangements between two or more governmental units within the metropolitan district.
4. Extension of state administration to include local government functions which are metropolitan in scope, or the supervision by the state of functions performed by local governmental units within the district.
5. Extension of federal administration with regard to certain local functions.[7]

None of the five expedients, however, offers a realistic prospect of permanently curing metropolitan ills, although any one might mitigate the pain temporarily. Jones himself evaluates them as "stop gaps, as complements to a more comprehensive scheme of integration, or as expedient stepping stones to a comprehensive unit of local government for the entire metropolitan area." [8]

Jones' second set offers greater promise (provided it is ever put into effect) of solving metropolitan government problems:

1. Annexation of contiguous territory or consolidation of adjacent municipalities.
2. City-county consolidation.
3. Merger of special authorities with either the central city or the county.
4. Reorganization of the urban county, and transfer to it of metropolis-wide municipal functions.
5. Establishment of a federated municipal government for the metropolitan area, with relationships between the satellite communities and the central city analogous to those between the states and the federal government.
6. Creation of a metropolitan city-state having the same political status as the present states of the union.[9]

---

[7] Victor Jones, *Metropolitan Government* (Chicago: University of Chicago Press, 1942), p. 87.

[8] *Ibid.*, p. 121.

[9] *Ibid.*, p. 87.

The present prospects for implementing these six changes are not good, and some of the consequences are unfortunate. Opposition to annexation or consolidation would probably thwart any attempt to bring the entire metropolis under one government. Because the metropolis frequently extends beyond the central county, city-county consolidation would be inadequate to integrate the entire metropolitan area. Special authorities tend to diffuse responsibility as well as to increase the number of government units. A reorganized and strengthened county government can suffice in cases where the metropolis is coterminous with a county. A federated metropolitan scheme might provide an acceptable compromise between separatists and "single government" enthusiasts. Finally, creation of metropolitan states appears remote—although potentially the most effective of these schemes.[10] Although these suggestions were made more than twenty-five years ago, little progress has been made toward instituting any of them.

Some change is under way, as cities are coming to provide health, transporation, and other services to their tributaries. A creeping alteration of local government has been taking place in recent decades: The legal limits of a city are decreasing in importance as boundaries of its services and even of its control. Because the largest incorporated community in a metropolitan region generally occupies a central position and usually dominates the economic and social life of the area, and because the central city has a fully developed set of machinery for policy decisions and administrative implementation, increasing numbers of urban activities are conducted with little or no reference to the "walls of the city." This obsolescent concept, which once strictly confined the compass of a city government to persons and things inside its corporate limits, is being replaced by a wider view of city functions. "Instead of a tight corporate community providing definite services and functions for its own membership, the city is now a somewhat fuzzy and indefinite association, supplying a mixed and indeterminate range of services to an amorphous and indeterminate constituency." [11]

10 *Ibid.*, p. 154.

11 York Willbern, *The Withering Away of the City* (Birmingham: University of Alabama Press, 1964), p. 91.

○ *Legislative Representation*

In addition to problems of government within metropolitan areas are those stemming from the changing urban-rural composition of the population. When state legislative bodies were created, the apportionment favored rural areas; since the United States was then overwhelmingly rural, this action was reasonable. Today, however, seven-tenths of the population is urban, but rural areas are still allocated a majority of the seats in state legislatures: In 1965 about three-fourths of the legislators were elected by little more than one-fourth of the people—those living in rural areas. A clear majority of the American people are governed by lawmakers they did not vote for and over whom they have no balloting control. This condition prevails in every state and will continue to prevail until states put into effect the Supreme Court decision of 1964 requiring that all state legislative houses be apportioned on the basis of population.

Legislative malapportionment is a kind of gerrymandering by inertia. This subordination of citizens to political units not their own is made more severe by chronic failure to reapportion, which creates a culture lag in which rapid changes in urbanization are not met with corresponding changes in political apportionment. Some states have not been reapportioned for fifty years. Most state constitutions provide for periodic reapportionment, but legislators ignore the law and courts do not enforce it; when an attempt is made, it is usually opposed by the party in power (why change a winning lineup?). A rural representative may serve 10,000 inhabitants, whereas an urban one may represent 1 million; this inequity by which rural people are much better represented is the national norm. As a result, state funds more often benefit rural districts than urban ones, a case of the demographic tail wagging the dog. Urban residents pay most of the state's bills but receive less than an equivalent amount in benefits. Rural dominance of state legislatures would perhaps be less objectionable if they would permit cities to conduct their own affairs; but cities are often treated as incompetent, having to obtain permission from state legislatures to install parking meters, to keep bicycles off the sidewalks, or to alter the city license fee on unspayed dogs.

Yet rural and suburban visitors complain if they do not receive downtown services. Central cities are plagued by daytime citizens who stream in from surrounding areas five days a week, require police, fire, water, street cleaning, and other facilities, but rarely pay their share of the cost. Few people have any concept of the dollar outlay for the services central cities provide for commuters, who normally pay no local property tax; this is a part of the justification for city sales and income taxes. It also helps explain why cities so often have to go on the Federal dole. It seems that metropolises are being played for suckers by their country cousins, and there is little prospect for significant change, at least in the near future.

Nevertheless, there are signs of change. The Department of Agriculture was established in 1862; 103 years later the Department of Housing and Urban Development was added, after a four-year effort by Presidents Kennedy and Johnson. This new Cabinet-level department will only gradually and partially alter urban circumstances of life. Certainly it has not yet undertaken comprehensive city or metropolitan planning.

○ *Metropolitan Planning Agencies*

Two big questions facing regional planners are "Is metropolitan planning a legitimate function of government?" and "Are its costs prohibitive?" Planning buffs counter by rephrasing: "If government does not do it, who will?" and "Are the costs of failure to plan prohibitive?" Perhaps a more practical question is "Which government unit will do the planning?"

Certainly metropolitan planning should supplement local planning rather than replace it. Area-wide plans can take responsibility for those functions too widely pervasive for any one component city to handle: for example, transportation, major parks, control of water and air pollution, and drainage and flood control. To date, metropolitan planning agencies vary considerably in both purviews and provenances.

The first county planning commission in the United States opened in 1923 in Los Angeles, taking advantage of a liberal home-rule charter that (in contrast to the legal situation in most states) did not require enactment of state enabling legislation. The Los Angeles County Regional Planning Commission promotes coordinated planning among the county's seventy-odd cities and 7 million people, provides municipal-type services to unincorporated areas (thereby indirectly discouraging them from incorporating), and purveys services by contract to incorporated places. Through its Lakewood plan, the county furnishes dozens of suburbs with police and fire protection, libraries, prosecutors, engineers, dog catchers, and as many as thirty-five other services. The county offers better municipal services than many incorporated cities do and for this and related reasons is one of the strongest and most effective counties in the nation.

> County-city contracts place Los Angeles County in a relatively unusual leadership role. By voluntary action, most of the cities have contracted with the county government to perform a broad array of functions for them. Although other counties in California, and in some other states, have developed this type of intergovernmental relationship, Los Angeles continues to be the leading example.[12]

In 1926 the National Capital Park and Planning Commission was formed to preserve and advance the social and aesthetic virtues of the District of Columbia, Montgomery and Prince Georges Counties in Maryland, and Arlington and Fairfax Counties in Virginia. Although its role is purely advisory, its reports are well worth considering, as for example, the comprehensive plan of 1950.[13] In 1964 the commission proposed that future development be channeled into six corridors radiating from Washington, D.C., for forty to fifty miles, each corridor to contain four or five cities separated by stretches of greenery; the wedges of open space between the corridors would provide nearby recreational areas.

The outstanding American example of a limited-purpose regional metropolitan agency is the Port of New York Authority. A self-supporting quasi-public agency created by the States of New York and New Jersey in 1921, it deals with the terminal and transit facili-

---

[12] Winston W. Crouch and Beatrice Dinerman, *Southern California Metropolis* (Los Angeles: University of California Press, 1963), p. 199.

[13] National Capital Park and Planning Commission, *Comprehensive Plan for the National Capital and Its Environs* (6 vols.; Washington, D.C.: Government Printing Office, 1950).

ties of the port. It builds and operates tunnels, airports, piers, bridges, and truck and bus terminals, supporting these endeavors through tolls and rental of concessions—with exceptional financial success. Although its purview is restricted officially to transportation, certain of its actions have consequences for other questions as well—for instance, the clearance of the slum inhabited by Rosa (see Chapter 8).

The nongovernmental Regional Plan Association of New York has broader functions. This privately operated organization was formed in 1929 to cope with problems created by haphazard growth in the twenty-two counties and 400-odd municipalities of metropolitan New York, in accordance with the ten-volume report issued by the Committee on the Regional Plan of New York and Its Environs.[14] From its permanent office in downtown New York the association issues bulletins, newsletters, and plans relating to zoning, housing, highways, manufacturing, public buildings, business, parks, land values, parking, neighborhoods, and public services. Its professional planners act as consultants to municipal planning agencies throughout the metropolitan area. In 1956–1959 the Regional Plan Association cooperated with Harvard University in a demographic and economic study of the greater New York region.[15]

In Florida, a 1957 referendum established Dade County (the Miami SMSA) as the first metropolis in the United States to put the comprehensive urban county idea into operation. The new government, which included twenty-seven municipalities, was empowered to

1. construct expressways, regulate traffic, and own and operate mass transit systems and transportation terminals;
2. maintain central records, training, and communication for fire and police protection;
3. provide hospitals and uniform health and welfare programs;
4. furnish parks and recreational areas;
5. establish and administer housing, urban renewal, flood and beach erosion control, air pollution control, and drainage programs;

---

[14] Committee on Regional Plan of New York and Its Environs, *Regional Survey of New York and Its Environs* (10 vols.; New York: Regional Plan Association, 1927–1931).

[15] Edgar M. Hoover and Raymond Vernon, *Anatomy of a Metropolis* (Cambridge, Mass.: Harvard University Press, 1959); and Vernon, *Metropolis 1985* (Cambridge, Mass.: Harvard University Press, 1960).

6. regulate or own various public utilities; and
7. engage in industrial promotion.[16]

By unifying many public utilities and services, resulting in greater uniformity and presumably avoiding much of the usual wasteful duplication of departments and personnel, this unique attempt brought order into one chronically chaotic American metropolis. Whether it is a harbinger of things to come or a solitary exception to public resistance remains to be seen.

Closer to having a true metropolitan government is Toronto, which launched a "supergovernment" in 1954 to rule the central city and its thirteen suburbs. Governed by the mayor of each suburb and thirteen officials from the city of Toronto, Metropolitan Toronto "presents the best case for metropolitan government in existence on the North American continent." [17] Local authorities still collect taxes, distribute water, operate schools, pave streets, maintain fire departments, and administer similar operations. "Metro" issues debentures for the local municipalities, plans arterial roads, operates the sources of water supply, approves school construction, administers the courts, supervises law enforcement, licenses artisans and tradesmen, and operates a park and a golf course.

Attempts to set up metropolitan governments have often failed, sometimes in the initial planning stage and sometimes in referendums. Analysis of one such rejection by voters—the proposed consolidation in 1958 of the governing bodies of the city of Nashville, Tennessee, and its surrounding county—disclosed that, although residents of the central city voted for the proposal, citizens in the rest of the county opposed amalgamation. Contributing to this defeat were fears of higher property taxes, increased centralization of government, and extension of the city political machine throughout the county—all motivated by one critical underlying factor: the division of the county's residents into cosmopolitan and local elements, each of the two groups having a different conception of the proper "basic community" to be fostered and trusted. In Tennessee and elsewhere, unless these two disparate conceptions can be reconciled, public support for

---

[16] Bollens and Schmandt, *op. cit.*, pp. 460–1.
[17] Webb S. Fiser, *Mastery of the Metropolis* (Englewood Cliffs, N.J.: Prentice-Hall, 1962), p. 121.

metropolitan integration will not be forthcoming from the total region.[18]

Coordination of metropolitan and local planning seems best achieved if the over-all direction by the metropolitan agency is supplemented and qualified by allocating to each municipality the control over those activities pertaining to its own residents. To the regional agency should be assigned those functions that transcend city limits: supervision of rapid transit, bridges, freeways, air and water pollution, sewage disposal, open space, and hospitals. Some functions might be assigned either to municipal or to metropolitan agencies: library service, fire protection, food inspection, law enforcement, social welfare, and higher education. Possibly the best compromise today between local and central authorities, and the most impressive achievement of the twentieth century in metropolitan planning, is to be seen in and around London.

○ *The Greater London Plan*

Confronted with an overcrowded and bomb-devastated capital city during World War II, the English wisely began to plan reconstruction of London before the war ended. Realizing a need to cope with choking metropolitan congestion and peripheral sprawl, and having Letchworth and Welwyn as illustrations of the benefits of making their beautiful countryside accessible to urban residents, the British adopted a postwar program with a dual objective: relieving overcrowding in metropolitan centers and building more garden cities. Toward these mutually compatible ends, Patrick J. Abercrombie and his associates designed elaborate plans to rebuild war-torn London, reduce its population, create a greenbelt around the metropolis, and disperse industry. The resultant Greater London and London County Plans, put into operation immediately after World War II, were described by an American sociologist as "probably the most comprehensive, realistic, and daring adventure in city planning." [19] They suc-

---

[18] Daniel J. Elazar, *A Case Study of Failure in Attempted Metropolitan Integration* (Chicago: University of Chicago, 1961), mimeographed, pp. 100–6.

[19] Wilbur C. Hallenbeck, *American Urban Communities* (New York: Harper, 1951), p. 553.

ceeded in preserving and reconstructing established areas and decentralizing a million people.

The County of London Plan, pertaining to the city and its immediate environs,[20] is intended to remedy five defects: traffic congestion, substandard housing, inadequate and badly distributed open space, jumbled industrial development, and the urban sprawl extending outward in ribbons of suburbs. Both residential and industrial decentralization are important parts of the county plan. The densely settled central city, for which there is a separate plan, is surrounded by three bands: an inner ring of apartments at a density of about 200 people per acre, the middle boroughs of two-thirds flats and one-third houses with about 135 per acre, and the outer boroughs of one-third flats and two-thirds houses with 100 per acre. A major feature is the creation of neighborhood units of 6,000 to 10,000 residents, each with its own school, parks, playgrounds, and community center. Three circumferential arterial highways expedite traffic movement.

The Greater London Plan deals with all or parts of nine counties.[21] Its primary aims are to discourage further industrial and population growth in the London region and to provide for better distribution of existing industry and housing. The region is divided into four rings: the inner county just discussed, a suburban ring in which density declines from seventy-five to fifty people per acre with increasing distance from the city center, a recreational greenbelt with a nominal density of zero, and a country ring of agricultural land through which are distributed eight new satellite towns of approximately 50,000 population each. Businesses and industries moving out from the central city are encouraged to settle in these new towns, which are not intended for commuters. Two outer circumferential roads supplement the central county's three inner-ring roads. Open space, both in the greenbelt and elsewhere, is scrupulously protected against encroachment by builders.

A revolutionary contribution of the Greater London Plan is its insistence on firmly controlling the growth of the London metropolitan region—territorially by the greenbelt's making sprawl impossible, demographically by setting limits on density in each band, and indus-

---

[20] J. H. Forshaw and Patrick Abercrombie, *The County of London Plan* (London: Macmillan, 1945).

[21] Abercrombie, *The Greater London Plan* (London: H. M. Stationery Office, 1944).

trially by providing factory sites in the new towns beyond the green-belt. The underlying and pervasive theme of containment of London was effected by viewing the entire region as a single metropolitan entity having a dominant center, a peripheral protective greenbelt, and a set of satellite cities. These last two conceptions are distinctive and nearly unique aspects of metropolitan planning; never before had an entire metropolis been treated as a unit and a coordinated plan actually put into effect. Ebenezer Howard would have admired this synthesis, for he remarked a few years before his death that, when he began writing, practically no one had any conception of regional planning and "a colossal mistake might be made if in starting new towns the importance of their relationships has not been sufficiently recognized." [22] Not only is each new town and its encircling greenbelt treated as a unit, but these new communities designed to maximize social and economic well-being are also integral parts of a grander scheme encompassing thousands of square miles and more than 10 million people.

Results have been gratifying. London was thinned out, a greenbelt four to twelve miles wide rings the city (although cut by dozens of transportation routes and dotted with previously existing structures), and eight new towns have been built, which in most respects "have materialized in full accord with expectations." [23] Most new-town residents work in the town, although a few commute, and community facilities are generally impressive, if slow in construction. In most new towns, urban amenities are provided without the crush and clatter of "the great wen." Not all new towns are situated within the orbit of metropolitan London, others being in Scotland, Northern Ireland, Wales, and central and northern England. Although initially reluctant to move to these towns created by central fiat, industries have shown increasing willingness to take advantage of the attractive sites, freedom from transportation bottlenecks, and stable labor supplies. Shopping centers in new towns attract patronage from neighboring older communities, however, thus aggravating parking problems.

[22] Ebenezer Howard, "Planning Problems of Town, City, and Region," *Papers and Discussions at the International City and Regional Planning Conference* (Baltimore: Remington, 1925), p. 8.

[23] Donald L. Foley, *Controlling London's Growth* (Berkeley: University of California Press, 1963), p. 107.

Although the new towns combine with older ones to form a regional network of sorts, little resemblance can be found with such rigidly geometric paradigms as Walter Christaller's. Spacing is not uniform, and there are only two intentional size levels in Howard's scheme as modified by Abercrombie: more than 1 million and about 50,000 (of course, pre-existing municipalities disrupt this simple model). Garden cities and new towns are in greater accord with central-place theories, serving both as distribution centers for surrounding agricultural territory and as market centers for smaller towns. Of course, Zipf's $M = RS$ thesis (postulating, as explained in Chapter 7, a smoothly graduated relationship between the sizes and numbers of cities) is wholly at variance with the garden-city concept and its practical expression in the new-towns program.

○ *Lessons for Other Nations*

British regional planning offers lessons for planners in other countries, including the United States. The planning of greater London unquestionably would not have been so successful without an integrated set of well-formed and mature ideals setting forth the desired mode of development. Although compromises are often necessary and sometimes desirable (and many were made by the English planners), regional planning is not likely to be thoroughly effective if it is as highly responsive to the tugs and blandishments of political factions as is common in the United States.

The American and English situations contrast in other respects. American officials making planning decisions tend to regard 360-degree metropolitan overspill as natural and almost inevitable; they place considerable confidence in the virtues of wide highways going in all directions to placate motorists; they accept or even encourage extremely high density and congestion at the center of the urban complex; they often gaze fondly on strings of suburbs sporting low-density tracts of single-family houses; they idealize grass-roots planning and are suspicious of national or state control; they share with the American public a resistance to the British practice of having the central government deal directly, frequently, and responsibly with local government; they place great reliance on zoning restrictions in preference to the heavy British reliance on compensation to property owners who are compelled to abandon the prospect of lucrative development of their land; and they lack the powerful British tradition of executive-administrative discretion.[24] Because of these differences, the likelihood of creating systematically ordered metropolises surrounded by inviolable public greenbelts uncluttered by outdoor advertising and suburban scatter seems all but nil in the United States. As in all cross-cultural borrowing, the new social context can render ineffectual an idea that seems so meritorious in another culture.

Other nations also differ from the English in cultural disposition and in degree of enthusiasm for self-sufficient towns severed from traditional bonds with regional centers. For example, the historic, financial, educational, recreational, political, and artistic dominance of Paris in French life does not encourage population dispersion into independent (garden) cities. Instead, the French government decided in the 1960s to accommodate the increasing Parisian population by encouraging two kinds of new communities, some large and some small. Suburbs are to be bolstered by industrializing nearby villages at the same time that eight new satellite cities, with 150,000 to 750,000 population each, are founded.

The Soviet Union has produced its own modification of the garden city–new towns principle, responding perhaps to one of the few explicit planning recommendations made by Marx and Engels—"the gradual abolition of the distinction between town and country by a more equitable distribution of the population over the countryside." Moscow and other metropolises are intentionally limited in growth, and people and industries are to be settled in satellites, of which eighteen have been proposed in the vicinity of the capital but outside the greenbelt. These new communities vary from 30,000 people to as many as 300,000, and apartments rather than single-family houses are the norm. The basic unit for residential areas is the microdistrict, a 5,000-to-20,000-person Soviet version of the neighborhood unit familiar in European and American plans.

Whatever their ideological dissimilarities, contemporary industrial nations generally adopt essentially similar solutions to metropolitan

[24] *Ibid.*, pp. 156–8.

problems, principally because the problems and objectives are similar from city to city. Differences do persist, but leaders of all countries agree on the need to strive for such desiderata as healthful living conditions, efficient transportation, and manageable municipal budgets. Variation is considerable, however, in the less practical ideals and utopias discussed in the chapter that follows.

chapter 14

UTOPIAN COMMUNITIES

EVERYONE DREAMS, AND SOME MEN DREAM OF IDEAL CITIES. WHEN they write down these dreams, the results are called "utopias." Utopians, Samuel Johnson said, are idealists "who listen with credulity to the whispers of fancy and pursue with eagerness the phantoms of hope." [1]

Curiously, most utopias have been constructed in the form of ideal cities or metropolitan regions, a preference noted by Lewis Mumford: "Utopias from Plato to Bellamy have been visualized largely in terms of the city." [2] Given our commitment to urban life, the next step may be the design of Anthropolis, the City of Man, embracing a mixed bag of ever changing human environments designed for optimum livability.

---

[1] Samuel Johnson, *Rasselas, Prince of Abyssinia* (1759; Oxford: Chapman, 1927), p. 7.

[2] Lewis Mumford, "Utopia, The City and the Machine," *Daedalus*, 94 (Spring 1965), 271; reprinted in Frank E. Manuel (ed.), *Utopias and Utopian Thought* (Boston: Houghton Mifflin, 1966), p. 3.

That utopian models are not always enthusiastically endorsed is intimated by the derivation of the word by Thomas More from the Greek *topos* ("place") and a pun on *eu* ("good") and *ou* ("not"). Whether they be eutopias, dystopias, or simply—and more practically —newtopias, these ideal communities bear on the planning of cities and regions if not the delectation of mankind. As Oscar Wilde said: "A map of the world that does not include utopia is not worth glancing at, for it leaves out the one country at which humanity is always landing. And when humanity lands there, it looks out, and seeing a better country, sets sail. Progress is the realization of utopias."

○ *Extrapolation From Reality*

But most utopias are never realized; in fact, their authors would probably be vastly surprised if their works were turned into brick and wood. Never intended to be built, many of these utopian communities are logical or imaginative exercises worked out on paper for the delight of readers—or sometimes only of their creators. Others are thin but effective covers for criticism of the weak points of contemporary society and culture that could not be published (under the tight control existing in most countries during the last several centuries) unless couched in fictional form, for satire has a way of biting hard enough to stimulate reprisals. Still others serve as controllable worlds for their authors, who, dissatisfied with a world they never made, decide to make their own, and publication is incidental or even objectionable. Nonetheless, some utopias were created as blueprints from which a better society could be modeled; they are the most relevant for planning. An indirect but not always unintended use is to provide an alternative to action: An effective legislative device is to delay action until a model has been prepared; when it is completed, the model may serve to block efforts to go out and do something. Yet some utopias are exactly the reverse both in intent and in outcome, serving as prods to action and bibles for social movements.

Some of these conflicting and ambiguous intentions can be seen in a single work of art. Aristophanes' burlesque extravaganza *The Birds* is at once a light comedy and a serious satire, complaining against man's lack of freedom in Greek cities and caricaturing the totalitarian smugness and joyless security of the fictional utopias that were in fashion at the time. This play of 414 B.C. portrays a fantasy city offering an escape from Athenian law courts and politics to "the least material of all regions, the air, the realm of the birds" [3]—a cloud-cuckoo-town free from care and strife. Yet this ideal *polis* remains connected with reality through the depiction of characters often associated with town building: opportunists, slackers, sycophants, sophists, and—perhaps worst of all—intellectuals. Longing for complete change in social conditions in order to form an ideal society is also portrayed in other plays by Aristophanes, most notably *Ecclesiazusae* (*Women in Council*) of 392 B.C., a broad satire on ideal communistic republics (some scholars claim it is specifically directed against Plato's *Republic*, of which Aristophanes may have heard through Plato's informal lectures) that ironically contains the germs of a meliorist plea for a communistic city-state.

In common with other instruments of inspiration, both pragmatic and unworldly utopias have had a checkered history. Following a long but intermittent heritage of utopian works, headed by Plato's *Republic* of the fourth century B.C., a conspicuous outpouring of utopias occurred in Italy and England during the sixteenth and seventeenth centuries, the most prominent being Thomas More's *Utopia* in 1516, J. V. Andreae's *Christianopolis* in 1619, Tommaso Campanella's *City of the Sun* in 1623, Francis Bacon's *New Atlantis* in 1627, and James Harrington's *Commonwealth of Oceana* in 1658. Thereafter, a fallow period ensued until the late nineteenth century, when utopian musings once more became abundant.

During the last century, many utopian novels were published, notably Samuel Butler's *Erehwon* ("nowhere" spelled backward) in 1872, Edward Bellamy's *Looking Backward* (Ebenezer Howard's inspiration) in 1888, Aldous Huxley's dystopic *Brave New World* in 1932, James Hilton's *Lost Horizon* (Shangri La) in 1933, and one of the most famous dystopias, George Orwell's *1984*, in 1949. William S. Gilbert and Arthur Sullivan even wrote an operetta called *Utopia, Limited* in 1893: "Utopia's quite another land; in her enterprising movements, she is England—with improvements." Most Renaissance utopias were fairly small, consisting often of only a single town, but

[3] Victor Ehrenberg, *The People of Aristophanes* (New York: Schocken, 1962), p. 57.

modern utopias frequently comprise entire countries or hemispheric blocs. In both periods, the ecological facets were subordinate to the prime objective: a perfect or at least an improved society. Two modern novels merit special mention: Austin T. Wright's *Islandia* (1942) is set on a large island much like Australia with a predominantly agricultural cast, an appealing ordering of human activities, and a weak urban structure; Burrhus F. Skinner's *Walden Two* (1948) describes the kind of community that could exist in the United States if contemporary knowledge of psychology, especially learning theory, were applied. (Skinner, a psychology professor at Harvard University, is the inventor of Skinner boxes and a pioneer in developing teaching machines.)

The next wave of utopias may well be of the genre known as science-fiction, now maturing away from its initial technologically imaginative space-horse operas whose characters held social values that had become obsolete long before the present day. While much science-fiction remains reactionary, viewing change—especially social change —as harmful, the trend today is toward social science-fiction (for instance, a recent play took as a theme the civil rights of androids), which is at least more sophisticated and may eventually initiate utopian contributions. (A "contribution" has already been made to criminology by a short story in which jail sentences were codified to fit the criminal's life span: Imprisonment was lengthened for creatures with life spans of, say, 700 years and shortened for someone with an expected lifetime of fifteen years.)

One of the most marked current scientific trends, the substitution of machines for human beings, encourages the evaluation of utopias as man-machine systems. Two famous psychologists, nondirectivist Carl Rogers and behaviorist B. F. Skinner, engaged in a debate on *1984* and *Walden Two* as utopian systems.[4] Beginning from different goals —the desire to maximize power in *1984* and to let men be happy in *Walden Two*—the leaders in both novels employed scientific means to further the chosen end. By exposing individuals to prescribed socializing conditions and establishing a social organization designed to produce the types of behavior that are most highly valued, the utopian leader uses his power either to diminish human worth (*1984*) or to maximize individual freedom (*Walden Two*). In *1984* power is

[4] Carl R. Rogers and Burrhus F. Skinner, "Some Issues Concerning the Control of Human Behavior," *Science*, 124 (November 1956), 1057–65.

wielded viciously without regard for the rights of individuals, but in *Walden Two* it is controlled largely by a plan to which each person has access. All systems, whether mechanical or human, need occasional repairs, but *1984*'s system is unreliable, and most of the novel's drama resides in accounts of repairmen at work to eliminate defective components—people. Although occasional lapses are inevitable in any utopian or ongoing urban system, their correction should not require large armies of repairmen who use psychological conditioning to enforce conformity of individual responses to specified stimuli or, that unavailing, apply the more forcible method of destroying defective parts.

Drastic as this punishment may sound, it is consistent with most utopian thought, for utopian thinking is law-making thinking. Although at first encounter utopias exert an almost irresistible appeal to defenders of freedom, thorough analysis exposes a persistent authoritarian and coercive spirit. Utopias tend to be marvelously uniform and compulsorily changeless. After all, anyone who figures out the best way to do something is not likely to accept substitutes, for any deviation from the best is bound to be inferior. For the same reason, everything should be identical in order to be perfect.

○ *The Nature of Utopian Thought*

Utopias are planned, not spontaneous. And, as the planning effort is usually directed toward applying an explicit theory of the purpose of man and the mode of achieving the good life, it includes devices to maintain an insulated set of values, preserved against innovation, often by cultural isolation. "Expected and observed behavior coincide —else it is no utopia." [5] Utopian organization generally requires nearly absolute conformity of individual behavior to the dominant societal goals. Subordination of the individual to the good of the community may take such forms as drastic enforcement of laws, strict status hierarchies, abolition of private property, and assignment of work by a central committee. Although not everyone must follow an

[5] Theodore Caplow, *Principles of Organization* (New York: Harcourt, 1964), p. 291.

identical daily routine, members are practically compelled to hold the same beliefs and act according to prescribed social norms. Confirmation of this contention is found in the irony that the perfect counter-utopia is anarchy: For example, the antiutopian Abbey of Thélème in François Rabelais' *Gargantua and Pantagruel* was operated according to the motto "Do as you wish."

Utopias are essentially authoritarian, favoring powerful control over individual actions; however, although this control is sometimes exerted through the government, it is more often intended to be accomplished by extreme socialization, instilling in each person through the educational system and reinforcement by peers the basic tenets to which that particular utopia is dedicated. Total fidelity is facilitated if the nuclear family is weakened. Because some of the conditions of a utopia may be fulfilled within a happy family, the family becomes a threat to the larger social order. Therefore many utopias undermine the nuclear family and encourage members to see the utopia as a family; it is not coincidental that members address one another as "Brother" or "Sister." Of the four examples of "real utopias" cited by Theodore Caplow—the Oneida community, convents of cloistered nuns, Israeli kibbutzim, and Hutterite brotherhoods—all four drastically alter the family structure customary in the Western world and adopt "Brother" and "Sister" as the prevailing mode of address, which doubtless plays a part in the success the four specimen utopias have had in suppressing internal conflict and transforming the personalities of their members.[6]

Imaginative though utopias are, they are not as varied as might be expected. "When one reads several utopias consecutively, he is struck by the monotony of the human imagination." From this opening paradox, Raymond Ruyer proceeds to list typical characteristics of social utopias.[7] Almost all utopias are as symmetrical as a French formal garden: Social classes form neat pyramids, and cities are made up of gridiron plans and identical houses. "There is in every utopian a sleeping Le Corbusier. Utopia consists of treating psychological and social problems as problems of architecture and city planning." Utopian cities do not grow as do actual communities, for they are not alive. Instead they are static and homogeneous, and their members

[6] *Ibid.*, pp. 299–315.
[7] Raymond Ruyer, *L'Utopie et les utopies* (Paris: Presses Universitaires, 1950), pp. 41–54.

are interchangeable parts, not daring to express dissent in this totalitarian system. Education is a fetish: Elaborate systems promote extraordinarily specific objectives, socializing new generations far more completely than do actual cultures. Authoritarian control is intense; it is not surprising that democracy owes little to utopian fancies. Utopians lack confidence in natural equilibrium, believing that they are avoiding their duty if they leave something to spontaneous dynamics. Also, "the architect of a world does not like to see his materials amuse themselves." Authoritarianism leads readily to collectivism: "Utopians have a horror of chance, disorder, and individual competition." A perfect society must be isolated; fragile masterworks are best protected against contamination from the outside world by locating them on remote islands or in hidden valleys—or in future times. Curiously, many utopias seem to have been designed by ascetics: Miserliness is admired, and waste is abhorred; among men of system, nothing is useless. Utopian lives are comfortable, but luxury is detested as irrational—for who needs frilly clothes or chrome-encrusted automobiles? The purpose of life is collective happiness, and utopian morality is based on quiet pleasure—but not ecstasy. Unhappiness stems from the stupidity of man and thus is curable.

This belief that man's salvation on earth lies in his own hands, coupled with a tendency toward rigid allocation of people and space, lends itself to city planning schemes. Utopian writers may be inflexibly deterministic and sometimes wildly revisionist, but planners generally are constrained to manipulate space within bounds set by existing political frameworks and social values. A utopia is a vision of some ideal future condition, whereas planning is a practical process for reaching a future condition—and not necessarily an ideal one. Utopianists are in the comfortable position of being able to ignore the harsh realities of the processes by which their ideals are to be attained —and of course such disregard of the means virtually ensures that their ends will never come to be, for the visionary's fate is to be disappointed. Planners, however, manage to achieve success in varying measures. It is the planner's task to improve, not to perfect; consequently, it is his fate, too, never to be content.

○ *Utopianists as Planners*

The utopian versus the practical in planning has been amplified by Thomas Reiner in a six-part analytical scale of planning solutions from idealization to practicality:

1. Idealized designs, as Renaissance ideal cities with rigid patterning exemplifying imposition of will on the environment.
2. Idealized schemes with definite land use patterns, as Howard's Garden City, 1898.
3. Hypothetical sites, as Wright's Broadacre City, 1945.
4. Ideal community with a real site, but not concerned with actual problems the area faces, as Garnier's Cité Industrielle, 1918.
5. Plan for a specific site, but not constrained by usual limitations placed on planners and considerations of acceptance, as Justement's plan for Washington, 1946.
6. Master plans prepared to serve actual clientele, as the Modern Architectural Research (MARS) Group plan for London, 1942.[8]

Although ideal communities may themselves never come into being, their models hold an essential place in the history of planning, for they suggest directions to be taken in research and can occasionally be adapted to real situations. The neighborhood unit is an example: William Dean Howells' 1894 anticity utopia, *A Traveler from Altruria* (ironically, written and published in New York City) extols the neighborhood, prefiguring Clarence Perry's neighborhood unit concept by thirty-five years. As the leading character says, "Neighborliness is the essence of Altrurianism." Howells called for removal of cities so that true neighborhood feeling could spring forth; a generation later, city planners set out to accomplish much the same result by remodeling rather than destroying the metropolis.

Another example of utopian and practical thought combined to advantage is control over environment: the domed (and doomed) undersea city of Atlantis dreamed of by the ancient Greeks adumbrated the Astrodome built in 1965 to enable the Houston baseball

[8] Thomas A. Reiner, *The Place of the Ideal Community in Urban Planning* (Philadelphia: University of Pennsylvania Press, 1963), pp. 21–2.

team to play a traditionally outdoor sport in any weather by supplying artificial light, heating, cooling, and even synthetic grass. Several authorities expect plastic-canopied cities to appear by the year 2000, especially in areas of harsh climate—like polar regions—or severe air pollution—like Los Angeles today or, in the near future, any large city. Buckminster Fuller claims that technologists could construct a plastic bubble one mile high and two miles in diameter for about $200 million—an outlay that now seems prohibitive but soon may be justified by the year-round climate control it makes possible. And if the land surface becomes insufficient, the ocean may provide succor: The Marine Resources Planning Committee of the University of California at San Diego envisions a multistoried hotel in the ocean extending from sea level to a depth of 8,000 feet; lower levels would house defense personnel, and the upper levels would include luxury apartments for civilians, some of whom could commute to jobs on land via freeways built over the ocean.

This correspondence—albeit a fluctuating one—between fictional models and real communities extends from the present time back to antiquity. The oldest major utopia, Plato's *Republic,* seems to have been inspired by a utopian experiment in Sparta. The second best-known model, More's *Utopia,* resembled the Inca empire so closely that some scholars have conjectured that More's narrator may have been an actual person who had traveled in Peru. Usually, however, the correspondence is reversed—the actual community follows rather than precedes the fiction. Harrington's *Oceana* inspired William Penn's stately design for the quasi-utopian colony he called Pennsylvania in 1682. Bellamy's *Looking Backward* influenced the garden-city movement in England and the United States. And quite a number of sects built small communities patterned after fictional idealizations.

Utopian conceptions are more relevant for creative than for corrective planning. Most planning action is corrective: preparing and revising zoning ordinances and maps, siting freeways, rehabilitating blighted areas, and similar day-to-day care of existing cities. Creative planning, on the other hand, involves the setting up of something that was not there before: a new town, a greenbelt, a subdivision, or a neighborhood. The first four of Reiner's types are utopian; the last two are creative plans.

During the Renaissance heyday of utopias, several town styles were offered. In 1516 the confirmed punster Thomas More gave the ambiguous name "Utopia" to his imaginary island containing a network of fifty-four city-states of 6,000 families each, which, with the large families envisioned by More and common to the times, might reach 40,-000 people. Each city was walled, almost square, about two miles on each side, and contained four neighborhoods with market squares and uniform three-story row houses. By a primitive form of nuisance zoning, offensive land uses were banned from the city and situated in the agricultural hinterland, with which cities were closely integrated.

Among the oldest technologically realizable projects was the "City of Tomorrow" conceived by Albrecht Dürer early in the sixteenth century. Surrounded by a series of three heavily fortified walls, Dürer's guild city was divided into rectangular quarters defined by straight streets and buildings set in barracks-like lines. Each trade was relegated to a separate section.

A century later came Johann V. Andreae's "Christianopolis," the most fully described utopian city of the period. The square, fortified city was divided into quarters by four streets originating in a central quadrangle, where a great temple and marketplace were located. The town was formed of a series of concentric squares. As in Dürer's proposal and in many modern plans, land uses were strictly separated into districts.

Tommaso Campanella's "City of the Sun" resembled both More's cities and Christianopolis. Seven concentric rings, the outermost two miles in diameter, were cut by four right-angle streets oriented to the cardinal points of the compass, thereby forming twenty-eight sections of varying size. These circles and sectors were remote harbingers of the superficial forms, but not the causal reasoning, of the twentieth-century Park-Burgess and Hoyt schemes.

Most utopian writers of the seventeenth century gave little attention to the layouts of their cities, concentrating almost exclusively on the economic and political systems. Bacon and Harrington offer scarcely a word concerning spatial makeup of their cities. Those few authors who did take the trouble to describe city design generally imagined small walled circular or square shapes with large central plazas. With no expectation of ever seeing their communities come into being, authors probably felt there was little point in providing details of street and building locations; anyway, their primary interest was in social and political reform. Partly because of their lack of physical details, direct effects of Renaissance utopias on city planning are negligible, but indirectly they probably have inspired considerable armchair reflection upon city structure—both how it was and how it might be.

○ Planners as Utopianists

Toward the end of the nineteenth century, a revolutionary principle of town design was advanced by a Spanish engineer, Arturo Soria y Mata, who in 1882 devised the idea of the linear city. A single massive road many miles in length would carry people, goods, and utilities to residential bands extending 200 yards on either side; beyond the residential strips, which would also be served by minor transverse streets, would be woodlands and farms. Soria actually began to build a linear city about thirty-five miles long, but financial troubles halted construction after one-fourth was built. Although it antedated the self-propelled internal-combustion vehicle, his plan nonetheless attempted to organize a city around transportation—in Soria's day trains and streetcars—and might well be adaptable to the age of the motor car. But association with the repellent "ribbon" development of gas stations and used-car lots along highways out of cities places the linear city among disreputable bedfellows; consequently, except for sporadic suggestions from avant-garde planners, as in schemes unsuccessfully proposed for Moscow in the 1930s and in the rejected radical MARS plan for London in 1942, few serious attempts have been made to adapt Soria's idea directly to twentieth-century communities.

The linear principle, however, was reborn during the 1960s in the plans of the highly successful Greek engineer and architect Constantinos A. Doxiadis for such cities as Islamabad, the new capital of Pakistan. On either side of a wide axial boulevard are gridiron segments divided into decentralized neighborhoods. As the city's population increases, new subcommunities and their component neighborhoods are to be added by extending the "axis of growth." In this way, provision is made for growth, and urban beauty and efficiency will not be destroyed by the urban fourth dimension—time. To avoid the strangulation he believes is implicit in concentric expansion, Doxiadis prefers to design cities that can expand in only one direction; he calls this new urban form "dynapolis." [9]

In 1924 Le Corbusier (pseudonym of Charles Edouard Jeanneret-Gris) published designs for a "City of Tomorrow" of 3 million population: Its central 600-foot commercial towers spaced at quarter-mile intervals were surrounded by 100-foot apartment towers separated by parks, and the whole was encircled by greenbelt, industrial districts, and garden suburbs. Roads were supplemented by an underground railway system with a station under each block of towers. Every residential tower comprised a little neighborhood with ready access to shops on the ground floor and the parkland separating it from the next "garden tower neighborhood." By providing considerable park space, Le Corbusier held densities near the core to fifty dwelling units per acre. The over-all pattern expressed Le Corbusier's respect for the modern need for movement as well as, less practically, his passion for abstract geometry. The French architect's 1925 "Plan Voisin" for Paris and 1933 "La Ville Radieuse" were characterized by staggered rows of skyscrapers on stilts with ample landscaped space between them. Although none of these communities was ever built, his "Cité Radieuse," a fourteen-story, self-contained apartment building in Marseille, with its own shopping center, recreation facilities, and clinic, was built in 1945.

Le Corbusier's American counterpart in fame was Frank Lloyd Wright, the iconoclastic creator of "Broadacre City," an idealized version of a midwestern prairie town. Conceived in the 1920s and published in 1932, but never actually built, Broadacres provided a minimum of one acre of land to each family and an average of two acres per family. Factories, offices, and stores were distributed in a polynuclear pattern. Wright emphasized superhighways, and residents would be dependent on automobiles. Despite this contemporary touch, the community was agrarian in spirit, espousing the notion that cultivation of land is the firmest basis for a good life.

Modern planners have worked with a number of urban designs, most of which are sophisticated modifications of paradigms first applied to cities by Hippodamus, Vitruvius, and other ancient planners. Square or rectangular cities in gridiron patterns have been constructed hundreds of times. Concentric circles also have been familiar

[9] Constantinos A. Doxiadis, *Architecture in Transition* (New York: Oxford, 1963), pp. 99–106.

for centuries. Dividing cities into quarters or smaller sectors is not only planned, but also, as Homer Hoyt contended, a natural development. Star-shaped cities of varying numbers of points have been advanced frequently, as have hexagonal and octagonal outlines. Some plans are attenuated to fit such topographic conditions as a mountainside or a lake; they are then referred to as linear cities. Polynucleation within cities has its counterpart in the satellite systems of metropolitan regions. Many designs make generous allowance for open space, and some have both residential and commercial buildings designed in intimate conjunction with parklands. Density varies from Wright's agrarian dream to the thickly packed high-rise slabs of some science-fiction contributions. Also, density may be either relatively uniform or highly variable from section to section within the community.

⬡ *Communities Actually Built*

Possibly the most effective utopian planner of all time was Ebenezer Howard, who inspired a national policy for urban planning culminating in the actual construction of more than a dozen towns. Like other successful dreamers, Howard wrote at a propitious time and struck a proper balance between his own ideas and those borrowed from his predecessors.

> One wonders how much of the persuasiveness of Howard's ideas lies in the reminiscence of a golden past, in sheer nostalgia for small communities in a rural setting, for simple joys and virtues missed in a metropolitan milieu. And how much of the attractiveness comes from the foreshadowing of a modern utopia, from the apparent reconciliation of technology and nature, town and country, place of residence and workplace, workers and employers, the needs of children and the imperatives of the balance sheet? [10]

The new towns inspired by Howard's garden-city thesis were not the only utopian conceptions to turn into fact. In the nineteenth century, tens of thousands of native-born Americans and thousands of

[10] Lloyd Rodwin, *The British New Towns Policy* (Cambridge, Mass.: Harvard University Press, 1956), p. 24.

immigrants abandoned their homes to join scores of widely varying religious and political groups for the purpose of establishing independent communities. Some leaders were religious zealots desiring to practice their beliefs without risk of contamination from people of other faiths; some were intellectual enthusiasts striving to live according to some unorthodox ideology, such as complete equality for all persons, abolition of money and property, or a new form of marriage; others saw the new communities as opportunities to get rich quick at the expense of their followers. The followers themselves were motley collections of Emersonian rationalists, devil-may-care adventurers, neurotic malcontents likely to contribute to the failure of any enterprise, self-seekers expecting a free ride at the expense of the more idealistic colonists, practical men viewing their utopia as another business endeavor, and European peasants seeking a farm village in the new world. "Marching across the continent with the planners of cities dedicated to Mammon—the grid surveyors, the town speculators, the creators of railroad towns, and the other men of affairs— were the reformers, the utopians, and the pariah religious sects in their restless quest for kingdoms of paradise on mortal earth." [11] Almost all the colonies foundered within a few years, but a few, notably the Shaker and Oneida colonies, managed to survive and even to prosper for several decades or longer. These experiments are of considerable interest to students of American social and urban development, for some utopianists were innovators in methods of education, women's rights, prohibition, antislavery, furniture design, and, usually only incidentally, urban structure. Although they designed and built cities, most utopianists were so unworldly that their urban products failed to match in interest or originality their sometimes bizarre doctrines of social reform.

George Rapp, a German immigrant and religious reformer who led the Harmony Society, founded Harmony, Pennsylvania, in 1803; New Harmony, Indiana, in 1814; and Economy, Pennsylvania, in 1825. Practicing an ascetic life of toil and self-denial, the Harmonists designed their communities in a conventional rectangular grid totally lacking in inspiration.

The Harmonists vacated New Harmony in 1825 to sell the town to Robert Owen, the English factory owner who had made such a success

[11] John W. Reps, *The Making of Urban America* (Princeton: Princeton University Press, 1965), p. 439.

of the New Lanark textile mills and town near Glasgow. After writing a book advocating drastic changes in the urban and social structure of England, each proposed town to contain 1,200 persons sharing the products of their cooperative agricultural and industrial labor, Owen determined to put his ideas in practice in the United States. Although quite specific about the internal arrangements of buildings and their uses in his book, Owen was faced in New Harmony with a pre-existing village with which his favored quadrangle system was not compatible. Further plagued with an unrealistic policy of accepting any colonist who chose to volunteer (therefore having to build a new community from unbalanced personnel lacking several essential occupational skills and being perhaps overly supplied with temperament), Owen's experiment ended three years later, whereupon he returned to England and established several moderately successful communities.

Owen's French contemporary Charles Fourier, hoping to reorganize society along socialistically rational lines, settled people in phalanxes. The basic unit was the phalanstery, a vast hotel-like building housing 1,600 people and containing all the necessities of life and surrounded by agricultural areas. Several phalanxes were founded in France and some forty in the United States in the 1840s, but few lasted more than a year. The most successful were at Red Bank, New Jersey, and Brook Farm, Massachusetts.

Another Frenchman, Etienne Cabet, founded the Icarian Society and sent a group of followers to Texas in 1848 to establish a communistically organized community. Cabet, however, like many other socialists a trusting and therefore poor businessman, was hoodwinked by Texas realtors and did not receive land for money. The following year the humbugged immigrants struggled hopefully northeastward to Nauvoo, Illinois, which the Mormons had abandoned in 1847. But unlike the uncompromisingly monotonous square city layout of the Mormons, Cabet's vision included broad streets embellished with beautiful monuments, and it anticipated later development of the superblock containing a neighborhood unit. The venture survived until Cabet's dictatorial tactics provoked serious dissension and led to his removal from the directorship in 1856.

The Icarians' predecessors in Nauvoo, the Mormons, originated in 1830 in upstate New York and were thereafter forced by people intolerant of their views to move from one area after another. On their way they founded communities in Kirtland, Ohio; Far West, Missouri; and Nauvoo before finally settling in Salt Lake City. Taking their cue from Numbers 35 and Leviticus 25, the Mormons built rectangular cities divided into square blocks. Nauvoo and Salt Lake City became the most prosperous towns in their respective states during Mormon occupancy. Salt Lake City, however, despite its beautiful natural setting, remains (according to many persons) one of the ugliest cities of its size in the nation.

The Oneida community, a communistic religious society founded by John Humphrey Noyes in 1848 in central New York, survived until Noyes' leadership faltered in 1880. Accepting the familiar gridiron street pattern, Oneida's colonists devoted their pioneering spirit to social rather than ecological invention. "Complex marriage" permitted cohabitation according to personal taste, but restricted conception to stirpiculture, the eugenically controlled production of healthy and intelligent offspring. Despite its economic success and lack of internal friction, outside antagonism to the unorthodox marital system compelled Noyes to move to Canada in 1880, after which the community lost its distinctive communistic and marital flairs.

More than 200 communities were founded by fiery preachers, faith healers, and fanatical believers, including the Altruists, Straight-Edgers, Society of the Woman in the Wilderness, and the Spirit Fruit Society. This near-incredible collection of religious sects offered city planners the monotonous spectacle of one gridiron plan after another. Ecologically if not theologically, their common property was regularity.

As their base was charisma rather than dogma, these communities died when their leaders died, left, or lost their charisma; followers then dispersed to other settlements of multifarious convictions. The somewhat disillusioning fact that most members of these religious groups seem to have been more influenced by their leader's personality than by his—or their own—theological convictions was compounded by other dysfunctional discrepancies between their official and actual behavior. Also, the core members of each community generally were idealists who apparently believed so strongly in the mission or gift of their leader that they had difficulty comprehending that outsiders might think differently—or worse, as they so often did, antagonistically. These religious utopians shared with many other impassioned liberals a belief that good will and the power of love will suffice to improve the world; consequently they were often so unsuspecting that they were victimized by astute real-estate agents and other shrewd businessmen.

Furthermore—and also like people of strong reformist convictions today—they usually were poorly organized, trusting to good intentions to succeed when a system was needed. Although the idea that everyone should love his fellow men—or at least should cease hating those who disagree or deviate in their political or sexual convictions —is one of the most admirable of all possible human attitudes, in fact the world is controlled not by love but power and governed not by goodness but by organized and disciplined action. The nineteenth-century utopian colonists possessed too much ingenuous goodness and too little common sense to effect their often inexplicit intentions.

For these reasons, the utopianists' ultimate impact on American planning was modest; except for the Mormons, none made any memorable impression on the contours of towns. Despite this rich legacy of fundamentalist and socialist hopes, the overwhelming majority of the nation's cities stubbornly pursued their sinful and capitalist ways.

chapter 15

CITIES OF THE FUTURE

"IT IS MEN WHO MAKE A CITY—NOT WALLS, OR SHIPS," THUCYDIDES
observed. The number of men in the world is a fundamental determinant of urban growth—past, present, and future. With the world due
to double in population by the end of the twentieth century and with
increasing proportions of people living in cities in both industrial and
in underdeveloped regions, we can look forward—whether with enthusiastic hopes or distressed sighs—to a substantial increase in the
number of cities and city people. Large cities will grow even larger,
small ones will become large, and rural villages will turn into small
cities. Furthermore, even the people who do not live in urban areas
will, through the influence of the mass media of communication and
rapid transportation, become more and more urban in their living
and thinking. If present trends continue—although, of course, they
may not—the traditional rural subsistence agriculture may vanish in
all but a few regions of the world, to be replaced by cities or giant
metropolises and conurbations. Although the world may never be-

come totally urban, the urban proportion seems likely to reach a majority in every country. City growth appears destined to continue as long as there is population increase, and demographic standstill can be visualized only by the exercise of a powerful imagination.

○ *Expected World Urbanization*

If the total world population continues to increase toward the 6 or 7 billion projected for the end of the century, and if the urban population continues to grow faster than the rural population, there will be more people living in cities in the year 2000 than there were in the whole world in 1965. Providing for the needs of these people will require far more extensive attention than is now given to food supply, transportation, housing, water supply, waste disposal, fire and police protection, entertainment, schools, parks, and so forth. One-fifth of the world's people—well in excess of 1 billion people—will probably be living in metropolitan areas of 1 million-plus inhabitants, and another fifth may be living in cities of 100,000 to 1 million, making an estimated total of more than 2.5 billion people in metropolises. And if another fifth of the world's people reside in smaller urban places, the total urban population may reach nearly 4 billion. By comparison, the total population of the world in 1965 was about 3.3 billion, of which barely more than 1 billion were urban.

Distribution of these figures by continents for 1960 and corresponding estimates for 2000 are supplied in Table 5. All continents are expected to increase both their number and their percentage urban, but in some cases the proportionate urban-rural changes will be relatively slight. The greatest burst of urban people should occur in the predominantly rural continent of Asia, which not only is the most populated continent (greater than all the other continents combined) but should increase its proportion in both large and small cities to the point of having more than half of the world's urban population by the end of the century.

Of course, any statements about the future must be made with reservations. The future increase in urbanization in already predominantly urban countries is fairly clear, but estimates for developing

TABLE 5. World Population by Size of Place and Continent: 1960 and 2000

YEAR AND CONTINENT	MILLIONS OF PEOPLE LIVING IN PLACES OF GIVEN SIZE				PERCENTAGE DISTRIBUTION				
	1 Million and More	100,000 to 1 Million	Other Urban*	Rural Areas and Villages*	1 Million and More	100,000 to 1 Million	Other Urban*	Rural Areas and Villages*	Total
1960									
Anglo America	67	52	47	31	34	26	24	16	100
Latin America	25	26	41	116	12	13	20	55	100
Europe (including U.S.S.R.)	80	109	152	298	13	17	24	46	100
Asia	102	102	151	1,296	6	6	9	79	100
Africa	6	14	18	213	2	6	7	85	100
Oceania	4	3	3	6	25	19	19	37	100
World total	284	306	412	1,960	10	10	14	66	100
2000									
Anglo America	125	115	41	32	40	37	13	10	100
Latin America	148	148	59	238	25	25	10	40	100
Europe (including U.S.S.R.)	189	265	208	284	20	28	22	30	100
Asia	774	735	425	1,935	20	19	11	50	100
Africa	41	88	36	352	8	17	7	68	100
Oceania	8	8	3	10	27	28	10	35	100
World total	1,285	1,359	772	2,851	21	21	12	46	100

* The community size distinguishing "urban" from "rural" is usually between 2,000 and 5,000 inhabitants, depending on the data-collection practices in the various nations.

Adapted by permission from Homer Hoyt, *World Urbanization*, Urban Land Institute Bulletin No. 43. Copyright 1962: Urban Land Institute, Washington, D.C., pp. 48–9.

nations are shaky. Aside from difficulties besetting attempts to predict the demographic futures of individual countries, the world political, economic, and technological situation will influence all nations in one way or another: Cities may or may not grow at the same rate in times of war as in periods of peace, and improvement or stagnation in the level of living may also play a part in urbanizing the population. Further, some nations conduct infrequent and methodologically unsophisticated censuses from which urban distribution trends can be deduced only with difficulty and doubts. For these reasons, demographers generally project rather than predict; that is, they simply extend present trends as literally and unimaginatively as possible, without making judgments about the probable courses of cold wars, economic melioration, technological advances, or other social events affecting city growth. The figures in Table 5 for the year 2000 thus are not attempts to guess at what actually will be the case; rather, they are "if . . . then" statements: If the percentage increase continues as it now is, then the population will be as indicated. Of course, if the circumstances of life cause growth rates to alter, then the future population figures also will alter. The moral should be clear: When contemplating urban population estimates, let the reader beware, for the events of the world have a way of changing in unanticipated directions.

Regardless of fluctuations in these projections, there is no question that the world and most of its regions will experience massive urbanization in the rest of this century. However conservative one may be, he cannot ignore the indications that the next few decades will add as many urban people to the world as have all the preceding millennia. A foremost demographer, Kingsley Davis, has suggested that "there is no apparent reason why [the world] should not become as urbanized as the most urban countries today—with perhaps 85–90 per cent of the population living in cities and towns of 5,000 or more and practicing urban occupations." [1]

Another indication of how far the world has proceeded toward near-total urbanization is that, in the most urbanized nations, the term "urban" is being redefined in the popular press. From the classic view of an urbanite as anyone who does not live in an isolated farmhouse or tiny agricultural village, Americans have changed to the point

[1] Kingsley Davis, "The Origin and Growth of Urbanization in the World," *American Journal of Sociology*, 60 (March 1955), 437.

where many people no longer think of a clerk in a record shop in a community of 30,000 people as "urban"; by this new definition, one must live in a city of at least 50,000 people and preferably 100,000. Sponsors of this view are forgetting man's history; for most of human existence (and in many underdeveloped nations of the world today) residents of a community of, say, 8,000 people possessed characteristics sufficiently different from those of less dense areas to merit a distinctive label—to wit, "urban." These contemporaries are making not an urban-rural but a metropolitan-small city distinction. Apparently the United States has now become so thoroughly urbanized in thought as well as settlement patterns that the traditional notion of rural life has lost its meaning to many persons; in short, we are an urban civilization.

○ Life Styles in Future Conurbations

Continuing urbanization seems almost inevitable during the rest of our lifetimes, and the question arises as to what the cities of the world will be like a half-century or so hence. There will undoubtedly be more conurbations similar to, although far from identical with, that of the northeastern seaboard of the United States. Indeed, many industrial nations already have one or more conurbations, and incipient newcomers can readily be discerned elsewhere.

The future internal pattern for megalopolis might resemble Los Angeles' sprawling collection of contiguous satellites and suburbs lacking a truly focal downtown center, the whole characterized by a more uniform density than is now usual in metropolitan regions. The auto-age community par excellence, Los Angeles exemplifies the advantages and discomforts of permitting everyone to drive his car to any part of the metropolitan complex at sixty-five miles an hour. With this degree of mobility, then employment, shopping, and recreation clusters are almost inevitably widely scattered throughout the area. In fact, "downtown" to Angelenos usually means not a mass of tall buildings as in New York, but the "interchange," where several freeways come together—but even this "snake pit" is losing its centrality because the freeway system is being redesigned so that drivers can make connections to other freeways without having to pass through the central interchange. Although it is doubtful that many cities will reach the total decentralization in which every residential cubicle has equal access to shops (through a system of tubes, perhaps?) and athletics and entertainment (through television, of course), it does seem that the traditional sharp peaks in property values and pedestrian traffic in a few centrally located blocks may be on the way out. Whether we like it or not—and many do not—Los Angeles may be the forerunner of the urban world of tomorrow.

Which of these two trends—the growing together of two or more existing cities or metropolitan sprawl outward of one huge supercity —will best characterize urban growth in the rest of the twentieth century is problematic. Both unquestionably will occur, and perhaps one day Angelenos may reverse the old cliché, "a hundred suburbs in search of a city," by deprecating other regions as "a dozen small metropolises in search of a supercity."

New modes of transportation may prevail. If everyone drives an air-cushion vehicle, paved streets will be unnecessary, and thoroughfares may become grassy malls. Or, surface automobiles may be eliminated in favor of aerial commuting powered by individual rockets strapped on each person's back.

Almost as beloved as a man's automobile is his house, which too may change. If population should increase to the point of making the single-family house too prodigal a use of space so badly needed for roads and parking lots, apartment living could become the norm for everyone but the exceedingly rich; what such an eventuality would do to city and regional planning, and especially the degree of separation of land uses, is uncertain. A few engineers have suggested tall frameworks for detachable apartments; when a tenant wants to move, he disconnects the utility lines and hires a crane to lift the apartment onto a railroad flatcar—a development not really far removed from the gigantic mobile homes that are too large to be towed by a family car and that have expandable sides and retractable patio covers. Engineers already use prefabricated room modules to rehabilitate tenements over a weekend.

At Montreal's Expo 67, precast concrete flats and duplex apartments of one to four bedrooms, overlooking outdoor gardens on the roofs of units diagonally below, formed the terraced twelve-story Habitat 67 exhibit—a twentieth-century version of the pueblos of the sixteenth-century Indians in New Mexico and Arizona. Habitat 67, designed by architect Moshé Safdie, consists of preassembled steel-reinforced concrete boxes hoisted into place by giant cranes, forming an irregular pyramid reminiscent simultaneously of children's blocks, Indian cliff dwellings, and wayward cubism. Assembly-line production could reduce construction costs to a level that might make Safdie's idea a practical solution to the housing miseries of rapidly urbanizing underdeveloped nations.

More imaginative yet is the proposal of R. Buckminster Fuller to house as many as 1 million people in a single pyramid-shaped edifice so constructed that each of its 300,000 families has a 2,000-square-foot apartment plus a 1,000-square-foot sunlit terrace. Inspired by Le Corbusier's forward-looking dictum that "a house is a machine to live in," Fuller's highly rationalized tetrahedral "city of the future" consists of a hollow three-sided pyramid two miles along each base line, with public gardens inside on the ground level, community parks and shopping centers on each side of every fiftieth floor, and dwelling units honeycombed in the three outer walls. This open-trusswork mountain would be self-contained and, because of its relatively light weight, could float on the ocean, thereby solving—albeit only temporarily—the problem of a limited supply of land. In addition, Fuller envisions covering these as well as traditional cities with huge geodesic domes offering such a combination of strength and lightness (geodesic spheres more than one-half mile in diameter are of negligible weight in proportion to the weight of the air they enclose) that proper control of air temperature would enable them to float in the sky. In this manner, people could live in prefabricated mile-diameter clouds, freed from subjection to the storms of nature and the fumes of industry. Fanciful as this vision may appear, its inventor claims that both the tetrahedron and the sky dome are within the technological and economic capabilities of major industrial nations. Although skepticism may be justified, we would be wise to inform ourselves of how far-fetched the jet airplane, the heated and air-conditioned automobile, and the appliance-filled home seemed when our grandfathers were young.

But whatever technology may bring, the possible doubling of the American urban population by the year 2000 will necessitate major modifications of the urban physical environment, including approximately twice as many houses, schoolrooms, workplaces, and miles of roads. If we are not careful—and perhaps even if we are—these 50 or 60 million new dwelling units will inundate the countryside with miles of suburbs sprawling outward from metropolitan centers in what may constitute, if we retain the present balkanization of metropolitan areas into scores or often hundreds of petty jurisdictions, a haphazard collection of communities whose most systematic interrelation may be through a spidery network of highways.

○ *Getting About Amid Urban Sprawl*

The villain in this play is the automobile. Cherished for its capacity to provide the individual with the ability to move wherever he wishes whenever he wishes, the automobile is driven in such numbers as to seriously restrict the mobility it purportedly provides, especially during the inchworm pace of the twice-daily rush hour. Car ownership offers the blessing of living more or less wherever one pleases, instead of being confined within walking distance of mass transit. Because owning a car is nearly universal in the United States, builders scatter suburban tracts over wide areas, the location often being determined more by the price demanded by landowners than by residential practicality. Commuters drive long distances, shopping housewives and school-bound children may face lengthy rides, and the cost of installing water and sewer lines and other public utilities is excessive in such scattered subdivisions.

Open space is being destroyed at a fearful rate. Conversion of Long Island's potato farms into Levittown, southern California's orange groves into pastel bungalows, and midwestern golf courses into apartment developments constitutes a removal of farms from production and parkland from recreation. The nearest open countryside is farther from the city dwellers, some of whom have to drive for hours in traffic jams to reach woods or meadows.

If this is America's present version of livability, what of the future? Will there be more leapfrogging of formless tracts of ranch houses scattered behind impressive shopping centers with their imposing expanse of white-striped parking lots? And will twice as many urban residents drive long distances on weekends in search of scenery, only to find that parking lots are full at the state park or that the public beach is filled to capacity? Already many people resist driving on weekends because of the crowded highways, and the national parks are to be avoided if you do not like crowds. Although many of these problems result from population growth per se rather than from its urban distribution, steps can be taken to meliorate urban overcrowding.

One solution is the English-inspired greenbelt, which freezes the boundaries of the city so that open space is permanently available at a reasonably close distance; but if this approach is to be adopted in the United States, action must be immediate, for most land close to cities is already built upon. Another possibility is the star pattern of ecology described by Richard Hurd at the beginning of the century; railroad commuting from fairly distant suburbs could be encouraged, taking care to leave open space in wedge-shaped interstices. A third recommendation is to decentralize urban workplaces and retail stores while building up the centrality function of satellite communities throughout the metropolis—another return to the past, this time to the polynuclear pattern common to the older European and Asiatic cities. Still another prospect is virtually to eliminate commuting to work or shops by providing dwelling units, work places, and stores within a single building, as in the huge apartment slabs of Le Corbusier. With increasing pressure to find solutions, urban problems will be attacked by more and more scholars and civic leaders; perhaps financially effective and socially and aesthetically satisfying proposals will result from this effort.

Of all the suggestions for improving metropolitan areas—or at least keeping them from deteriorating in the face of the impending rapid growth—one of the least frequent procedures is to canvass the public. With all the surveys of opinions taken in this country, it is remarkable that so little effort has been devoted either to official referendums or to informal questionnaires about the organization of cities. It is the present residents who stand to benefit or suffer most from changes in their city, and it seems appropriate that they voice their preferences about how the growth of their city should be channeled: For example, should zoning and other civic legislation encourage or discourage high-rise apartments, heavy industry, or a municipal golf course? An exception to this prevailing lack of opinion surveys is an occasional inquiry regarding residents' reactions to redevelopment of their immediate area, thereby offering hints of grass-roots encouragement of or resistance to urban renewal projects.[2] Another exception is the recent canvassing by the Twin Cities Metropolitan Planning Commission, in which 4,600 citizens of the Minneapolis area were asked their preferences regarding type of housing (detached single-family, row houses, or apartments), desirability of access to the downtown district, the optimal compactness-versus-spread of the metropolitan region, and the best form of regional government. Not that it should be assumed that all citizens are equipped with the knowledge to make meaningful statements on such subjects; in fact, many residents couldn't care less. Still, recognition of the troubles besetting cities is spreading, if only because of the difficulties residents encounter in trying to navigate thoroughfares that obviously are no longer able to handle existing, let alone prospective, volumes of automobiles.

Much of the congestion engulfing cities derives from the circumstance that street layouts generally were designed years before cars attained such large displacement, regarding both combustion chambers and shadows cast on the pavement. Both automobile size and ownership increase so fast that planners' efforts to think ahead usually result in keeping barely abreast of the flow, new freeways being virtually obsolete by the time they are completed. Although a shift away from the private automobile to mass transit might be helpful, such a change seems unlikely in the near future, for people have become attached to the comfort and privacy of their own cars. And, as expediting traffic stimulates the hopeless cycle of more cars being driven to work and therefore more demand for freeways and multitiered garages, a lasting solution to this problem is difficult to come by.

Similar problems are developing in newly industrializing nations, where rapid urbanization and eager purchases of autos are creating the same kind of transportation clogging as that in industrial nations. Added to over-all population problems, urban congestion reduces economic efficiency by increasing overhead costs. If effectively used, however, modern transportation facilities may be forces for dispersal as well as concentration, providing relief from overcentralization and

[2] Morton Rubin, Louis H. Orzack, and Ralph Thomlinson, "Resident Responses to Planned Neighborhood Redevelopment," in Marvin B. Sussman (ed.), *Community Structure and Analysis* (New York: Crowell, 1959), pp. 208–34.

encouraging the planning of new communities so designed as not to be engorged by automobile traffic on obsolete roads. Eventually all cities in all nations will have to face up to the challenge of great quantities of private cars in ever increasing motion.

○ *Pollution of Environment*

The subject of traffic congestion brings up the correlative—and consequent—topic of air pollution. For many years, southern Californians have wiped the smarting teardrops of smog from their eyes. Smog has become so bad that in 1966 the chief of the California Division of Environmental Sanitation wrote an article declaring that the air of California and the gasoline-powered engine are incompatible and that consequently gas-driven motor vehicles should not be permitted after 1980, when they should be replaced by electrically powered or other vehicles that do not emit dangerous hydrocarbons and nitrous oxides. Given the industrial and urban growth in store for California, he claimed, pollutants put out by factories alone, even if maximally controlled, would overburden the ability of the state's air to absorb waste. Beginning in 1967, the power utilities in the Los Angeles basin were prohibited from installing any new oil or gas-fired boilers or replacing old ones. This phasing out of thermal power plants will be facilitated by increases in nuclear power sources.

Reading about the problems of Los Angeles may give the impression that smog is a newly invented trial for mankind, but its presence was decried (although without use of the word, coined from "smoke" and "fog" in the late nineteenth century) in London by John Graunt in 1662,[3] and, as long ago as 1273, the English government passed a smoke-abatement law. The French author, politician, and putative steak fancier Chateaubriand wrote of a trip in 1822, "Soon I saw before me the black skullcap which covers the city of London."

Nor is southern California the only twentieth-century sufferer. West Virginia has experienced severe smog for many years, and New York called its first air-pollution alert in 1966. A report issued by the

[3] John Graunt, *Natural and Political Observations Made Upon the Bills of Mortality* (1662; Baltimore: Johns Hopkins University Press, 1939), p. 76.

United States Public Health Service in 1967 emphasized that "all large cities—and many small communities, too—have serious air pollution problems." Based on eight quantitative criteria, the highest scores were recorded, in order, for New York, Chicago, Philadelphia, Los Angeles, Cleveland, Pittsburgh, and Boston.

New York's smog, like London's, is of a different chemical quality from that in Los Angeles; it contains a higher proportion of sulfur dioxide from the burning of coal and fuel oil for heating and industrial purposes. New York has for several decades had a reputation for dirty, gray air that blackens shirt collars and leaves marks on the skin at the tops of one's shoes, and as long ago as 1845 a New York physician complained that the foul air of the city caused New Yorkers' blood to become overburdened with noxious impurities. A report on the 6,000 to 7,000 persons waiting on the sidewalk to enter the 6,200-seat Radio City Music Hall to see the 1966 Christmas show illustrated both the overcrowding in New York and the dirt in the air: To the wistful question "Is that a snowflake?" came the answer "No, Mother, it's a piece of soot." [4]

Chemical pollutants are not readily eliminated or controlled, but soot in the air can be handled. Pittsburgh, where motorists sometimes needed headlights at noon and where residents could wear light-colored pants an extra day because the soot formed a simulated crease-line down the front, was transformed into a relatively clean city by an aggressive program largely consisting of persuading factory owners to clean up the smoke issuing from their chimneys.

The manner in which smoke and industrial chemicals affect public health is not fully known, but research is gradually confirming the suspicion that persons exposed to smog over a decade or more may be adversely affected. Although Norman Cousins' "a breath of death" seems unduly inflammatory, supporting evidence is supplied by the two classic cases of deaths from air pollution: Donora, Pennsylvania, and London, England. In Donora, when a 1948 thermal inversion held smog over the city for three days, 6,000 persons were reported ill (including more than half of all inhabitants over age sixty-five), and twenty died. In London in 1952, excess mortality during a one-week smog attack amounted to between 4,000 and 5,000 persons, and older bronchitis patients served clinics much as the canaries that miners

[4] "The Talk of the Town," *The New Yorker*, 42 (December 24, 1966), 25.

once carried to give early warning of noxious gases: Veteran broncho-pulmonary sufferers noted discomfort six to twelve hours before others detected the onset of the smog episode. Except for extreme cases, however, it is probable that prolonged exposure to polluted air only aggravates existing ailments, especially chronic lung diseases like emphysema. Recognizing that injurious effects may result, leaders of smog-bound cities are attempting fitfully to control pollution by two steps: requiring factories to convert to a more expensive but safer fuel at times when smog threatens, and requiring crankcase and exhaust devices to be installed on automobiles.

Pollution in our effluent society is not confined to the air, for water is also seriously affected. In many areas, water from kitchen faucets comes already supplied with detergent foam from the thousands of washing machines whose drains lead eventually into fresh-water sources. If it continues unchecked, this fouling of our own nest may soon reach proportions disastrous enough to justify Tom Lehrer's advice to visitors to the United States from underdeveloped areas lacking filtration plants and pasteurization: "Don't drink the water and don't breathe the air." [5]

○ *Los Angeles*

If the cities of the present are increasingly beset by air pollution, hordes of automobiles, and suburban sprawl, might not the cities of the future be characterized even more by these man-made irritants? For a model, where else is one to turn but Los Angeles, that "tobacco stain on the landscape" whose presence is signaled to airline visitors by a gray pall pierced by mountain tops. But it takes money and people to manufacture smog, and in the crowded city of the angels the dual magnetism of the gold of sunlight and of dollars has created a new kind of city. Whether in seriousness or caricature, this urban laboratory reflects not only present trends but also the aspirations and fears of many residents of other cities. Since World War II, most United States metropolises have been duplicating—with necessary

[5] "Pollution," words and music by Tom Lehrer. Copyright 1965 Tom Lehrer. Used by permission.

concessions to differences in climate and topography—the Los Angeles habits of home building, transportation, and the like.

This urban pioneering is not surprising, as California has for many years represented the realization of utopia to people, from the "California or Bust" migrants crossing the continent in wagon trains to the elderly woman enthusiast of a religious utopia who identified the four "neutral points" on the earth from which the salvation of mankind might emerge: 1) Palestine, 2) California, and 3) and 4) "with a distant and transfigured expression she slowly answered, 'no one knows.' " [6]

In 1781 Spanish missionaries traveled up from Mexico and founded a small village that they named El Pueblo de Nuestra Señora la Reina de Los Angeles de Porciuncula (The Town of Our Lady Queen of the Angels of Porciuncula—the name of the church in Italy in which St. Francis is buried). In 1848 the town of 1,600 inhabitants became a part of the United States, and the gold rush of 1849 converted the sleepy village into a rip-roaring frontier settlement and gave it the reputation for prosperity, toughness, and violence that it has today. The railroad rate war of 1885–1887, during which passage from Kansas City to Los Angeles could be had for $1, brought thousands of settlers to the city and created the first of many real-estate booms. Growth was also encouraged by the discovery of oil in 1890, the expansion of the citrus fruit industry in the 1890s, the development of motion pictures in the 1920s and 1930s, the mushrooming of aircraft factories during World War II, the growth of foreign trade after the war, the expansion of the electronics and aerospace industries in the 1950s and 1960s, and, throughout the twentieth century, a flocking to the area of numerous industrial plants and sybaritic seekers of sunshine. By 1965 its 7 million inhabitants had made it the second largest metropolis in the United States and possibly the fastest-growing metropolitan area in the world.

As befits the world center of the automobile cult, the airplane industry, and aerospace endeavors, the metropolis of Los Angeles is widely dispersed. Its property of spreading sideward, with only an occasional concrete thrust toward the sky, results in a scarcity of man-made landmarks and perhaps merits burlesquing as a growing megalopolitan fungus. Few apartment buildings interrupt the vistas of

[6] Robert V. Hine, *California's Utopian Colonies* (San Marino, Calif.: Huntington Library, 1953), p. 178.

single-family houses, oil-well derricks, low-lying factories, motels, supermarkets, and hamburger and taco stands scattered almost randomly mile after mile between ocean, mountain, and desert. Seen from the air, the freeways at night seem almost living things, as twisting dragons of headlights advance inexorably toward intersection with another freeway. Many commuters drive as far as thirty-five miles each way, and a few cover sixty or seventy miles every morning and evening on these ubiquitous freeways, perhaps enjoying the benefits of having their convertible tops down in January and being able to drive one hour south from home to water ski on Saturday and one hour north on Sunday to ski in the snow.

Squandering space as has perhaps no other city on earth, Los Angeles is so spread out and bus and taxi fares consequently so high that residents can justify their propensity for going everywhere by car. On their way, they see (when smog permits) mountains in the distance and drive through stretches of greenery (or, in the rainless summer, brownery) instead of the stone canyons of New York, never missing the absence in their city of a meaningful ecological form. Enthusiasts applaud Los Angeles' vigor and sun-drenched, verdant expanse; opponents note the tastelessness of Forest Lawn's "most magnificent cemetery in the world" and the city's disquieting absence of "heart." *New York Times* reporter Harrison Salisbury, returning from his first visit to Los Angeles, paraphased Lincoln Steffens' commentary on Soviet Russia to remark: "I have seen the future, and it doesn't work"; Los Angeles migrant Clifton Fadiman replied, "*We* have seen the future—and it plays." But the stimulation of Los Angeles does work in its crude and expansive fashion; more appropriate concerns might be "How long will it continue to prosper?" and "How many other cities will follow its lead?"

Many will follow, say some observers, for Los Angeles is the "prototype of supercity" [7] and "the ultimate city of our age," deeply imbued with willfulness in battling nature and "to a rare degree the product of technology." [8] Although built on a near-desert, it may be "the most luxuriously materialistic" of the world's main cities, and the optimistic residents tend to live in the future.[9] Adding nearly a

---

[7] Richard Austin Smith, "Los Angeles," *Fortune*, 71 (March 1965), 99.

[8] Christopher Rand, *Los Angeles: The Ultimate City* (New York: Oxford, 1967), p. 3.

[9] *Ibid.*, pp. 3–4.

thousand inhabitants a day and expected to go on gaining indefinitely, L.A. (even its most chauvinistic supporters are not offended by the acronymic abbreviation) should double its population long before the end of the century and may in the twenty-first century become the largest metropolitan agglomeration in the world.

The erratically shaped central city is surrounded by a county containing nine other cities of 90,000 or more and sixty-seven smaller incorporated places. Little more than 100 miles north and south along the Pacific Coast (two and three hours' driving time, respectively) are Santa Barbara and San Diego, which some Angelenos include as parts of the L.A. hinterland. That this 230-mile strip will soon become one giant conurbation—a smaller version of the Atlantic Coast conurbation—is certain, but whether or not additional communities will become attached to this monster is debatable, for mountains separate the L.A. basin and coastal strip from the interior valleys, and San Francisco is too far north for contiguity. Nearby deserts, however, are being settled with the aid of air conditioning and other benefits of technology.

The outer fringes are expanding rapidly, the inner suburbs have almost no vacant land remaining, and "rice paddy" terraces are being slashed into the slopes of nearby canyons and mountains to gain costly building lots, but the central city is not thriving, and the downtown district is even more moribund than those of most other American metropolises. Los Angeles County, once the nation's leader in agricultural production, has been converted bit by bit into thousands of rectangular superblocks, often subdivided into strict gridiron patterns and uniform lots but sometimes gracefully platted into curving cul-de-sacs that discourage through traffic and make the streets safer for children. Whether one regards them as suburbs or slurbs, in these areas several million Angelenos live—and it may be the way of life for much of the rest of the world before long.

But even as other areas are adopting the ranch-house sprawl, L.A. is turning to high-rise living, partly because unused land is becoming scarce and therefore expensive and partly because increased congestion is slowing commuter speeds on the freeways from the previous seventy-mile-an-hour average to forty or fifty or, near the city center, a creeping ten or fifteen. Another discernible trend is the rise of satellite communities—Long Beach, Torrance, Pasadena, Santa Monica, and Pomona among others—with their huge shopping centers, major employment opportunities, and daily newspapers challenging the *Los Angeles Times* for dominance in their own territories. The metropolis is thus unitary yet fragmented; the single entity as seen from the outside is in reality broken into several dozen interacting subcommunities.

To keep going and growing, the Los Angeles metropolitan area has to make use of considerable technological expertise; to deal with its manifold complexities, it has by force of necessity become "the technological city par excellence" and the "climax of modern urban mechanization." [10] Water must be imported into this arid area; floods, fires, and earthquakes have to be fought; waste products must be thrown off harmlessly; housing construction dare not lag; and freeway traffic has to be kept moving.

Here, if anywhere, is autopia. Cars are both idolized and respected in southern California, and huge amounts of space are provided for them on multilaned streets and acres of parking lots. With its widespread obsession with luxury and sports cars and hot rods, the culture is not hospitable to mass transportation by the proposed monorail or other medium; whether or not residents can shake the automobile habit in the near future is doubtful. And whether or not other new metropolises, once introduced to the entrancing, if not always real, freedom of movement offered by motor cars, can resist their lure is yet unknown; if not, the world is due for a series of Los Angeles's, complete with freeways, customized Detroit musclecars, English sports cars, and helicopter-radioed "sigalerts" warning of dread traffic obstructions. It may never, however, reach the extreme of the fictional Los Angeles hero who lived almost entirely in his automobile, conducting business over his mobile telephone, eating and sleeping in his car, and keeping constantly on the move, even to the extent of efficiently figuring out the fastest way to get through each section of town regardless of whether or not he had a destination.[11]

Like other big cities, Los Angeles has large numbers of minorities; its Negro, Japanese, and Mexican populations are among the three largest in the Western hemisphere. The infamous Watts riot of 1965 notwithstanding, minority-group privileges and acceptance have been improving, albeit—as everywhere—slowly. Of course, other ethnic groups—American Indians, Chinese, Italians, Russians, Jews, and so

[10] *Ibid.*, p. 67.
[11] Stanley Crawford, *Gascoyne* (New York: Putnam, 1966).

forth—are resident in the area, but their tendency to reside in separate districts is slight; indexes of segregation for ethnic groups in Los Angeles County show only Negroes to be highly segregated, with Mexicans and Orientals moderately segregated, and all other groups hardly differentiable ecologically.[12] Whether or not Negroes will ever be distributed uniformly throughout the metropolitan area is problematical, an issue in which Los Angeles may also represent the future racial structure of cities. It can be said definitely, however, that social equality is increasing—although very belatedly and far too slowly—in education and employment, a trend that may well take place elsewhere.

○ *Horror or Fulfillment?*

Increasing city size and density have been caricatured in what Arnold Auerbach has called "the alternate-people plan," by which residents of overcrowded cities would be divided into two groups: Monday-Wednesday-Friday and Tuesday-Thursday-Saturday.[13] MWFs would wear red badges entitling them to be away from home on those three days but making them subject to arrest if discovered on the streets on other days; TTSs would wear blue badges conveying the same privileges and penalties on their days; Sundays and holidays would be free to both groups. Confronted with intolerable overcrowding ("everywhere people were jostling or waiting to jostle"), civic leaders considered several recommended solutions (for example, traffic lights reading WALK, DON'T WALK, and LEAVE TOWN) before adopting this two-platoon system, to the benefit of all. Perhaps future paleontologists will discover that the missing link between the apes and civilized man is us.

But however city life may come to be ordered in the future, its present form fascinates many people. True city lovers—and they are many—choose to live in cities because they offer privacy, variety,

---

[12] See for example Eshref Shevky and Marilyn Williams, *The Social Areas of Los Angeles* (Los Angeles: University of California Press, 1949), p. 54.

[13] Arnold M. Auerbach, "The Alternate-People Plan," *Harper's*, 226 (January 1963), 33–5.

excitement, heterogeneity, tension, specialized shops, exuberance, personal freedom, gusto, and intellectual challenge. "Even the touch of Sodom and Gomorrah intrigues them; they may never go to a nightclub, but they enjoy the thought that if ever they were of a mind, there would be something interesting to go out to. 'No matter what goes on,' says a Chicago man, 'it goes on *here.*' " [14]

Like other startling growths, major world cities can be discussed in interminably contradictory ways. Every sententious evaluation has its opposite, and both views are expressed with oracular vehemence. This Janus role is played perhaps best of all by Los Angeles, where Grant Wood characters mix with mushroomburger eaters at all-American drive-ins and where *was* and *to be* mix indiscriminately with *now*, maximizing human living in a kaleidoscopic confusion of motorized displacement. "Unyokable adjectives fit L.A.—drab, surprising; absurd, impressive; politically conservative, politically experimental. A paradise of paradox." [15]

Encomiums and obloquy aside, Los Angeles appears to be in the vanguard of urban development. But whether it is leading the rest of the world toward something very good or very bad is even more uncertain than whether or not other cities will follow.

When Frank Lloyd Wright was asked what he thought of Los Angeles, he replied that the only way to help it would be to demolish the city and completely rebuild it; regrettably, Wright offered no suggestions on the manner of rebuilding. An English city planner almost as well renowned, Frederic J. Osborn, characterized the "rationalized congestion" of Los Angeles as "the hashish dream of a fanatical motorist." [16] On the other hand, a permanent resident of Los Angeles, Aldous Huxley, remarked that it has the greatest potential of all the places he had ever known, but whether this is a potential for horror or for fulfillment he could not tell.[17]

[14] William H. Whyte, Jr., "Are Cities Un-American?" in The Editors of Fortune, *The Exploding Metropolis* (New York: Doubleday, 1958), p. 19.

[15] Clifton Fadiman, "Party of One: Mining-Camp Megalopolis," *Holiday*, 37 (October 1965), 8.

[16] Frederic J. Osborn and Arnold Whittick, *The New Towns: The Answer to Megalopolis* (New York: McGraw-Hill, 1963), p. 149.

[17] Rand, *op. cit.*, p. 195.

SELECTED READINGS

Readers who want to do research on a narrowly defined topic should consult the books and articles mentioned in the relevant footnotes; the indexes of subjects and names are useful for this purpose. Those who would like to explore further the material of a particular chapter are offered the following works, listed chapter by chapter.

The fifteen chapters of this book are not precisely separable, and many of the suggested readings could be entered under several chapter headings. To avoid undue length of this list, however, each book is included only once, under whichever heading seems to represent its greatest contribution. Many of these volumes, in fact, might well be listed under some such category as "General Studies of Urban Life" because of the wide range of subjects they discuss; rather than using this broad catchall, I have chosen to locate each bibliographic entry not according to the average of its over-all content but according to my conception of its greatest intellectual strength. Although articles are omitted in the interest of brevity, many are included indirectly through edited "readers." Asterisks identify the books most strongly recommended as "starters."

CHAPTER 1. *Space as a Social Force*

This group of books supplies evidence both for and against an ecological approach to social phenomena in general and to urban patterns and events in particular. The comprehensive survey by Beaujeu-Garnier and Chabot touches on many of the topics discussed in the fifteen chapters of this book; Ardrey argues that territoriality is central to the behavior of animals, birds, fish, insects, and men; Hawley's work advances the case for human ecology; and Burgess and Bogue have gathered under one cover abridged versions of many of the graduate theses written over the past forty years in the Department of Sociology at the University of Chicago— the one department that has probably contributed more than any other to our ecological knowledge of cities. That departments other than sociology have also been urban-oriented is indirectly apparent in the fact that the University of Chicago Press has produced an overwhelmingly large percentage of the books in this bibliography.

*Ardrey, Robert, *The Territorial Imperative*, 1966.

*Beaujeu-Garnier, Jacqueline, and Georges Chabot, *Traité de géographie urbaine*, 1963.

Burgess, Ernest W. (ed.), *The Urban Community*, 1926.

*Burgess, Ernest W., and Donald J. Bogue (eds.), *Contributions to Urban Sociology*, 1964.

Faris, Robert E., and H. Warren Dunham, *Mental Disorders in Urban Areas*, 1939.

George, Pierre, *Précis de géographie urbaine*, 1961.

*Hawley, Amos H., *Human Ecology*, 1950.

Johnson, James H., *Urban Geography*, 1967.

Laurenti, Luigi, *Property Values and Race*, 1960.

Park, Robert E., Ernest W. Burgess, and Roderick D. McKenzie, *The City*, 1925.

Wynne-Edwards, V. C., *Animal Dispersion in Relation to Social Behavior*, 1962.

Zipf, George K., *Human Behavior and the Principle of Least Effort*, 1949.

CHAPTER 2. *How Ecological Facts Are Known*

Crucial to any subject are its quantitative data and its qualitative information, as well as the research techniques used to analyze facts in such a way as to elicit their inferences as reliably and thoroughly as possible. Gibbs sets forth some pertinent methodological tools, Hauser and Schnore provide a dozen excursions into the frontiers of urban research, and the other books (except Bogue's and Thomlinson's) supply masses of statistical data. Articles and books about all branches of urban sociology are summarized in several of the twenty-three areas of sociological specialization reported in the periodical *Sociological Abstracts*.

Bogue, Donald J. (ed.), *Needed Urban and Metropolitan Research*, 1953.

Bogue, Donald J., and Calvin L. Beale, *Economic Areas of the United States*, 1961.

Bunge, William, *Theoretical Geography*, 1962.

*Gibbs, Jack P. (ed.), *Urban Research Methods*, 1961.

*Hauser, Philip M., and Leo F. Schnore (eds.), *The Study of Urbanization*, 1965.

International Statistical Institute, *International Statistical Yearbook of Large Towns*, since 1961.

International Urban Research, *The World's Metropolitan Areas*, 1959.

Passoneau, Joseph R., and Richard S. Wurman, *Urban Atlas*, 1967.

Schnore, Leo F. (ed.), *Social Science and the City*, 1968.

Sociological Abstracts, since 1953.

Thomlinson, Ralph, *Sociological Concepts and Research*, 1965.

United Nations, *Demographic Yearbook*, since 1948.

CHAPTER 3.   *The Nature and Rise of Cities*

Knowledge of the historical development of cities in various regions of the world is prerequisite to a complete understanding of why modern cities are ordered as they are. Mumford provides his usual erudite and witty historical overview, Sjoberg definitively summarizes the present state of knowledge of the beginnings and current conditions of non-industrial cities, and the other books discuss one or another period in the long history of city growth.

Beresford, Maurice, *New Towns of the Middle Ages*, 1967.

Fustel de Coulanges, N. D., *The Ancient City*, 1889.

Ghurye, Govind Sadashiv, *Cities and Civilization*, 1962.

Glaab, Charles N., and A. Theodore Brown, *A History of Urban America*, 1967.

Gutkind, E. A., *International History of City Development*, several volumes, since 1964.

*Mumford, Lewis, *The City in History*, 1961.

Pirenne, Henri, *Medieval Cities*, 1925.

*Sjoberg, Gideon, *The Preindustrial City*, 1960.

Weber, Adna F., *The Growth of Cities in the Nineteenth Century*, 1899.

Weber, Max, *The City*, 1921.

Weimer, David R. (ed.), *City and Country in America*, 1962.

Woolley, Leonard, *Excavations at Ur*, 1954.

CHAPTER 4. *Ways of Life in Cities*

What modern cities are like constitutes a huge subject, embracing such sweeping subtopics as the differences between urban and rural life, the social organization within cities, and the variations among different types of cities. Questions of this magnitude cannot be answered completely in any one book, and the volumes cited here should be supplemented by those in other sections of this bibliography, especially Chapter 10. The Vidich and Bensman paperback is a readable account of the mixed social structure and attitudes to be found in a small community in upstate New York, and Gans, Hollingshead, Lynd, and Warner attempt to uncover the fundamental workings of larger towns in other parts of the United States.

Baltzell, E. Digby, *Philadelphia Gentlemen*, 1958.
Chabot, Georges, *Les villes*, 1958.
Cox, Harvey, *The Secular City*, 1965.
Cuber, John F., and Peggy B. Harroff, *The Significant Americans*, 1965.
Duncan, O. D., and Albert J. Reiss, Jr., *Social Characteristics of Urban and Rural Communities: 1950*, 1956.
Gans, Herbert J., *The Levittowners*, 1967.
Geddes, Patrick, *Cities in Evolution*, 1949.
Hollingshead, August B., *Elmtown's Youth*, 1949.
Lynd, Robert S., and Helen M. Lynd, *Middletown*, 1929.
Lynd, Robert S., *Middletown in Transition*, 1937.
Srole, Leo, and others, *Mental Health in the Metropolis*, 1962.
Strauss, Anselm L., *Images of the American City*, 1960.
*Vidich, Arthur J., and Joseph Bensman, *Small Town in Mass Society*, 1958.
Warner, W. Lloyd, and Paul S. Lunt, *Social Life of a Modern Community*, 1941.
Whyte, William H., Jr., *The Organization Man*, 1956.

CHAPTER 5. *Metropolitan Regions*

Metropolitan areas and their components—the central city, usually a satellite or two, and always an encircling ring of bedroom suburbs—are becoming increasingly important as larger and larger segments of the population of so many nations move into them. Dickinson's geographic view of European and other metropolitan regions is supplemented by Duncan's coverage of the regional relationships of fifty major American cities; the largest superregion (the northeastern seaboard megalopolis) is described at length by Gottmann.

Bogue, Donald J., *The Structure of the Metropolitan Community*, 1950.

*Dickinson, Robert E., *City and Region*, 1964.

Dobriner, William M. (ed.), *The Suburban Community*, 1958.

Dobriner, William M., *Class in Suburbia*, 1963.

*Duncan, O. D., W. Richard Scott, Stanley Lieberson, Beverly D. Duncan, and Hal H. Winsborough, *Metropolis and Region*, 1960.

Fisher, Robert M. (ed.), *The Metropolis in Modern Life*, 1955.

George, Pierre, and others, *Études sur la banlieue de Paris*, 1950.

*Gottmann, Jean, *Megalopolis*, 1961.

Hawley, Amos H., *The Changing Shape of Metropolitan America*, 1956.

McKenzie, Roderick D., *The Metropolitan Community*, 1933.

Martin, Walter T., *The Rural-Urban Fringe*, 1953.

Scott, Mel, *The San Francisco Bay Area*, 1959.

Seely, John R., Alexander Sim, and E. W. Loosley, *Crestwood Heights*, 1956.

Spectorsky, Auguste E., *The Exurbanites*, 1955.

Wood, Robert C., *Suburbia*, 1959.

CHAPTER 6.   *Urban Growth and Settlement*

Cities grow through births (minus deaths) and migration (from other cities, rural areas, and other nations); both of these demographic processes are influenced by, and in turn influence, a number of other social forces and events. Schnore documents major urban demographic trends in the United States, which Thomlinson puts in perspective by examining migration theories and other dynamics of population movement. The periodical *Demography*, published by the Population Association of America, contains articles on all aspects of population, including the growth and properties of urban areas.

Chevalier, Louis, *La formation de la population parisienne au xixe siècle*, 1950.

Demography, since 1964.

Freedman, Ronald, *Recent Migration to Chicago*, 1950.

Gilmore, Harlan W., *Transportation and the Growth of Cities*, 1953.

Handlin, Oscar (ed.), *Immigration as a Factor in American History*, 1959.

Kennedy, John F., *A Nation of Immigrants*, 1964.

Morrill, Richard L., *Migration and the Spread and Growth of Urban Settlement*, 1965.

*Schnore, Leo F., *The Urban Scene*, 1965.

Taeuber, Conrad, and Irene B. Taeuber, *The Changing Population of the United States*, 1958.

*Thomlinson, Ralph, *Population Dynamics*, 1965.

Wilkinson, Thomas O., *The Urbanization of Japanese Labor*, 1965.

CHAPTER 7. *Networks of Cities*

Geographers have contributed a vast literature to the study of the inter-relationships between cities and their hinterlands, other cities, and the world about them; in this context, cities are often viewed as mediators between their residents and the rest of the world, both human and inanimate. Isard presents the techniques (frequently mathematical) of what he calls "regional science," and Murphy condenses geographic thinking about cities into one volume. The potential but as yet incompletely realized contribution of computer simulation to urban ecology is implied in the readings collected by Guetzkow and Shubik.

Boskoff, Alvin, *The Sociology of Urban Regions*, 1962.

English, Paul W., *City and Village in Iran*, 1966.

Gottmann, Jean, and Robert A. Harper (eds.), *Metropolis on the Move*, 1967.

*Guetzkow, Harold (ed.), *Simulation in Social Science*, 1962.

Haggett, Peter, *Locational Analysis in Human Geography*, 1965.

*Isard, Walter, *Methods of Regional Analysis*, 1960.

Losch, August, *The Economics of Location*, 1954.

Mayer, Harold, and Clyde Kohn (eds.), *Readings in Urban Geography*, 1959.

*Murphy, Raymond E., *The American City*, 1966.

Shubik, Martin (ed.), *Game Theory and Related Approaches to Social Behavior*, 1964.

CHAPTER 8. *The Shape of Urban Areas*

The dozen theories and approaches described in this chapter represent important attempts to explain why each type of person or activity is located in a particular section of the city. Most of the following books offer the classic hypotheses contributed by their authors, and Theodorson has brought together and republished additional original expositions of ecological theses.

Firey, Walter, *Land Use in Central Boston*, 1947.

Gist, Noel P., and Sylvia F. Fava, *Urban Society*, 1964.

Harris, Chauncy D., *Salt Lake City*, 1940.

Hoyt, Homer, *The Structure and Growth of Residential Neighborhoods in American Cities*, 1939.

Park, Robert E., *Human Communities*, 1952.

Quinn, James A., *Human Ecology*, 1950.

Ratcliff, Richard U., *Urban Land Economics*, 1949.

Shevky, Eshrev, and Marilyn Williams, *The Social Areas of Los Angeles*, 1949.

Shevky, Eshrev, and Wendell Bell, *Social Area Analysis*, 1954.

*Theodorson, George A. (ed.), *Studies in Human Ecology*, 1961.

Tryon, Robert C., *Identification of Social Areas by Cluster Analysis*, 1955. .

Zorbaugh, Harvey, *The Gold Coast and the Slum*, 1929.

CHAPTER 9. *International Contrasts*

Comparison of urban structure and ecological patterns in modern and early cities of various societies supplies invaluable empirical material for testing the cultural and temporal universality of ecological hypotheses. The paperback by Breese reports the relatively scanty research results in India and other developing and urbanizing nations, whereas Dickinson's comprehensive analysis of sites and functions of West European cities is based on a vast amount of accumulated scholarship.

*Breese, Gerald, *Urbanization in Newly Developing Countries*, 1966.

Carcopino, Jerome, *Daily Life in Ancient Rome*, 1940.

*Dickinson, Robert E., *The West European City*, 1952.

Dore, Ronald P., *City Life in Japan*, 1958.

Geertz, Clifford, *Peddlers and Princes*, 1963.

Hauser, Philip M. (ed.), *Urbanization in Asia and the Far East*, 1957.

Hayner, Norman S., *New Patterns in Old Mexico*, 1966.

Jones, Emrys, *Towns and Cities*, 1966.

McGee, T. G., *The Southeast Asian City*, 1967.

Miner, Horace, *The Primitive City of Timbuctoo*, 1965.

Reissman, Leonard, *The Urban Process*, 1964.

Spiro, Melford E., *Kibbutz*, 1956.

Turner, Roy (ed.), *India's Urban Future*, 1962.

Van den Berghe, Pierre L., *Caneville*, 1964.

Wiser, William, and Charlotte Wiser, *Behind Mud Walls: 1930–1960*, 1963.

Wylie, Laurence, *Village in the Vaucluse*, 1964.

Yazaki, Takeo, *The Japanese City*, 1963.

CHAPTER 10. *Neighborhoods and Other Subareas*

All cities are divided into parts distinguished by race, nationality, religion, or other characteristics of their residents; some of these parts are far more meaningful to their residents than is the city as a whole. The reader by Hatt and Reiss contains sixty-two selections treating this and related facets of urban life and the people who live it, and the other books discuss various aspects of neighborhoods, neighboring, and those larger sections of cities often called "districts" or "quarters."

Caplovitz, David, *The Poor Pay More*, 1967.

Caplow, Theodore, Sheldon Stryker, and Samuel E. Wallace, *The Urban Ambience*, 1964.

Cavan, Sherri, *Liquor License*, 1966.

Drake, St. Clair, and Horace Cayton, *Black Metropolis*, 1945.

Duncan, Otis Dudley, and Beverly D. Duncan, *The Negro Population of Chicago*, 1957.

Gans, Herbert J., *The Urban Villagers*, 1962.

Goldstein, Bernard, *Low Income Youth in Urban Areas*, 1967.

*Hatt, Paul K., and Albert J. Reiss, Jr. (eds.), *Cities and Society*, 1957.

Keller, Suzanne, *The Urban Neighborhood*, 1968.

Sussman, Marvin B. (ed.), *Community Structure and Analysis*, 1959.

Taeuber, Karl E., and Alma F. Taeuber, *Negroes in Cities*, 1965.

CHAPTER 11. *City-Planning Principles*

One organized attempt to do something positive to cure urban ills is known as city planning—a vast field of contemporary action derived from centuries of development, particularly in several European countries. Gallion and Eisner have written a lucid and profusely illustrated exposition of the history and principles of urban planning, to which the case studies and other articles that first appeared in *Scientific American* constitute an interesting supplement. *Ekistics* is published monthly under the direction of the controversial and very active planner, C. A. Doxiadis of Athens, and contains abstracts of articles on a wide range of topics.

Abercrombie, Patrick, *Town and Country Planning*, 1943.
Ashworth, William, *The Genesis of Modern British Town Planning*, 1954.
Bardet, Gaston, *Le nouvel urbanisme*, 1948.
Ekistics, since 1955.
*Gallion, Arthur B., and Simon Eisner, *The Urban Pattern*, 1963.
Giedion, Sigfried, *Space, Time, and Architecture*, 1947.
Haverfield, F., *Ancient Town Planning*, 1913.
Hiorns, Frederick R., *Town-Building in History*, 1956.
Howard, Ebenezer, *Garden Cities of Tomorrow*, 1902.
Lubove, Roy, *Community Planning in the 1920's*, 1963.
Orlans, Harold, *Utopia Ltd.*, 1953.
Osborn, Frederic J., and Arnold Whittick, *The New Towns*, 1963.
Parkins, Maurice, *City Planning in Soviet Russia*, 1953.
Rodwin, Lloyd, *The British New Towns Policy*, 1956.
*Scientific American, *Cities*, 1965.
Stewart, Cecil, *A Prospect of Cities*, 1952.
Tunnard, Christopher, *The City of Man*, 1953.

CHAPTER 12.   *Planning Practices and Problems*

Today's city planners are faced with imposing day-to-day problems of zoning, land use, housing, slums, transportation, and the like; however, few planners take the time to write about their experiences in facing these threats to urban well-being. Abrams draws from his extensive practical experience in many countries to write about housing deterioration and renewal, and Jacobs imaginatively scores the provocative counterpoint of the decline and regeneration of neighborhoods having human scale and purpose. The *Journal of the American Institute of Planners* is the official organ of the national professional association.

*Abrams, Charles, *The City Is the Frontier*, 1965.
Anderson, Martin, *The Federal Bulldozer*, 1964.
Breese, Gerald, and Dorothy E. Whiteman (eds.), *An Approach to Urban Planning*, 1953.

Chapin, F. Stuart, Jr., *Urban Land Use Planning,* 1957.

Colean, Miles L., *Renewing Our Cities,* 1953.

Dahir, James, *Communities for Better Living,* 1950.

Duncan, Beverly D., and Philip M. Hauser, *Housing a Metropolis,* 1960.

*Jacobs, Jane, *The Death and Life of Great American Cities,* 1961.

Journal of the American Institute of Planners, since 1935.

Lynch, Kevin, *The Image of the City,* 1960.

Mumford, Lewis, *The Highway and the City,* 1964.

Owen, Wilfred, *The Metropolitan Transportation Problem,* 1966.

Rapkin, Chester, and William G. Grigsby, *Residential Renewal in the Urban Core,* 1960.

Stein, Clarence S., *Toward New Towns for America,* 1951.

Tunnard, Christopher, and Henry Hope Reed, *American Skyline,* 1955.

Wilhelm, Sidney M., *Urban Zoning and Land-Use Theory,* 1962.

Woodbury, Coleman (ed.), *The Future of Cities and Urban Redevelopment,* 1953.

CHAPTER 13. *Metropolitan Planning*

Pleas for comprehensive regional planning are voiced by political scientists as well as by planners and sociologists, but, except for Greater London, hardly any metropolis is actually being planned as a regional unit. Mumford contributes a classic statement of the case for planning on a regional basis, and Elias, Gillies, and Riemer have collected fifty-five polemical arguments disputing the most appropriate action to improve metropolitan living.

Bollens, John C., and Henry J. Schmandt, *The Metropolis,* 1965.

Chinitz, Benjamin (ed.), *City and Suburb,* 1964.

*Elias, C. E., Jr., James Gillies, and Svend Riemer (eds.), *Metropolis,* 1964.

Foley, Donald L., *Controlling London's Growth,* 1963.

Fortune, The Editors of, *The Exploding Metropolis,* 1958.

Hirsch, Werner Z. (ed.), *Urban Life and Form,* 1963.

Jones, Victor, *Metropolitan Government,* 1942.

Kaplan, Harold, *Urban Political Systems,* 1967.

*Mumford, Lewis, *The Culture of Cities,* 1938.

Vernon, Raymond, *Metropolis 1985,* 1960.

Walker, Robert A., *The Planning Function in Urban Government,* 1950.

Webster, Donald H., *Urban Planning and Municipal Public Policy,* 1958.

CHAPTER 14.   *Utopian Communities*

Utopian ideals have contributed fresh ideas to the real-life planning of cities, even to the extent of specifying the building of a few towns. Articles from a recent issue of *Daedalus* devoted to perfect societies were edited by Manuel, the anthology by Negley and Patrick extracts writings of the major inventors of imaginary societies, and Skinner's quasi novel portrays a utopian community whose design flows explicitly from modern behavioral psychology.

Boguslaw, Robert, *The New Utopians*, 1965.

Goodman, Percival, and Paul Goodman, *Communitas*, 1947.

*Manuel, Frank E. (ed.), *Utopias and Utopian Thought*, 1966.

Mumford, Lewis, *The Story of Utopias*, 1922.

*Negley, Glen, and J. Max Patrick (eds.), *The Quest for Utopia*, 1962.

Nordhoff, Charles, *The Communistic Societies of the United States*, 1875.

Reiner, Thomas A., *The Place of the Ideal Community in Urban Planning*, 1963.

Reps, John W., *The Making of Urban America*, 1965.

Ruyer, Raymond, *L'utopie et les utopies*, 1950.

*Skinner, B. F., *Walden Two*, 1948.

CHAPTER 15.   *Cities of the Future*

With a large population increase and a flocking to urban areas, cities are bound to become both larger and more numerous—and if suburban sprawl and environmental pollution continue to be inescapable by-products, urban life may well become nearly intolerable. Eldredge's megatome brings together seventy-one diverse articles suggesting many different ways to deal with our rapidly urbanizing world, and Rand describes the existing city most often nominated as the prototype of the twenty-first-century city, but whether this exemplar calls for tears or cheers is anyone's guess. The best guesses regarding world and national population growth during the rest of the twentieth century have been prepared by the United Nations Population Division.

Berry, Brian J. L., and Jack Meltzer (eds.), *Goals for Urban America*, 1967.

*Eldredge, H. Wentworth (ed.), *Taming Megalopolis*, 1967.

Ewald, William R. (ed.), *Environment for Man*, 1967.

Hall, Peter, *The World Cities*, 1966.

Mayer, Albert, *The Urgent Future*, 1967.

*Rand, Christopher, *Los Angeles: The Ultimate City*, 1967.

Rodwin, Lloyd (ed.), *The Future Metropolis*, 1961.

*United Nations, *World Population Prospects*, 1966.

NAME INDEX

SUBJECT INDEX